Studies in N

THE SHOW TO
END ALL SHOWS

THE SHOW TO
END ALL SHOWS

Frank Lloyd Wright
and The Museum of Modern Art, 1940

Edited by Peter Reed and William Kaizen

With an Essay by Kathryn Smith

The Museum of Modern Art, New York

EDITOR-IN-CHIEF
John Elderfield

ADVISORY COMMITTEE
Mary Lea Bandy
John Elderfield
Peter Galassi
Michael Maegraith
Kynaston McShine
Peter Reed

Studies in Modern Art is prepared by the Research and Scholarly Publications Program of The Museum of Modern Art, which was initiated with the support of a grant from the Andrew W. Mellon Foundation. Publication is made possible by an endowment fund established by the Andrew W. Mellon Foundation, the Edward John Noble Foundation, Mr. and Mrs. Perry R. Bass, and the National Endowment for the Humanities' Challenge Grant Program.

Produced by the Department of Publications, The Museum of Modern Art, New York

Edited by David Frankel
Designed by Amanda Washburn
Production by Elisa Frohlich
Printed and bound by Conti Tipocolor s.p.a., Florence, Italy

This book is typeset in Gotham, Kennerly, and Neutraface. The papers are 135-gsm Gardamatt and 130-gsm Pigna Ghiaccio

Library of Congress Control Number: 2004114393
ISBN: 0-87070-055-3

Published by The Museum of Modern Art
11 West 53 Street
New York, New York 10019
(www.moma.org)

Distributed in the United States and Canada by D.A.P., New York
Distributed outside the United States and Canada by Thames & Hudson Ltd, London

Cover: Frank Lloyd Wright. Cover design (detail) for the publication planned to accompany the exhibition *Frank Lloyd Wright: American Architect*, The Museum of Modern Art, November 12, 1940–January 5, 1941. Back cover and frontispiece: Wright with a model of the Herbert F. Johnson House ("Wingspread") in the exhibition *Frank Lloyd Wright: American Architect*. Page 10: final page of Walter Curt Behrendt's essay "Frank Lloyd Wright," edited in Wright's hand

Printed in Italy

7
Acknowledgments

8
Preface by John Elderfield

10
Introduction by Peter Reed and William Kaizen

12
THE SHOW TO END ALL SHOWS
Frank Lloyd Wright and The Museum of Modern Art, 1940   Kathryn Smith

65
LETTERS AND TELEGRAMS
Introduction by William Kaizen

104
ORIGINAL MANUSCRIPTS
Introduction by Peter Reed

Frank Lloyd Wright   Walter Curt Behrendt   116

Frank Lloyd Wright   Walter Curt Behrendt as edited by Frank Lloyd Wright   125

To My Critics   Frank Lloyd Wright   134

Frank Lloyd Wright: His Influence in America   Talbot Hamlin   137

Wright's Influence Abroad   Henry-Russell Hitchcock   143

Builder and Poet—Frank Lloyd Wright   Fiske Kimball   151

The Early Impress of Japan on Wright's Art   Grant Manson   154

"Museum of Modern Art Opens Large Exhibition
of the Work of Frank Lloyd Wright"   John McAndrew   159

Structure and Design in the Work of Frank Lloyd Wright   Richard Neutra   160

My Frank Lloyd Wright   Alvar Aalto   166

Untitled   Harwell Hamilton Harris   167

1940: Frank Lloyd Wright   Ludwig Mies van der Rohe   169

To Meet—To Know—To Battle—To Love—Frank Lloyd Wright   Edgar J. Kaufmann, Sr.   170

Untitled   Liliane Kaufmann   180

Untitled   Edgar Kaufmann, Jr.   181

185
PLATES
Introduction by William Kaizen

209
APPENDIX
Biographical Reference   229

Trustees of The Museum of Modern Art   240

ACKNOWLEDGMENTS

This publication would not have been possible without the enthusiastic support and encouragement of John Elderfield, The Marie-Josée and Henry Kravis Chief Curator, Department of Painting and Sculpture. Sharon Dec, Assistant to the Chief Curator, facilitated many aspects of the project.

Research for a publication such as this brought us in touch with many individuals and institutions outside the Museum. In addition to her substantial essay, Kathryn Smith provided scholarly advice and an in-depth perspective on the subject. She was a diligent colleague. We are grateful for the cooperation of the Frank Lloyd Wright Foundation. Our associates at The Frank Lloyd Wright Archives at Taliesin West assisted in many ways, not least by providing images and documents, and by responding to our numerous queries. We would especially like to thank Bruce Brooks Pfeiffer, Director; Margo Stipe, Registrar and Art Collections Administrator; and Oskar Muñoz, Assistant Director. Research was also facilitated by Ken Rose, Assistant Director of the Rockefeller Archive Center; Janet Parks, Curator of Drawings and Archives, Avery Architectural and Fine Arts Library, Columbia University; and Lynda Waggoner, Director of Fallingwater and Vice President, Western Pennsylvania Conservancy, and her colleagues Cara Armstrong, Curator, and Clinton Piper, Museum Programs Assistant.

A number of individuals and institutions generously and graciously granted permission to publish original documents in this volume. We owe special thanks to Susan Anderson, Philadelphia Museum of Art Archives; Beth Dodd, Curator, Alexander Architectural Archive at the University of Texas, Austin; Markku Lahti, Director of the Alvar Aalto Foundation; Lynda Waggoner of Fallingwater; Mosette Broderick; Talbot F. Hamlin; Dirk Lohan; and Dion Neutra. For assistance in obtaining photographs we are grateful to Howard Bossen, Kai Gutschow, Ray Hall, Bruce Kellner, Al Krescanko, Wilma Slaight, Edgar Tafel, and Robert Wojtowicz.

Many colleagues at The Museum of Modern Art assisted this project. The Museum's Archives and Library staff were enormously cooperative, and we thank Michelle Elligott, Museum Archivist; Michelle Harvey, Associate Archivist; and Jennifer Tobias, Librarian, Collection Development. Erik Landsberg, Head of Collections Imaging, Rosa Smith, Senior Archiving Technician, and Roberto Rivera, Administrative Assistant, coordinated requests for many illustrations. Tina di Carlo, Assistant Curator, and Christian Larsen, Curatorial Assistant, Department of Architecture and Design, also deserve our thanks. Stephen Clark, Associate General Counsel, and Nancy Adelson, Assistant General Counsel, patiently advised us on matters relating to rights and permissions, which seem to grow ever more complicated.

Finally, the Museum's Department of Publications under the direction of Michael Maegraith, Publisher, played a key role in producing this book. Amanda Washburn, Senior Book Designer, brilliantly and beautifully resolved the complicated relationship between contemporary and archival texts. Elisa Frohlich, Associate Production Manager, oversaw many details related to bookmaking and coped admirably with our changing schedules. Although working behind the scenes with extraordinary patience and skill, David Frankel, Managing Editor, was in fact at the forefront of this publication. He worked closely with Kathryn Smith and us, not only improving our writing but also enhancing all aspects of the book from cover to cover.

—Peter Reed and William Kaizen

PREFACE

Studies in Modern Art was founded in 1991 to publish scholarly articles focusing on the collection of The Museum of Modern Art and on the Museum's programs. It was the creation of two convergent motivations. First was a long-developing consensus that a vehicle should be found to foster scholarship and publication on the Museum's collection and programs as well as on the individual research interests of the Museum's staff. Such scholarship and publication did already take place, but not as consistently as was wished, in part owing to the enforced deadlines of loan exhibitions and in part because there was no formally established program to encourage it. Second was the generous offer of the Andrew W. Mellon Foundation, subsequently complemented by the Edward John Noble Foundation, Mr. and Mrs. Perry R. Bass, and the National Endowment for the Humanities, to support scholarly work at the Museum. It was consequently decided to establish a Research and Scholarly Publications Program, which, as one of its principal endeavors, would publish a scholarly journal, *Studies in Modern Art*.

The Museum published seven issues of *Studies in Modern Art* through 1998, when it embarked on a large-scale end-of-century program, "MoMA 2000," whose aim was to prepare for a new museum building by reviewing and reconsidering the collection in exhibitions that were accompanied by their own series of publications. *Studies in Modern Art* seemed duplicative of that series, so production was temporarily suspended, although it was also decided that the opening of the new building would be an appropriately auspicious moment to begin publishing the journal once again. The publication of this eighth issue does indeed coincide with the opening of the new Museum of Modern Art.

The pause in publication will not change the original mandate and mission of *Studies in Modern Art*, but that mandate will expand in two directions that had always been anticipated but never fully realized. First: the Museum's collection and programs cover, in the main, all the visual arts in the period from 1880 to the present (and in photography from the medium's invention to the present). Consequently, a mandate to encourage scholarship and publication in this field is, effectively, to do so for the study of modern art in toto. While continuing to honor the terms of our foundation by favoring scholarly articles that bear directly on works of art in the Museum's collection and on the Museum's programs, then, we will now more frequently publish on subjects in the period of the Museum's collection and programs but less specifically attached to them. Second: it was understood from the start that our mission would include the encouragement of research and publication by scholars not only from the Museum's own staff but outside the Museum, and every issue published thus far has included at least one outside contribution. Again, we will continue to honor the terms of our foundation by favoring internal contributions, but in the future we will also publish external contributions more frequently. In both of these directions but most especially the second, we will give absolute precedence to the publication of scholarly articles of the highest quality and interest for the study of modern art.

One programmatic feature of this series will change. Hitherto, each and every volume of *Studies in Modern Art* has had a unifying theme. This policy was intended to help focus research within the Museum, attract specialist outside contributors, and result in useful works of reference on particular subjects. These reasons remain valid ones for producing thematic volumes, and such volumes will continue to appear. However, the liability of a series composed exclusively of thematic volumes is that it affords no opportunity for the encouragement of research and the publication of important scholarly articles on subjects that do not fit the volumes that are being planned. Consequently, we now intend to produce portmanteau volumes as well as thematic ones, the balance between the two depending upon the submissions and commissions that would justify each kind of book.

As it turns out, the present issue is a thematic one, and does concern itself specifically with the Museum's programs—indeed, being devoted to the exigencies attendant on the Museum's Frank Lloyd Wright exhibition of 1940, and to the book that was intended to accompany it, *Studies in Modern Art* 8 concerns an architect of capital importance to the Museum's history and exhibition program. It is edited by Peter Reed, Curator in the Museum's Department of Architecture and Design, and by the outside scholar William Kaizen, and their Introduction immediately following this Preface discusses the scope and purposes of the volume. I would only add to their remarks that their collaboration on *The Show to End All Shows* has given *Studies in Modern Art* an auspicious rebirth.

—John Elderfield
The Marie-Josée and Henry Kravis Chief Curator
Department of Painting and Sculpture

(typ. style is not)
style itself has not;

himself, ~~a~~ style has become offensive, and most of all ~~his personal one.~~ *individual style*

is needed as the most precious of democratic privileges

This is out of the An offensive wrong conclusion.

This does not diminish the value of his artistic achievement. On the

contrary, it clearly brings out the remarkable fact that the form, in which

Wright for the first time expressed the idea of an organic architecture, is a

individual *his buildings* *inspiring*

thoroughly ~~personal~~ ~~creation~~ creation of his own, and as such ~~deserving~~ our

fullest admiration and gratefulness as it opened to us a fresh source of that

the practice of principle and

fine delight that goes with the enjoyment of beauty. *What form have this*

we evolved on their own?

Frank Lloyd Wright is one of the most imposing figures from the past

individual

period of individualism who has lived on into our time, a ~~personality~~ of such

overwhelming greatness as we will not see soon again. As an artist he is

and romantic guided by principles that are not personal but

emotionalist. It is for that reason that the younger generation is inclined to

idolize ~~have~~ ~~so~~ ~~have applied for admission to his~~ *following a*

~~distrust~~ him. ~~In their judgment he passes as a romantic, which only means that~~

Youth crowds the occasions upon which he speaks

although *seems to have*

the world today ~~has~~ begun to lose the sense for that kind of romantic beauty

as an expression of principle which

he has to offer as the most precious gift of his extraordinary talent. But

democratic State

even if the form in which he presented his ideas should prove to be evanescent,

and the individual be replaced by the totalitarian or communistic or

socialistic idea of architecture

the principle on which his work is founded will continue to be upheld in all

future efforts directed toward making architecture again a living art.

my meaning and implied untruths concerning myself and my work

Behrend has either ignorantly or deliberately twisted

If the Museum values this opinion enough to paste it across the face of my exhibition there

is going to be no exhibition

INTRODUCTION

In 1940, The Museum of Modern Art staged a retrospective of the work of Frank Lloyd Wright, the great American architect, then in his seventies, who had experienced a professional rebirth over the previous decade after many years of relative invisibility. Wright was a full collaborator in the organization of the project, which he intended, he said, to be "the show to end all shows." To accompany the exhibition, *Frank Lloyd Wright: American Architect*, the Museum planned a publication in the form of a *Festschrift*, commissioning essays from many of the best-known architectural figures of the day—Alvar Aalto, Henry-Russell Hitchcock, Jr., Richard Neutra, Mies van der Rohe, and others. Wright, however, took issue with parts of the book, complimentary though they were, and after an incendiary exchange of correspondence, including the architect's threat to cancel the entire exhibition, the show went forward but the book did not.

Several years ago the manuscripts that had been commissioned for the aborted publication, and other archival documents, came to light at the Museum after decades of being segregated from other historical records—perhaps an indication of how sensitive the debacle had been. Now, for the first time in one volume, the Museum is publishing the entire surviving group, along with a full selection of the letters and telegrams written by Wright, the Museum, and others during the Museum's and the architect's collaboration-cum-collision. Accompanying these period documents is an extensive essay by the noted Frank Lloyd Wright scholar Kathryn Smith, who provides a full account of the exhibition, both as it was and as it was intended to be—including, for example, an unrealized plan to build one of Wright's Usonian Houses in the Museum's garden. To place the events of 1940 in context, Smith explores Wright's relationship not only with the Museum but with the architectural profession, his critics, and other exhibitors of his work in the years leading up to the exhibition.

There are gaps in the surviving documentation of *Frank Lloyd Wright: American Architect*. Most notably, installation shots of the exhibition have disappeared; photographs of the show were taken, but they are missing from both the Museum archives and the most significant collections of relevant papers. Despite all efforts to track them down, their whereabouts remains a mystery. Another gap is a definitive exhibition checklist: many documents prepared by the Museum's registrar record the vast amount of material (models, drawings, and photographs) that Wright sent to the Museum, but much is not known about exactly what made it into the galleries. The Appendix in the present book contains several key documents related to the planning and contents of the exhibition.

At the heart of this extraordinary story, with its successes and failures, are the competing agendas between architect and museum. Wright, busily pursuing new commissions during this resurgence in his career, wanted to present his work in his own way, in a context he would define with as little outside critique or interpretation as possible. The Museum wanted to promote Wright as the "greatest living architect" and so to claim America's prominence in modern architecture. The reexamination of the story in *The Show to End All Shows* offers a look inside the organization of a major museum exhibition, demonstrating the difficulties it entails, even, or perhaps especially, when its subject is still alive and well.

—Peter Reed and William Kaizen

Frank Lloyd Wright at Taliesin, Spring Green, Wisc.

THE SHOW TO END ALL SHOWS
Frank Lloyd Wright and
The Museum of Modern Art, 1940
Kathryn Smith

In November 1940, when negative reviews of the Frank Lloyd Wright retrospective at The Museum of Modern Art appeared in the press, no one was more surprised than the architect himself. After all, he had chosen the material and designed the installation to be, in his words, "the show to end all shows." Yet for Geoffrey Baker of the *New York Times*, the "slipshod arrangement" lacked "dramatic clarity" and "historical perspective."[1] Labeling it "a real disappointment" and "a bewildering mélange," other critics often cited the absence of a catalogue as partial explanation for the confusion they encountered.[2] It was not publicly known that an ambitious book had been planned—by John McAndrew, the curator of the Museum's Department of Architecture—only to be canceled just days before being sent to the printer. Intending to document the architect's historical influence as well as his continuing role as a source of inspiration to a younger generation, McAndrew had included both historians and prominent modern architects as authors. Acutely aware of the importance of Wright's impact on European architecture before and after World War I, he had selected the German émigré Walter Curt Behrendt, former editor of *Die Form* and author of the seminal *Der Sieg des neuen Baustils* (The victory of the new building style, 1927), to write the principal essay. Yet Wright, on previewing the text, had violently objected to certain passages: "BEHRENDT HAS EITHER IGNORANTLY OR DELIBERATELY TWISTED MY MEANING AND IMPLIED UNTRUTHS CONCERNING MYSELF AND MY WORK," he protested in a scorching telegram. "IF THE MUSEUM VALUES HIS OPINION ENOUGH TO PASTE IT ACROSS THE FACE OF MY EXHIBITION THERE IS GOING TO BE NO EXHIBITION."[3] As a result of the ensuing standoff, the Museum shelved the book, explaining there was no longer sufficient time to deliver it for the opening.[4]

The catalogue was only one aspect of an elaborate program that Wright and McAndrew had formulated in their initial meetings. Extensive correspondence survives to document the scope and content of the principals' intentions. With both a historical point of view and a thematic dimension, the show was conceived to highlight the architect's achievements in residential planning, structural experimentation, organic form, and urbanism. As a symbolic, if not literal, recognition of his central importance to modern architecture after a decade of struggle to overcome financial bankruptcy and rebuild his reputation, this showcase in New York took on heightened significance for the seventy-three-year-old architect. So, after forcing the Museum to abandon the publication, Wright quickly took over all remaining aspects of the show, virtually ignoring McAndrew's careful preparations. Recalling a large exhibition of his work that he had organized in 1930, he designed almost identical freestanding easels and model bases. In addition to a comprehensive display of his drawings, he was intent on presenting his most recent work in color. To that end, he supervised the construction of almost a dozen new, polychromatic models, commissioned large-format transparencies, and narrated a color film about his architecture and design school, the Taliesin Fellowship. Combined with several older models and hundreds of black-and-white photographs, the show surveyed the full fifty years of Wright's architectural practice in an installation of his own design.

Finally, the most innovative feature of the exhibition plans was to be the construction of the first model house to be displayed by an American museum.[5] Wright had wanted to build a Usonian House—a prototypical residence for the American middle class—in the Museum's Sculpture Garden along 54th Street. Not only did he seek to build a full-scale experimental structure in the heart of midtown Manhattan, but, in seeming ignorance of the bureaucratic difficulties, he specified a fully functioning plumbing system and radiant heat. Although the proposal survived months of planning that went as far as a complete set of working drawings, in the end it too was aborted, the victim of legal technicalities over the use of the land behind the Museum.

Even in its truncated form the Museum's retrospective was a coup for Wright, after a decade-long campaign to revive his career. The first twenty years of his practice had produced the revolutionary Prairie Houses and such experiments in modern materials and austere abstraction as Unity Temple (Oak Park, Illinois, 1905–8) and the Larkin Company Administration Building (Buffalo, 1902–6), but from 1909 to 1929 he had been preoccupied with domestic strife, financial hardship, and extended periods of work in Japan and California that had taken him away from his original client base. He had abandoned his family in 1910, and his continuing domestic turmoil ultimately resulted in two prolonged divorces, one of them complicated by endless legal entanglements and scandalous publicity. Having spent the greater part of those twenty years with few clients, mounting debts, and deep in bankruptcy—in his darkest hour, in 1926, he was locked out of his Wisconsin house and studio, Taliesin, by a bank foreclosure—he faced yet another obstacle in the Great Depression. But his determination and talent paid off; after the completion of the S. C. Johnson & Son, Inc., Administration Building in Racine, Wisconsin (1936–39), and the publication of the western-Pennsylvania country house Fallingwater (1934–37), designed for Edgar and Lilianne Kaufmann, Wright made the cover of *Time* in 1938. By 1939 his residential practice was thriving and his opportunities for public buildings were increasing. Even so, the Museum was forewarned that he would prove a difficult colleague in organizing the 1940 show.

American and European Exhibition Tour 1930–31

In the late 1920s and early '30s, Wright employed a number of strategies to resuscitate his career, founding the Taliesin Fellowship, giving public lectures, and writing books and articles. He gained the widest exposure, however, by organizing a traveling exhibition. The idea of mounting a show of his work recalled the earliest years of his practice, from 1894 through 1914, when he regularly selected his own material—drawings, photographs, and models—to

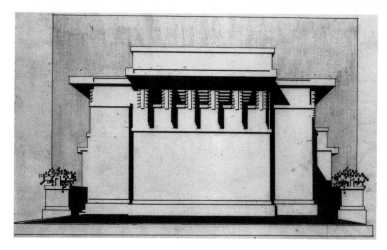

1. Frank Lloyd Wright. St. Mark's-in-the-Bouwerie Towers, New York. Project, 1927–1931. Model

2. Frank Lloyd Wright. Unity Temple, Oak Park, Ill. 1905–8. Elevation, c. 1930. Ink on tracing paper, 10 x 12" (25.4 x 30.5 cm). Frank Lloyd Wright Foundation

hang at the Chicago Architectural Club along with that of other members of this professional society. Wright's 1930–31 show, though, was far more ambitious, and it was a risky venture to initiate a circulating exhibition without any institutional or financial backing.

Wright saw his opportunity in 1930, when he was invited to speak at Princeton University. He made the most of this comparatively modest proposal: to the organizer, E. Baldwin Smith, who had suggested a series of eight lectures, Wright replied,

> But why eight lectures? In six days the world was made, on the seventh the work was visible and the maker no doubt viewing it,— let us assume with "the modest assurance of conscious worth": Could we not make it six? A seventh to consist of an exhibition I could appropriately arrange, of my own recent work illustrating the ideas and principles involved in the "course."[6]

Smith accepted immediately.[7] With Princeton committed, Wright began to seek additional locations, first in the United States and finally in Europe, resulting in a show that eventually traveled for most of two years.[8]

With this American and European tour, in 1930–31, Wright set the pattern for presenting his work that he would impose at the Modern in 1940. First, he personally selected the material: "over six hundred photographs, about one thousand drawings and sets of plans, and four models" (fig. 1).[9] In an effort to shape critical opinion, he exhibited not only his characteristically delicate renderings in colored pencil but also large-format black-and-white perspectives of six buildings he had designed before 1910, redrawn in a severe graphic style evoking the present European avant-garde (fig. 2).[10] The coupling of these particular buildings—the Frederick C. Robie House (Chicago, 1908-10), Unity Temple, the Larkin Administration Building, the Richard W. Bock House and Studio project (Maywood, Illinois, 1906), the Yahara Boathouse project (Madison, 1905), and the William H. Winslow House (River Forest, Illinois, 1893-94)—with the newly abstract style of the renderings was intended to reinforce the notion that Wright, the "father of modern architecture," had anticipated the radical forms of European modernism by decades.

3. Installation of Wright's traveling exhibition of 1930-31 at
The Art Institute of Chicago, 1930. The display racks Wright designed
for this exhibition are almost identical to those he designed in
1940 for his show at The Museum of Modern Art

4. Installation of Wright's traveling exhibition of 1930-31 at
The Art Institute of Chicago, 1930

To accommodate his preference for showing drawings and photographs separately, Wright designed a unique installation system of freestanding boxes: on the long sides, large boards set at an angle created easel-like supports for the drawings; on the short ends were pivoting vertical panels for photographs. The system—flexible enough to be broken into sections, crated, and reassembled in a variety of settings—was almost identical to the display panels he instructed MoMA to build a decade later (figs. 3, 4). His presentation style was not uniform: some drawings were matted, others mounted on boards, others simply pinned to the panels. Wright did not favor traditional salon-style hanging, nor did he adopt the installation methods of the European avant-garde, such as the Bauhaus teachers or Mies van der Rohe; rather, the overall effect was like stepping into his architectural studio (fig. 5).

The Princeton show was brief in duration (May 6–14, 1930), but through a letter-writing campaign to a network of friends and supporters Wright eventually secured eleven more sites, including New York, Chicago, Madison (figs. 6, 7), Milwaukee, Amsterdam, Berlin, Stuttgart, Antwerp (fig. 8), and Brussels.[11] In some venues, such as Chicago, Wright oversaw the installation personally, but he also instituted a procedure to ensure quality when he was absent, assigning an assistant to travel with the crates so as to repair models, supervise installations, and act as a guide for the public.[12]

Wright did not accompany the exhibition to Europe; instead he dispatched his German assistant, Heinrich Klumb, who was entrusted with coordinating the arrangements. Klumb assumed an unprecedented degree of control, owing, no doubt, to a unique combination of factors: his command of German, his geographic distance from Wright, and a strict budget that did not allow for unlimited use of the telegraph, a means Wright employed to send instructions to his staff. Klumb made an exhaustive list of contacts all across Europe, and Wright himself had written ahead to three supporters—H. Th. Wijdeveld, Heinrich de Fries, and Erich Mendelsohn.[13]

Liberties were taken with the exhibition design in Wright's absence. Installing the exhibition in Holland, Wijdeveld gave it a strong graphic style consistent with the

5. Frank Lloyd Wright. Frank Lloyd Wright Studio, Oak Park, Illinois. 1898.
This photograph of the library, taken in c. 1902–3, shows pivoting display
racks similar to those Wright designed for his exhibitions of 1930 and 1940

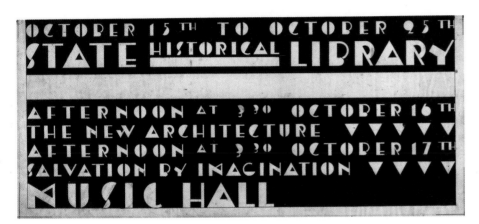

6. Poster for Frank Lloyd Wright lecture at
the State Historical Library, Madison, 1930,
accompanying his traveling exhibition of 1930–31.
The Frank Lloyd Wright Foundation

8. Poster for Wright's traveling exhibition of
1930–31 in its installation in Antwerp, 1931.
The Frank Lloyd Wright Foundation

7. Poster for the U.S. tour of Wright's
traveling exhibition of 1930–31.
The Frank Lloyd Wright Foundation

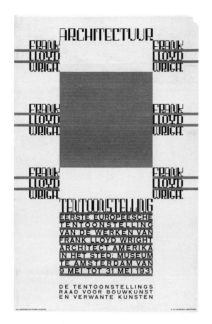

9. Poster by H. Th. Wijdeveld for Wright's
traveling exhibition of 1930–31
in its installation in Amsterdam, 1931.
The Museum of Modern Art

10. Installation of Wright's traveling exhibition of 1930–31 at
the Stedelijk Museum, Amsterdam, 1931

11. Installation of Wright's traveling exhibition of 1930–31 at
the Stedelijk Museum, Amsterdam, 1931

12. Installation of Wright's traveling exhibition of 1930–31 in Berlin, 1931

Amsterdam school (figs. 9–11), while in Berlin Klumb pared the material down considerably and mounted it with a certain geometric regularity (fig. 12). He was certainly more aware than Wright of the inevitable comparison to another exhibition, *Die Wohnung unserer Zeit* (The dwelling of our time), appearing concurrently at the German Building Exhibition. That spare and elegant installation by Mies and Lilly Reich elevated exhibition design to a modern art form in its own right.[14] "People are critical, in fact very critical, in looking at your work and even at the way of showing it," Klumb warned Wright. "The smallest error we would make in arranging and presenting it would have done much harm."[15] Despite Klumb's adjustments, Philip Johnson—in Berlin that summer making arrangements for The Museum of Modern Art's first architecture show—considered the installation "frightful." He wanted Mies to design the show in New York, and explained to the Museum's director, Alfred H. Barr, Jr., "We will at least have a simple and understandable arrangement."[16] The plan to use Mies did not materialize; instead Johnson designed the show himself, setting a new standard in exhibition design for the Museum.[17]

Wright's 1930–31 exhibitions were not accompanied by a catalogue, but when Wijdeveld enthusiastically welcomed the show to Amsterdam, Wright seized the opportunity. It was this Dutch architect who had produced the lavishly illustrated, elaborately designed, and sumptuously printed book *The Life-Work of the American Architect Frank Lloyd Wright* (1925), a compilation of issues of the magazine *Wendingen*.[18] In the intervening years Wright had conceived an ambitious book project of his own, growing out of a series of articles he had published in *Architectural Record* between 1927 and 1929. Charting the logical evolution of form and structure derived from his innovative use of both traditional and modern materials, the book, loosely arranged chronologically under topic headings—stone, wood, concrete, glass, and so on—was to survey his entire career. Having been turned down by several American publishers, Wright suggested to Wijdeveld that he produce this monograph as the catalogue for the European tour.[19] Wijdeveld willingly agreed, but evidently could not find support for such an expensive venture; the matter eventually was dropped.[20] It would be years before Wright finally abandoned the project, to be called *Creative Matter in the Nature of Materials*, but he held fast to the name, reviving the phrase "In the Nature of Materials" in 1940 as his own title for the retrospective at the Modern. He also used it for a book that he arranged to be published as a substitute catalogue for the MoMA show, though appearing two years later.[21]

13. Frank Lloyd Wright. Frederick C. Robie House, Chicago. 1908–10

Critical Reception in Germany

When Wright's exhibition opened in Berlin, the climate for it was not particularly receptive. By the early 1930s the debate over modernism among German architects and critics was intense. The building of the Weissenhof Housing Colony in Stuttgart in 1927 had accelerated the split between advocates of Expressionism and of *Neue Sachlichkeit* (New objectivity) in German architectural circles, and after Weissenhof the *Sachlichkeit* architects began to gain dominance, especially in Berlin.[22] Controversy over Wright's exhibition, staged at the Preussische Akademie der Künste, occupied the pages of newspapers such as the *Deutsche Bauzeitung*, the *Berliner Tageblatt*, the *Württemberger Zeitung*, and the *Frankfurter Zeitung*, as well as influential journals like *Die Form*.[23] Critics favoring the *Neue Sachlichkeit* were quick to note the anonymous character of the crisp machinelike forms in the Robie House (fig. 13) and Larkin Administration Building, but were repelled by Wright's ornamentation of even such a utilitarian structure as a gas station (fig. 14). Meanwhile writers who had mistakenly but admiringly seen him as the prophet of a new, classless social order in his works of the Prairie period condemned his recent projects for bourgeois summer resorts in California and Arizona—the Emerald Bay Summer Colony (c. 1923–24) in Lake Tahoe and the San Marcos-in-the-Desert Resort Hotel (Chandler, Arizona, 1928–29).[24]

One of the most positive and penetrating responses, by contrast, was by Behrendt (fig. 15). This architectural editor and writer had become aware of Wright when he was the only critic in Europe to review *Frank Lloyd Wright, Chicago* (1911), one of three books on Wright issued by the Berlin publisher Ernst Wasmuth.[25] After examining the picture book's illustrations and plans, Behrendt prophetically announced, "It seems . . . as if something significant is to be expected from [America], which will initiate a new development and regeneration in architecture." *Frank Lloyd Wright, Chicago* awakened in Behrendt an insatiable curiosity about American architecture, one made "even stronger after reading the excellent and profound introduction written by the London architect C. R. Ashbee."[26] Ashbee, ironically, had faced a predicament with Wright quite similar to the one in which Behrendt would end up twenty-seven years later: a personal friend of Wright's, he had been the architect's choice to write the introduction after Wasmuth had chosen "some German in Cologne," but Wright had objected to passages in the text, especially the asser-

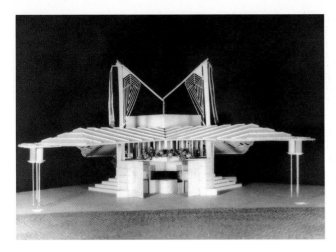

14. Frank Lloyd Wright. Standardized Overhead Service Station. Project, 1931. Model

15. Walter Curt Behrendt

16. Lewis Mumford

tion that Wright's designs had been influenced by Japanese art.[27] Wasmuth printed the introduction intact, but Wright excised the offending paragraphs from the American edition (confusingly given the German title *Frank Lloyd Wright: Ausgeführte Bauten*), which he distributed himself. Despite this act of censorship, Wright maintained warm relations with Ashbee, admitting to him some years later, "Whenever I think of my abuse of your friendship I am much ashamed."[28]

This episode, however, remained unknown to Behrendt, whose interest in Wright apparently deepened when he became associated with the American social historian Lewis Mumford (fig. 16), whom he met on a U.S. tour in 1925.[29] The two were drawn to each other through their common vision of a humane vernacular style in architecture. In writings arguing for social and architectural reform, they lauded industrial technology as a tool for a new society but rejected idolatry of the machine. They believed that a heroic artist could bring about a new style, but only by adhering to past traditions and continuities rather than through any abstract formalism.[30] Although Mumford, under Behrendt's influence, came to accept aspects of the European avant-garde, he still primarily championed Wright as the architect whose modernism was both progressive and humane.

Mumford had begun to write seriously about Wright as early as 1924, when the architect's reputation was at its nadir in the United States. In three major publications—*Sticks and Stones: A Study of American Architecture and Civilization* (1924); "The Social Background of Frank Lloyd Wright," in *Wendingen* (1925); and *The Brown Decades: A Study of the Arts in America, 1865–1895* (1931)—Mumford built up an argument for Wright's place in the modern movement that became commonly accepted.[31] In *The Brown Decades* Mumford not only emphasized Wright's work before 1910 but, unlike most commentators, also referred positively to his career between 1915 and 1930. The author was principally concerned, however, with a linear progression of influence in nineteenth-century American architecture, as when he wrote, "[Louis] Sullivan was the link between two great masters, [H. H.] Richardson and Frank Lloyd Wright; and with the development of Wright's architecture the last stage in the transition was made: modern architecture in America was born."[32]

Mumford applied his discourse to contemporary issues equally with "the usable past." As a result, he thrust himself in the middle of the debate arising from the American publication of Le Corbusier's *Towards a New Architecture*, in 1927.[33] His opportunity came when he reviewed Henry-Russell Hitchcock's book *Frank Lloyd Wright*, published by Cahiers d'art, Paris, in 1928. Battle lines were drawn when Mumford set up an opposition between Wright and Le Corbusier. In an argument that was singular for its time, Mumford stated,

> Mr. Wright is not the forerunner of Le Corbusier, but, in a real sense his successor. He has passed that painful step in learning when one is conscious of one's movements and one's instruments, and has reached that period in pure mechanical design when he can play with it, in short, the engineer has given way to the artist, and despite a hundred efforts to prove either that the engineer is the artist, or that engineering is the only possible type of art in the modern world, Mr. Wright's work exists as a living refutation of this notion. He had achieved Cubism in architecture before the Cubists, and he has gone on to an integral architecture which creates its own forms with, not for, the machine.[34]

Mumford saw a profound difference between Wright and the International Style. He not only understood Wright's expressive response to various native landscapes, he applauded it: "Mr. Wright is, definitely, our greatest regional architect, his Chicago houses *are* prairie houses, as his Pasadena homes are 'Mediterranean' ones, to harmonize with that climate and milieu."[35] At the same time, Mumford believed that Wright's architecture should serve as a means to a new modern vernacular rather than existing solely as the work of one individual genius.

While Behrendt seems to have assimilated certain of Mumford's views on American modernism, he also had an intellectual base in the German avant-garde. *Der Sieg des neuen Baustils*, the first book to announce the unified style of the European modern movement, set forth his manifesto of the *neues Bauen* (new building): in accepting industrial construction, rather than pure creativity, as the basis for modern architecture, he came closer than Mumford to advocating a rationalist formal language, and while he did not single out Mies, Walter Gropius, or any other architect as the heroic leader of the new movement, he nevertheless observed that the construction of *Siedlungen* (model housing colonies) invested the German avant-garde with a humane purpose. While Behrendt, more than any other critic in Germany, clearly understood Wright's aesthetic, he increasingly regarded him as of the old order.

Even so, at the time of Wright's Berlin exhibition in 1931 Behrendt became well-known in Germany for defending the American architect in the pages of the *Frankfurter Zeitung*. Simply the title of one of his essays, "Wright or Le Corbusier," fueled a good deal of debate,[36] but the article that set the tone for his future Wright criticism was a review of the Berlin show in the form of an extended critical analysis of the work from the Oak Park years of 1889 to 1910.[37] In his first paragraph Behrendt quietly passed over the exhibition because, he said, it did not clearly show Wright's real contribution, which could only be found in the structure of the architect's thinking. Instead of citing single buildings or refer-

17. Wright's house and studio Taliesin in 1911–14

ring to dates, Behrendt restricted his argument to the topic of the single-family dwelling, producing brilliant insights into Wright's radical transformation of space and form in the Prairie Houses (fig. 17). At the same time, however, he completely disregarded projects and buildings that did not fit his thesis, and ignored the doctrinaire formalism that emerged in Wright's work in the 1910s and '20s. Behrendt did not debate the change of direction in Wright's design, then, he merely sidestepped it. Yet on the whole, with the exception of an attack on Wright's use of ornament, his essay was adulatory: Wright, he boldly stated, as the "founding father of modern architecture," had made the "first independent contribution by the United States to Europe." Behrendt's approach in this essay would have consequences in the future: in 1940, when the Modern asked him to write an overview of Wright's entire career, his critical stance on the later work was all the more surprising for being previously unarticulated.

Behrendt's review notwithstanding, the negative reaction to the Berlin show reached Wright rather quickly in the form of dispatches of newspaper clippings.[38] He went on the offensive with an essay entitled "To My Critics in the Land of the Danube and the Rhine," dated July 23, 1931, and addressed to the newspaper most sympathetic to his cause, the *Frankfurter Zeitung*.[39] Copies were sent to Wijdeveld, Mendelsohn, and Klumb. Wright launched his attack against what he presciently called the "International Style."[40] He rejected the machine as a symbol in architecture, embracing instead the idea of individual imagination in the service of art. Distancing himself from the *Neue Sachlichkeit*, he warned, "Do not imagine, my architects and critics, that mathematics is music, although music is sublimated mathematics." While admitting that he had employed geometric abstraction, he maintained that it was not an end in itself. "As Artists it is our office not only to overcome the machine by intelligent use of that engine," he explained, "but by means of it, used as a new tool, to gratify the natural thirst of the human soul for beauty."

Wright's rebuttal reinforced the schism that had emerged between himself and the German architectural movement in the 1920s. The antagonism directed at him had put him on the defensive. As the modern movement grew stronger in Europe, and, later, as such leaders as Gropius and Mies eventually emigrated to the United States, his hostility would only grow. It is clear from Wright's reaction to passages in Behrendt's essay a decade later that they had taken him directly back to the harsh rejection he had suffered in Berlin. In fact his immediate response to Behrendt's 1940 essay was to revise "To My Critics . . . " and send it to McAndrew as his reply.

The "International Style" Exhibition at the Modern, 1931–32

Beginning with the Museum's first architectural show, *Modern Architecture: International Exhibition*, coorganized in 1932 by Johnson (fig. 18) and Hitchcock (fig. 19) with counsel from Barr (fig. 20), Wright's relationship with The Museum of Modern Art was fraught with ambivalence and difficulty. As astute observers of the architectural scene, the curators of the exhibition—widely known as the "International Style" show—sought to define modern architecture for a general audience by presenting the work of the European movement (Mies, Gropius, Le Corbusier, and J. J. P. Oud) and its adherents in America (Raymond Hood, Howe and Lescaze, Richard Neutra, and the Bowman Brothers) as a unified style. Wright's work did not fit the show's premise, and it seems clear there was originally no intention of including him.

Johnson, Barr, and Hitchcock (the latter less strongly) were all in general agreement that Wright's significance lay in the historical influence he had exerted on the younger generation. Early in 1931, during the planning stage of *Modern Architecture*, Johnson wrote to Mumford, "[Wright] is better than [Auguste] Perret or [H. P.] Berlage, more advanced if you will but he has nothing to say today to the International Group."[41] This rather echoed Barr's view in 1929 that "Frank Lloyd Wright is, of course, greatly admired as a pioneer who is no longer to be imitated."[42] Hitchcock's stance, however, was more equivocal. He had relegated Wright to the lesser category of "New Tradition" in his recently published *Modern Architecture: Romanticism and Reintegration* (1929), but Mumford had rightly detected his disillusion with Le Corbusier and his growing respect for Wright, remarking in a letter to the architect a month before the opening, "[Hitchcock] has almost become a disciple of yours, much though you might prefer to see him remain on the hostile side of the fence."[43] This shift in attitude, in a fluid climate, underlies Hitchcock's claim in the book that accompanied the 1932 show that

> there is already no question that Wright is one of the greatest architects of all time. As an American architect he completed the development of a national art initiated by Richardson. As a modern architect he first saw all the revision and replacement of traditional concepts which alone could bring a new architecture generally into being.[44]

But Hitchcock nevertheless concluded, "The day of the lone pioneer is past, the advance may be on a more general front at last. Throughout the world there are others beside Wright to lead the way toward the future."[45]

Wright's inclusion in *Modern Architecture*, problematic from the outset, came about in the end through the intervention of Mumford, who first persuaded Johnson to include Wright and then persuaded Wright to accept. As Johnson admitted at the time, "Wright was included only from courtesy and in recognition of his past contributions."[46] Nevertheless, in April 1931 Johnson wrote to Wright, asking him to submit a model of his choice.

Despite the clarity of the request, communication between Johnson, Wright, and Wright's staff would be confused almost until opening day. Over the nine-month period from April until December 1931, Johnson and Wright met only once and spoke briefly by telephone. Despite several attempts at closer contact, either illness or conflicting travel plans prevented it. Johnson spent the entire summer in Europe conferring with Gropius, Mies, and Oud; on his return to the United States, Wright departed for an extended trip to Brazil

18. Philip Johnson.
Photograph: Carl Van Vechten

20. Alfred H. Barr, Jr. Photograph: Jay Leyda

19. Henry-Russell Hitchcock

to judge a competition. The sixty-five-year-old architect believed he was turning matters over to Klumb, whom Johnson had met in Berlin while viewing Wright's exhibition. But Klumb was detained in Europe and Johnson's letters remained unopened.

For this and other reasons, Wright's first exhibition at the Modern was filled with conflict. First, it was not until a month before the opening that Wright professed to understand who else was to be included besides himself.[47] While he was willing to be shown in the company of the four leading European modernists, he withdrew when he was informed of the inclusion of Hood and Neutra, complaining, "MY WAY HAS BEEN TOO LONG AND TOO LONELY TO MAKE A BELATED BOW TO MY PEOPLE AS A MODERN ARCHITECT IN COMPANY WITH A SELF ADVERTISING AMATEUR AND A HIGH POWERED SALESMAN."[48] While liking Hood (the self-advertising amateur) personally, Wright dismissed him as a commercial architect merely copying the fashionable style of the day. As for Neutra (the high-powered salesman), who had apprenticed at Taliesin in 1924, he maintained that within only five years of arriving in the United States, Neutra had established a reputation not by designing—he had just one major building to his credit—but by writing, lecturing, and teaching. Wright was insulted to be placed in the company of these men, and still more to be regarded as their inferior. Fearing that the exhibition would cast Hood as America's most important modern architect if Wright withdrew, Mumford cabled him, "PLEASE RECONSIDER YOUR REFUSAL. I HAVE NO CONCERN WHATEVER ON BEHALF OF MUSEUM BUT AM INTERESTED IN YOUR OWN PLACE AND INFLUENCE."[49]

When Wright agreed to remain in *Modern Architecture* (fig. 21), he jumped into an architectural debate raging in New York between the traditionalists and the modernists as a prelude to the show's opening. In the spring of 1931, Johnson and Barr had organized the exhibition *Rejected Architects* as an alternative show to the Architectural League's fiftieth-anniversary exhibition. Johnson had also staged a protest in front of the Architectural League show, going so far as to hire picketers carrying signs directing the public to *Rejected Architects*.[50] In the same spirit, Wright agreed to participate in the "International Style" show on the condition that the Museum print and distribute his own essay "Of Thee I Sing," in which he attacked European modernism (fig. 22) and its defenders, whom he labeled *Geist der Kleinlichkeit* (spirit of the narrow-minded). This, of course, was a repetition of the strategy he had used the previous summer in Berlin, in sending an essay to the *Frankfurter Zeitung*, and he would repeat it again with McAndrew in 1940. An even clearer glimpse of his mercurial nature occurred when, just after refusing to participate in the "International Style" exhibition, he asked Johnson to take on an enlarged version of his 1930–31 traveling show.[51]

Wright could not afford to attend the opening of the "International Style" show,[52] but received his impressions from the *New York Times*, where, he wrote Johnson a few days later, "I learn I am there, not that I no longer count, but because I am historical, well, I am not hysterical, but smiling a somewhat sarcastic smile. The shameless and selfish essence of such promotion and propaganda that is back of this attitude is, in its essence, a fitting attribute of the exploit."[53] As a result, he initially refused to be included in the exhibition's tour.[54] In another harbinger of his protest against Behrendt in 1940, two weeks later he wrote

21. Frank Lloyd Wright exhibit in *Modern Architecture: International Exhibition*, at The Museum of Modern Art, 1932

22. J. J. P. Oud. Row of International Style houses, Weissenhof Housing Colony, Stuttgart. 1927

a more thoughtful three-page letter to Hitchcock correcting sixteen mistakes he had discovered in the writer's essay. Already armed with knowledge from Mumford that Hitchcock was more sympathetic to him than Johnson was, he softened his tone considerably, and alluded to a possible meeting in the future: "We see too little of each other, each for his own good? Some day we may remedy that if the 'bump' of principle doesn't break us. Perhaps I am going to pray someday that somebody convert me to pragmatism or shoot me."[55]

Reflecting the tenor of the times, the organizers embraced controversy over the show rather than trying to deflect it. Johnson, Barr, Hitchcock, and George Howe, as associate editors of the April 1932 issue of *Shelter*, devoted the entire magazine to a symposium planned by Barr at the Museum to discuss the "International Style" show. Not only did they refuse to restrict the pages to the symposium speakers (Hood, Howe, and Hitchcock), they also invited rebuttal from well-known opponents. Johnson obtained Wright's permission to include his essay "Of Thee I Sing," which, to the architect's dismay, they published with other critiques, by Arthur T. North, William Adams Delano, Chester Aldrich, and Kurt Lönberg-Holm, whose "Two Shows: A Comment on the Aesthetic Racket" juxtaposed all the curators' references to "style" with "an advertisement for toilet fixtures."[56] Incensed at the content of *Shelter*, Wright shot off a vitriolic three-page letter to Johnson, withdrawing from the show a third time and launching an attack:

> Russell's editorial is essentially Hitchcock. Sincerity is one of his limitations I am bound to respect. Evidently he had a good time making his collection and classifying it. If classifying were classic—Russell is a classic. But I fear he is an ass.[57]

Johnson's response was unemotional and diplomatic, which no doubt helped to keep Wright's material with the traveling exhibition. Hitchcock had less tolerance: in a letter of April 22 (which, however, he may have refrained from mailing), he retorted,

> I am sorry that in this question of whether your exhibits are or are not to remain in the Show you should descend to unanswerable vulgarity. I must say that at last I am

convinced that there is no further reason for attempting to remain on working terms with you. I regret now that we have ever begun to know you personally. But knowing you, I realize we could not otherwise have had dealings with you at all.[58]

Despite the acrimonious correspondence, Johnson's long, patient letter of explanation pointed out, "Please believe that I have appreciated your effort to remain friends despite the many misunderstandings which I sincerely regret."[59] In an earlier meeting in New York, Johnson had mentioned his intention to drive through the Midwest with Hitchcock in the summer to research an upcoming show on Chicago architecture. Wright invited them both as guests to his home. "Of course, you will be welcome at Taliesin at any time," he wrote cordially, "Any feeling I have in this whole matter is directly personal to no one."[60]

In fact the founding of the Museum—in 1929, when Wright was at a very low ebb—had marked a significant turning point for him. His objections to MoMA's support of the International Style architects may have grown the more bitter since he surely realized that no other institution could have more influence on his career. In any case his behavior throughout the "International Style" show was a clear warning for the future, but by 1940 Johnson had departed and Hitchcock was on the sidelines; Barr was still in a position of power, but a less influential one. (Under increasing pressure from the Museum's management, he would be dismissed as director in 1943.) Perhaps a clue to the reason the Museum proceeded with the 1940 retrospective in light of Wright's past history of unpredictable behavior can be gleaned from a declaration Barr made late that year: "At the beginning of our conversations here at the Museum, Mr. Wright announced: 'I am a very difficult man.' We agree, but we still believe him to be the greatest living architect."[61]

Three MoMA Exhibitions, 1933–38

Despite his tempestuous behavior during the "International Style" show, Wright's historical place in modern architecture, his increased production of innovative designs, the critical attention given his publications and theory, and the completion of the Kaufmanns' dramatic new house over a waterfall all guaranteed that he would continue to receive the attention of the Department of Architecture. Between 1933 and 1938, in fact, the Museum organized three exhibitions that presented Wright from various perspectives.[62]

In January 1933, just ten months after the close of the "International Style" exhibition, the Museum presented *Early Modern Architecture: Chicago, 1870–1910*, organized by Johnson and Hitchcock. As Terence Riley, present Chief Curator in the Museum's Department of Architecture and Design, would later explain,

> Barr had developed a twofold mission for the young institution: not only to present the best of the art of the day but also to establish a history of modern art that supported contemporary artistic theory. . . . Henry Hobson Richardson, Louis Sullivan, and Frank Lloyd Wright . . . are positioned as the principal protagonists in the aesthetic development of the Chicago school of architecture. . . . In fact, the exhibition may

even be considered a work-in-progress or as a prologue to the Museum's publication, in 1935, of *Louis Sullivan—Prophet of Modern Architecture* by Hugh Morrison . . . and, in 1936, Hitchcock's *The Architecture of Henry Hobson Richardson and His Times*.[63]

23. John McAndrew, c. 1950

Although the Chicago exhibition essentially charted the development of the skyscraper, it ended with Wright's Winslow House, opening the door to speculation that the Museum intended to follow through with a complementary project (an exhibition, a book, or both) that would present Wright as the seminal influence on modern architecture. Indeed, one week after the opening of Hitchcock's Richardson show in 1936, the Architecture Committee proposed a Wright retrospective for the fall of that year.[64] The show was eventually postponed with the idea of rescheduling it to commemorate Wright's seventieth birthday, in 1939, but the idea was not forgotten.[65]

The second exhibition came about without the involvement of either Hitchcock or Johnson (who departed the Museum in December 1934). Instead it was the initiative of McAndrew (fig. 23), who was appointed curator of the Department of Architecture on September 1, 1937.[66] McAndrew came to his post with a variety of credentials preparing him for the job. He had studied architecture at Harvard University, although he left without graduating; he had worked briefly in an architect's office in New York and had taught for a number of years at Vassar College. Through these associations he knew Hitchcock and had met Barr and Johnson in the late 1920s.[67] In November 1937 McAndrew became aware of a dramatic new country house, Fallingwater, that Wright was finishing for the department store magnate Edgar J. Kaufmann.[68] For McAndrew the discovery was timely: needing to fill a gap in the exhibition schedule left by the postponement of a major Alvar Aalto show, he acted swiftly, telegraphing Wright at the end of December to request permission to mount an exhibit using plans and text from a special Wright issue of the January 1938 *Architectural Forum*.[69] The architect shot back, "ALL RIGHT, JOHN, LET'S SEE WHAT YOU CAN DO."[70]

Details fell quickly into place and the Fallingwater show was slotted for January 25 through March 6, 1938. Coincidentally, both the exhibition and its accompanying publication conformed to Wright's ideal. The show was purely documentary: there was a brief text by Wright (excerpted from *The Architectural Forum*), floor plans and elevations, and twenty enlarged black and white photographs—including the iconic view by William Hedrich (fig. 24), in a stark new style of photography that accentuated the extraordinary engineering. In a continuing effort to avoid any suggestion of influence from European modernism, Wright pointed out in the publication that the ideas of Fallingwater "are in no wise changed from the early work." Further distancing himself from the International Style, he concluded, "The effects you see in this house are not superficial effects."[71] Fallingwater brought Wright national exposure, with a cover story in *Time* magazine[72] and widespread newspaper coverage. The Museum's exhibit was an extremely influential part of this attention, attracting 14,305 visitors in New York and tens of thousands more with a tour that stopped in ten cities.[73]

While the Fallingwater show was organized rather spontaneously, the third show to feature Wright was the result of many years of planning and negotiation. From May 24

24. Frank Lloyd Wright.
Edgar J. Kaufmann House (Fallingwater), Mill Run, Pa. 1934–37.
Photograph: Hedrich-Blessing

25. Installation of *Three Centuries of American Architecture*,
a traveling exhibition organized by The Museum of Modern Art,
at the Cleveland Museum of Art, 1938.
The model of Wright's Robie House appears at the lower right

until July 31, 1938, at the Galerie Nationale du Jeu de Paume, Paris, the Modern presented *Trois siècles d'art aux États-Unis* (Three centuries of American art). An encyclopedic survey of American painting, sculpture, architecture, photography, and film, the exhibition contained hundreds of artworks, photographs and models of buildings and other structures such as bridges, and screenings of films from the silent era through the 1930s. The architecture section, organized by McAndrew and his assistant, Elizabeth Bauer Mock,[74] was shaped by what the Germans called *Amerikanismus* and the French *américanisme*: the emphasis, in other words, was on mechanization and rationalist planning, as seen in the development of the skyscraper and in the careers of Richardson, Sullivan, and Wright (fig. 25). Photographs and models of these architects' projects were shown alongside images of the anonymous, vernacular and industrial American structures favored by modern European architects, such as grain elevators, iron bridges, and barns.

As the most comprehensive exposition of American architecture the Museum had ever presented, *Trois siècles d'art aux États-Unis* made the assertion that the current of influence once thought to have flowed from Old World to New had been reversed. In an accompanying essay, "Architecture in the United States," McAndrew made a direct link between American innovation and European modernism, explaining that "Wright's work was published in Germany in 1910 and 1911, long before it was widely known here. Mies van der Rohe, Gropius, Oud, and other leaders of modern architecture have acknowledged the inspiration they found in his courageous pioneer works. His influence in Holland was such that he could properly be counted one of the founders of the modern Dutch school."[75]

Although *Trois siècles* was intended for a French audience, it offers an important insight into a notion shaping subsequent exhibitions at the Modern: American painting and sculpture were considered derivative of European sources, but American architecture, photography, and film were seen as innovative and sui generis.[76] Discussing the general impression of the Museum as identified with "foreign art" in an internal memo two years later, Barr described "a tendency on the part of the public to identify art with painting and sculpture—two fields in which America is not yet, I am afraid, quite the equal of France; but in other fields—the film, architecture and photography, for instance, the United States would seem to be the equal or superior of any other country."[77] An indirect result of the Paris show was the idea of dedicating an exhibition exclusively to this idea, and by October of 1939 the Museum had formulated plans for a major show to that effect: *Three Great Americans: Frank Lloyd Wright, Alfred Stieglitz, and D. W. Griffith.*[78]

The Exhibition in Boston

By late 1939, when Wright's commissions were steadily increasing, the Modern finally fixed a firm schedule for his retrospective, in the 1940 fall season.[79] The exhibition had been in discussion since 1935, and by the time MoMA's plans became concrete it was no longer the only museum planning a large Wright show. By a stroke of luck, however, the other institution was the Institute of Modern Art, Boston—originally founded in 1935 as The Boston Museum of Modern Art, a branch of MoMA. The Institute had become independent in 1938 (thus the change in name), but close ties still bound the two museums. Three important trustees of the Institute had originated with the Modern: Barr; Paul J. Sachs, Barr's former professor and mentor at Harvard University and a MoMA trustee; and Jere Abbott, MoMA's first associate director. As a result, when the Institute's director, James S. Plaut, approached Wright in May 1939 to obtain his cooperation for "a one-man exhibition" that would open in November or December and circulate thereafter,[80] what could have resulted in conflict became collaboration, with the two institutions sharing costs for some photography and models. As Plaut concluded, "This is a splendid solution as it will enable us both to get twice as much for nothing or something like that."[81]

As it turned out, the Institute's exhibition was postponed; arrangements bogged down in the summer and fall, with both Plaut and Wright out of the country. When correspondence resumed, Plaut first rescheduled the show to January–February 1940 and then suggested a meeting.[82] It must have been during his ensuing visit to Taliesin, in the company of an Institute trustee, Nelson W. Aldrich, on the weekend of September 12–13, that Wright informed him of the pending exhibition at the Modern. Two weeks later, having returned to Boston, Plaut told Wright,

> I had several very pleasant meetings in New York with John McAndrew and Alfred Barr. I think it came to them as a complete surprise that we are contemplating the holding of a Frank Lloyd Wright exhibition prior to theirs, but they could not have been more amenable to the suggestion and cooperative in every way. I told them that it was our intention to do our exhibition along thematic lines rather than in the retrospective and historical way in which they will undoubtedly do theirs. They both approved of this difference in approach and are very anxious to have the material we use in our exhibition, though it may not be used by them in the same way.[83]

From the beginning, Plaut wanted Wright to deliver a lecture in Boston to coincide with the opening. An unintended consequence was a chance encounter between Wright and Gropius, who had immigrated from Germany in 1937 to teach at Harvard University.

26. Wright, Walter Gropius, and Ise Gropius at the members'
opening of the exhibition *Bauhaus: 1919–1928* at
The Museum of Modern Art, December 8, 1938. From
The Bulletin of The Museum of Modern Art 5, no. 6 (December 1938)

Although Gropius acknowledged a debt to the older architect's early work, Wright equated the former Bauhaus director with the International Style, and was aggressively antagonistic; one of his apprentices would later remember that he had refused to meet with Gropius in Madison in 1937.[84] But evidently relations later began to thaw, for a photographer captured the two in conversation at the opening of the *Bauhaus: 1919–1928* exhibition at the Modern on December 8, 1938 (fig. 26). The Boston exhibition was another opportunity for a meeting. As McAndrew confided to Mumford, "You may be glad to know that [Wright] has become reconciled to Gropius and even voluntarily proposed a toast to him at the grandest of the dinner parties."[85] In his memoir *Apollo in the Democracy*, written many years later, Gropius provided an insight into his rival's behavior: after the lecture, Gropius invited Wright back to his house, where they spoke freely. "He referred particularly to the fact that I had been made Chairman of the Department of Architecture at Harvard," Gropius recalled, "whereas he himself had never been offered such a position of influence when he was younger." When Gropius revealed the obstacles he had faced in obtaining commissions, Wright seemed bewildered. "His self-centeredness was irritating and at the same time disarming," Gropius concluded, "for he was hiding his hurt feelings behind a mask of haughty arrogance which gradually became his second nature."[86]

While Wright's reconciliation with Gropius may have been ambivalent at best, his association with Joseph Hudnut, Boston's other conspicuous champion of architectural modernism, he saw as unequivocally disastrous. Hudnut's involvement came about when Plaut was unable to secure his first choice for author of the principal essay in the show's publication. As he explained to McAndrew, "We are going to try to produce our catalogue along critical rather than documentary lines in an effort to trace the development of Wright's residential architecture and to evaluate each successive step."[87] To this end, Plaut asked Mumford to write a foreword of twelve to fifteen pages.

Unfortunately for both the Boston and the New York exhibitions, Mumford was engaged in a four-volume survey of Western civilization, *The Renewal of Life* (1934, 1938, 1944, and 1951). As Plaut told Wright a couple of weeks before the opening, "We tried to get Mumford to do a short preface to the catalogue, but he was too busy with his book, although he was very sympathetic to the idea."[88] Plaut then added, "Dean Hudnut has consented to write about a thousand words for us, and I hope that this will meet with your approval." The organization and content of the sixty-two-page publication were perfectly stated in its title, *Frank Lloyd Wright: A Pictorial Record of Architectural Progress. With notes selected from the published writings of the architect and a foreword by Joseph Hudnut, Dean of the Faculty of Design, Harvard University*. The bulk of the booklet consisted of photographs, and was, as Plaut explained, "thematic in character, and . . . restricted in scope to a general development of his residential architecture on the arbitrary premise that Wright is first and last a builder of homes—such successful monuments as the Larkin Building and Johnson buildings to the contrary notwithstanding."[89] This section was interspersed with quotations from Wright's writings of the 1930s.[90]

The two-and-a-half-page foreword is a complex document, but Wright perhaps understandably labeled it "the worst introduction I ever had."[91] He never recovered from what he saw as another damning critique. As the former head of Columbia University's architecture school and the dean of the design school at Harvard, Hudnut was in the forefront of the modern-architecture scene. He was publicly linked to the European avant-garde, to which he was drawn because it addressed urgent social issues and embraced technology, but he opposed functionalism in favor of a union of aesthetics and construction. Above all, Hudnut believed that modern architecture should directly reflect the experience and circumstances of modern life. In his foreword he defined Wright as "a poet" rather than "a logician," but admitted that the architect nonetheless fused "intuition and feeling" with "analytical experiment and invention." He admired Wright's "stratified space," which had its origin in function, but dismissed his forms as failing to "develop as inevitable necessities from his inventions." Finally, Hudnut could not come to terms with Wright's view of man and nature, concluding, "The genuine spirit of science, engaged in its eternal struggle with the forces hostile to man, addressed to a collective destiny, building patiently on foundations economically feasible, socially attainable, escapes him entirely; nor can he discover in the new architecture in which this spirit is manifest any quality other than sterility and a pernicious negation." Perhaps most offensive to Wright was the statement, "With all their assertion of modernity [Wright's houses] do not exist in a modern world integral with our time, our way of life."[92]

Wright was attracting record numbers of commissions in 1940, but only after years of financial hardship, and he could ill afford to have potential clients believe that he could not design a house suited to modern life. Hudnut's criticism made a searing impact on the architect, who was jealously guarding his recent successes. Ironically, the close cooperation between the Institute and the Modern, which had proved so harmonious for the curators, had unintended implications for Wright: he came to view the Boston show, which preceded the New York opening by nine months, as a dress rehearsal. Although there is no evidence that he objected to the Boston show itself, Hudnut's essay stayed in the forefront of his mind; as he told McAndrew later, "But for the suspicion aroused in me by the Boston experience all might have gone well. But for that I should have trusted you fully."[93] He became wary of McAndrew's choice of authors for the Museum's upcoming book and ultimately requested a preview before the essays were sent to the printer. After all the planning and research that went into the publication, it was doomed by the architect's fears of being dismissed by a proponent of the European avant-garde.

27. Frank Lloyd Wright

28. Alfred Stieglitz, 1932.
Photograph: Dorothy Norman

29. D. W. Griffith

Three Great Americans: Wright, Stieglitz, and Griffith

By late October 1939, as plans for the Boston show were being finalized, the program for the Museum's Wright retrospective was taking shape. First, the Trustees approved a trio of exhibitions under the title *Three Great Americans: Wright, Stieglitz, and Griffith*.[94] Although the grouping of these artists (figs. 27–29) was meant to convey a greater meaning than three independent presentations would have had (was meant to suggest, in other words, the preeminence of the United States in the arts of architecture, photography, and cinema), there appears to have been no attempt to coordinate the shows to match any overriding theme. Indeed, McAndrew's concept for the Wright retrospective was developed almost exclusively in concert with the architect alone.[95] The early exhibition proposal presented a straightforward chronological sequence: 1889–94, 1894–1911, 1911–35, the last years, and Broadacre City. The most important feature from Wright's point of view was a proposal to construct a full-scale Usonian House in the Sculpture Garden behind the Museum.[96] This ambitious plan to construct an experimental structure in the middle of midtown Manhattan, conceived without full knowledge of the legal and bureaucratic hurdles involved, would ultimately lead to misunderstanding and conflict. In 1939, however, these problems were in the future, and McAndrew reviewed the plans for the show with the architect over a two-day stay at Taliesin between October 20 and 26 of that year.[97]

With the architect committed to the retrospective, McAndrew turned his attention to the book. Wright's reputation for sensitivity to criticism probably affected the decision to conceive the publication as a Festschrift, comprising a series of essays and tributes of different lengths.[98] From the outset, McAndrew wanted both Mumford and Behrendt to write principal essays; like Plaut before him, however, he was unable to secure Mumford, no matter how often he tried.[99] At the end of January 1940, while preparing to spend two months in Mexico at work on the mammoth exhibition *Twenty Centuries of Mexican Art*, scheduled to open on May 15 of that year, he wrote to Mumford and Behrendt asking for an essay on a theme of their choice. Unfortunately Behrendt never received his letter, due to a change of address, and Mumford, hoping that progress on his book would allow him to participate, waited to reply until McAndrew's return from Mexico, so that the authors' participation remained unresolved for weeks.[100] When Mumford did respond, he explained he was too busy to undertake the project, noting that Behrendt was "in a better position . . . for he has actually seen more of Wright's buildings than I have."[101] The letter, opened by McAndrew's assistant, Janet Henrich, while McAndrew was still in Mexico, had a twofold impact: while alerting McAndrew that Mumford had declined, she immediately dispatched a follow-up letter to Behrendt.

Mumford was right about Behrendt's qualifications, for by 1940 this German critic had written one of the most laudatory and perceptive texts then in print on Wright's work. After emigrating to the United States in 1934 (the Nazis had dismissed him from his civil service position) to take a teaching post at Dartmouth College, New Hampshire, Behrendt visited the Midwest to see the architect's buildings. In 1937, when he published a popular textbook on modern architecture, *Modern Building: Its Nature, Problems, and Forms* (in which he extended themes from his earlier *Der Sieg des neuen Baustils*), he added a separate section on Wright. Speaking as a critic and reformer, he made a case for the radical architecture of the European avant-garde, primarily in mass housing; but a central tenet of his book hinged on the influence of America, specifically "that radiant triple star" so familiar to his close friend Mumford: Richardson, Sullivan, and Wright. Interestingly, for his new section on Wright Behrendt simply expanded the review of the architect's 1931 show in Berlin that he had published in the *Frankfurter Zeitung*. Although he wrote *Modern Building* six years later, and over twenty-five years after the design of the last building he illustrated or referred to in the text, he did not alter his arguments to include Wright's work between 1913 and 1937.[102] As a result, he ignored shifts in the architect's theory and style.

Behrendt repeated his earlier premise, "Wright's work is the first creation in the realm of architecture that can be regarded as an independent contribution of the American spirit to European culture."[103] Unlike almost any other writing of the time, this penetrating article went beyond a discussion of style to an analysis of the morphology of Wright's thinking, recognizing that the structural logic of nature was at the root of his architectural compositions. Concentrating on the revolutionary character of Wright's plans, Behrendt wrote, "In the projects in which Wright has achieved the maturity of his style, the rooms are arranged around the nucleus of the chimney part, like leaves of a plant around the stem. Radiating as if from a power center, they reach out into the garden and the landscape, opening themselves to the light and the view on all sides."[104] In one remarkable passage Behrendt also seized on the ephemeral element of light: "Wright treats light as if it were a natural building material. The graduated interplay of light and shade is to him an artistic medium of expression. And similarly, the air is evaluated as an element of form, is drawn into the concept of building. . . . With this inclusion of the air space in the formation, there is accomplished an intimate connection of the inside with outside, a new feature which from now on becomes the unmistakable characteristic of the modern house."[105]

Despite his admiration for Wright, however, Behrendt the reformer was committed to an architecture based on industrial technology rather than on art or tradition. He objected to Wright's use of ornament, and laid the blame on the generous budgets provided by affluent clients. Thus he qualified his praise by quoting Oud: "Wright the artist renounces what Wright the prophet proclaims."[106] He appreciated Wright in part as a figure from another time:

> The nineteenth century . . . was in art a period of great personalities. . . . In architecture probably the last of these . . . was Frank Lloyd Wright. His art is founded on the principle of general validity, the principle of organic structure which must be the guiding principle of the future, if architecture is again to be a living art. Yet the form in which Wright realizes and represents this general principle is unique: a personal creation, worthy of highest esteem, as a product of an exuberant imagination, full of grace and serenity, of gaiety and enjoyment of life, a form of such wealth as we shall not see soon again. The period of individualism which formed the background of his

art, giving the artist a full opportunity to develop his own personality to its utmost potentialities—this happy period is over. It was rudely ended by the World War.[107]

With the publication of *Modern Building* in 1937, Behrendt became one of the leading authorities on Wright in America. Seeming to overlook Behrendt's dismissal of his relevancy in favor of his adulation, Wright ordered the book in quantity for distribution to members of the Fellowship.[108]

In the spring of 1940, however, McAndrew, busy in Mexico, appears not to have informed Wright that he had asked Behrendt to write for MoMA's book. "Work upon the Wright exhibition has been seriously interrupted," the Modern's Architecture Committee reported on April 11, "by the Curator's taking charge of the installation of the Mexican exhibition."[109] Activity on the Wright retrospective was almost at a standstill. Eventually, in late May, it was Behrendt himself—while verifying facts—who informed Wright that he was writing an essay for the publication.[110] Immediately reminded of his experience with Hudnut only three months before, and also no doubt visited by lingering memories of the harsh criticism accompanying his 1931 Berlin exhibition, the architect sat down and wrote a warning letter to McAndrew even before replying to Behrendt: "Many felt that [Boston] show was put on with 'tongue in cheek' owing to the scandalous introduction by Gropius mouthpiece—Hudnut. . . . ," Wright explained. "Let's veer away from that sort of thing if we are heading into it. Once is enough." After posing the rhetorical question "Who sits in judgement?" he then pretended to read McAndrew's mind by jotting in the margin, "No, I am not getting a persecution complex—we, the people—are like that—that's all."[111] No response from McAndrew survives in the Wright or MoMA archives, so it is impossible to determine how he handled Wright's alarm; but with all the responsibilities following the opening of the Mexico exhibition on May 15, McAndrew did not turn his attention back to the Wright show itself until mid-June.

If Wright had had reservations about *Modern Building*, its publication had been outside his control; but a book connected to the first major exhibition of his work in his own home country was a completely different matter. When Wright imagined a book about his career, it would probably have been documentary: heavily illustrated with photographs (probably in color), plans, and perspectives, and supplied with descriptive text only, interspersed with quotations from his own writing. It is clear that McAndrew never consulted him about the Museum's publication, or even informed him of the numerous authors who had been chosen. When the architect learned, after the fact, of Behrendt's involvement, he was as gracious as possible. He wrote a short, straightforward letter answering the writer's queries and closed with, "I am glad that you are writing something. Undoubtedly it should have authority lacking in the perfectly silly foreword by Hudnut in the catalogue of the Boston show at the Museum of Modern Art last winter." In an attempt to affect the text positively, he added, "Why not come up and see me sometime?"[112] Wright's persuasive arguments had often turned adversaries into allies in the past. Behrendt did not respond to the offer.

30. Model of the Herbert F. Johnson House (Wingspread)
under construction by Wright apprentices
Curtis Besinger and Marcus Weston, summer 1940

Meanwhile another event was developing that would derail the Modern's plans for *Three Great Americans*: the cancellation of the exhibition's photography component. Alfred Stieglitz had been reviewing his work for the show with the future curator of the Department of Photography, Beaumont Newhall, when he became disenchanted with MoMA over a perceived slight and canceled his retrospective.[113] With his health in decline after a heart attack in 1938, he also admitted in a letter to Newhall on July 17, 1940, that he was physically unable to go through with it.[114] With Stieglitz's withdrawal, the original coherence of the three exhibitions was lost. Unfortunately, the pairing of Wright alone with a master of the silent screen took on a different meaning for the architect: the connotation of being viewed as an anachronism, or, as he put it to McAndrew, "a kind of 'Americana' extra, illustrated by a Griffith's bygone—etc."[115]

The Show to End All Shows

Since Wright was providing all the material for his retrospective, he had considerable control from the beginning. Shortly after McAndrew's visit in October 1939, he began preparations for new photography and models. To introduce the innovation of large-format color transparencies, he ordered apprentice Larry Cuneo to begin building a new photography studio at Taliesin.[116] By December he was seeking funds to support this project, so he asked McAndrew for money; when told the photo budget was set at $1,250, he requested all of it. McAndrew could not oblige, however, because the money would not be available until the next fiscal year, so Wright settled for a smaller advance.[117] Early in 1940 he instructed apprentices to begin construction on the more complicated models, including those for the Herbert F. Johnson House, "Wingspread" (Racine, Wisconsin, 1937–39; fig. 30); the Gregor Affleck House (Bloomfield Hills, Michigan, 1940); and Usonia I (Lansing, Michigan, 1939).[118]

As summer turned to fall, with Wright in Wisconsin and McAndrew and Barr in New York (although Wright made occasional trips east and McAndrew went more than once to Taliesin), they were, as things turned out, working at cross-purposes. Wright had an overpowering personality and a past experience of complete control over his exhibitions, and he wanted a show that would present his philosophy of architecture while promoting his most recent work. He hoped to tap the power and resources of the Modern to produce the most important exhibition of his work *he* had ever mounted—what he began to call "the show to end all shows"—and he brought all his skill at self-promotion to bear in his dealings with MoMA. The Modern, on the other hand, was seeking to provide a factual background and thematic dimension for one of two Americans, originators of a modern art form that had gone on to influence Europe. Equally important for the Museum was its obligation to the public—to organize its presentations so that an educated audience, as well as specialists, would come away enlightened.

As the weeks moved closer to the scheduled opening day—October 28[119]—events took a dramatic turn, resulting in bitter disappointment for both Wright and the Museum. In early September Wright began to focus with growing intensity on his agenda for the exhibition, his attention sparked by receipt of McAndrew's production schedule. Apparently ignoring McAndrew's efforts totally, he sought to take complete control over the program. "GETTING LOUSY WITH IDEAS CONCERNING CATALOGUE, SHOW, AND EXHIBITION HOUSE," Wright cabled McAndrew on September 10, "CAN YOU FLY UP WITH YOUR CATALOGUE ENGINEER AND WHAT MATERIAL YOU HAVE AND SEE WHAT WE'VE GOT." Later the same day he impatiently cabled again: "WANT TO SHOW YOU GENERAL SCHEME FOR CATALOGUE AND SHOW AND HOUSE. DROP EVERYTHING."[120]

31. Wright at Taliesin, 1940. He faces the model of Wingspread; behind him from foreground to background are models of Suntop Homes, Ardmore, Pa.; the S. C. Johnson & Son, Inc., Administration Building, Racine, Wisc.; and the Ralph Jester House, project for Palos Verdes, Calif.

McAndrew's brief trip to Taliesin two days later, between September 12 and 13, was more ominous than he realized at the time. First, Wright unleashed his ideas by giving McAndrew a tantalizing tour of dozens of models (fig. 31) and hundreds of unpublished drawings. Exploiting the curator's enthusiasm, he argued that his show should get more space; but McAndrew was compelled to explain that this was impossible, partly because the Griffith retrospective was slotted into several galleries, but also, he confided, because the Museum was working on a show known only to a few, "Exhibition X." Planned by Leslie Cheek, director of The Baltimore Museum of Art, and Mumford (unbeknownst to Wright), it had originated over the summer at the request of Abby Aldrich Rockefeller. With a program by Mumford and a design by Cheek, the exhibition, later known as *For Us, the Living*, was intended to tell "the American people of the dangers of Hitler's assault on the Free World and of the necessity for the U.S. to prepare itself for the inevitable war."[121] The innovative feature of the installation was to be the construction of an enormous gallery in the Sculpture Garden abutting 54th Street, the same size as the Museum itself, usurping the location for Wright's Exhibition Usonian House. The shock of hearing this news gave Wright pause; a few days later he would recall his momentary reaction, which was to consider canceling the show immediately. Telling the architect there was little room for change, McAndrew nevertheless cabled Barr requesting more space on the first floor.[122] The curator considered the matter so urgent that he asked Barr to telephone person to person; there is no record of whether or not this happened. Before he left, McAndrew dropped off at least two of the essays for the book, including Behrendt's. Wright read it within a day.[123]

What he discovered confirmed his worst fears. His aggression rising to the surface, he shot off his blistering cable warning "IF THE MUSEUM VALUES [Behrendt's] OPINION ENOUGH TO PASTE IT ACROSS THE FACE OF MY EXHIBITION THERE IS GOING TO BE NO EXHIBITION." The threat sparked a crossfire of telegrams and letters between New York and Wisconsin over the next five days. Unfortunately McAndrew's initial response inflamed matters still more: affirming that the Museum wanted to continue with the exhibition and book, he added, "WE HOPE WITH YOUR COOPERATION AND ADVICE." He also suggested that Wright cable information about what parts of the essay he disagreed with and the Museum "WILL TRY TO STRAIGHTEN MATTERS OUT."[124] This attempt to pacify the architect was destructive in the long run, as it implied that the Museum was inviting Wright to edit Behrendt's text. Handed this ammunition, Wright lost little time using it. First, he was outraged at the phrase "WE HOPE WITH YOUR COOPERATION AND ADVICE," demanding, "AM I TO UNDERSTAND FROM YOUR TELEGRAM THAT THE MUSEUM INTENDS TO CONTINUE WITH OR WITHOUT MY COOPERATION."[125] He then turned to Behrendt's essay, editing and rewriting passages, and on September 14 he instructed his apprentice Gene Masselink to retype the manuscript and mail it to McAndrew. The parts of Behrendt's essay that Wright objected to seem to have taken him back to the summer of 1931 in Berlin, when he had faced his harshest critics: as a personal retort, he revised his own text from that episode, sending it to McAndrew with the title, "To My Critics." Although well-meaning, McAndrew was clearly outmatched.

Having finished his work on the essay on September 14, and had time to think the matter over, on September 15 Wright turned to a campaign to obtain more space for his show. Realizing that his threat to withdraw, made only a few weeks before the opening, and McAndrew's conciliatory response to it had given him a powerful advantage, he began to soften his tone, but he did not back down. In two letters to McAndrew dated September 15 and 16, Wright laid out his case: he was surprised to have heard during the curator's visit about both the Griffith show and "Exhibition X." (The surprise seems genuine; perhaps he had not been previously told about them.) He was angry that these exhibitions were siphoning money from the budget and reducing the amount of space he needed for his show. "When you were here I thought I could go through with it," Wright explained to McAndrew, "though greatly disappointed to find that what was to be a concentration of the Museum's resources on a complete showing of my work was to be really several shows, encroaching on the space we needed to give a show in keeping with our powers and resources. I intended to make it the show to end all other shows of my work." Wright's upset seems justified: not only had McAndrew, after eight months of work, been unable to raise more than a fraction of the funds necessary to build the house in the Garden, but, more to the point, Wright had lost his Exhibition House site to the building required by "Exhibition X." Without naming names in the Museum, Wright appeared to look beyond McAndrew to those responsible for the lack of funds and space:[126]

> My only regret is—at the moment—that I seem to desert you at the last moment when you had evidently been having an uphill pull all the way. It is that "uphill pull" that I am resenting now. That there should still be (at this time) such back drag is quite too much when all is added together. But I hope we shall continue friends, John, just the same. I've never had much faith or respect for what the museum has come to represent so there is little lost there.

Meanwhile Wright was carefully structuring his argument so as not to withdraw definitively, as he continued to repeat, "By biding my time the whole matter might be greatly improved."[127] While Wright was biding his time, McAndrew was consulting Barr. The director told him that the Museum could not censor the essays, but "if Wright does not want a Festschrift on this basis we have no other alternative than to abandon it—but the decision is *immediate*."[128] McAndrew, under pressure to save a major exhibition that had already been publicized, crafted a letter on September 18 that solved the immediate problem but would cause fresh conflict in the future. In an effort to convince Wright to reconsider canceling the exhibition, he addressed two points: one was the publication, the other "Exhibition X." Unfortunately, what he told Wright about the publication was that the Museum had decided to cancel it since there was "no longer time to see an adequate catalogue through the press." He did not refer to the issue of censorship that Barr had brought up. In failing to face the issue squarely, McAndrew allowed Wright to believe that his objections to Behrendt's essay had had nothing to do with the decision to abandon the publication. This would become a bitter issue in the coming months, when the architect got a different impression from Barr. "Another surprise (in talking with Barr) was that you thought I had proscribed any catalogue at all," Wright complained to McAndrew after the opening, continuing,

> What I really expected (after you said that owing to my objection to gratuitous pre-mortem essays) there was no time to print the literary efforts you had collected with such good intention—to honor me I am sure—was that you would print the catalogue clean as you had already put the work of a real catalogue in upon it. I saw at the museum the feeling engendered by my objection to the ornamental part of it and suppose the feeling was, "well since he won't have the catalogue we wanted, let's see him get along without any."[129]

Wright either did not or pretended not to understand that without the essays, which constituted the bulk of the text, the only content remaining would have been the back matter—an illustrated catalogue raisonné and a bibliography.[130]

Next the Museum resolved several questions regarding Wright's request for more exhibition space and additional funding. "As to the space—we will give you the ground floor as originally planned (including the whole garden for the house)," he announced, "and in addition the five bays on the second floor facing the garden" (plate 2). The monies estimated for the Exhibition House—$5,500—had been raised and a contractor had been located who would build it at cost. Finally, "Exhibition X" had been canceled owing to questions of funding, clearing the way for Wright's show.[131] McAndrew told Wright, "The Museum wants to have the exhibition very much, and certainly does not want to make 'Americana' of your work, nor to bury you alive as an 'Old Master.' . . . May I beg you one last time to reconsider . . . I hope you will wire 'yes.'"[132]

McAndrew's letter explaining these points was delayed, and Wright became more agitated. He cabled, "IF SILENCE ASSENTS THAT MUSEUM INTENDS SHOW OVER MY HEAD WOULD LIKE INTERVIEW WITH MUSEUM AUTHORITIES WHEN I REACH NEW YORK NEXT WEEK WEDNESDAY."[133] That same day he also wrote another lengthy letter explaining that he needed to protect his future practice, because "Anyone reading the Behrendt piece as a preface to a voluntary showing of my work would consider these statements endorsed by me and would be foolish to ever employ me under any circumstances whatsoever."[134] McAndrew reassured by cable, "NO SHOW HERE WITHOUT YOUR CONSENT AND HELP. SORRY TO HAVE BEEN SLOW IN ANSWERING. LETTER WAS MAILED YESTERDAY."[135] Wright's next telegram arrived on September 20: "THAT EQUIVOCAL CATA-LOGUE GONE AGONY ABATED. AT WORK AGAIN ON EXHIBIT."[136] McAndrew was delighted. The result of Wright's confrontation with the Museum was the loss of the publication, but his tactics were successful: he gained the additional space he had been requesting, and, after months of uncertainty, he was assured that the Exhibition House would be built.

Behrendt's Essay: What Did Wright Object to and Why?

Much of Behrendt's essay was an updated version of the Wright section in his *Modern Building* book, published three years earlier. (That section itself, we have seen, expanded an earlier article in the *Frankfurter Zeitung*.) He did, however, introduce new themes central to his viewpoint: structural experimentation, low-cost housing (the Usonian House), and city planning (Broadacre City).[137] To prove Wright "a great genius, one of the greatest architects of all history," Behrendt structured his argument around several themes: the rejection of academic tradition in favor of a rationalist methodology; the transformation of the plan, elevations, and materials of building to adapt to a new social order; and the relentless pur-suit of a radical course of structural experimentation. He reserved his critical judgments for the final pages.[138]

On September 19, at the same time that his negotiations with McAndrew were coming to a head, Wright sent Behrendt a version of the essay showing the "presumptuous editorial amendments" that he had sent to the Museum five days earlier. Beyond taking minor exception to wordings and subtleties of interpretation, his fundamental disagree-ments boiled down to three: "You represent me as a reckless experimenter at the expense of my clients to gratify my own passion for mere experiment, and you misquote me and mis-understand my reference to the undesirability of *a* style (as any style whatever)—and finally you assume that I am a hangover from a past distrusted by youth today because of my personal style as a romanticist and therefore destined to disappear in the larger view of art which is impending."[139]

Behrendt had devoted a major section of the essay to the evolution of Wright's structural innovations, beginning with the Romeo and Juliet Windmill (Spring Green, Wisconsin, 1896) and concentrating especially on the foundation of the Imperial Hotel (Tokyo, c. 1912–23) and the concrete columns of the Johnson Administration Building. Wright took exception to the following statement:

> For the client it is no easy task to work with an architect who is such a passionate experimenter. . . . He has to be willing to put up with disappointment, inefficacy, weari-some detours, perhaps even failure. . . . A leaking roof matters little when a new build-ing material is tried out for the first time. The way to experience is through initial mistakes. In the development of Gothic construction the occasional collapse of vaults

of daring new construction was, as an experience, an important stimulant to further exploration.[140]

After a great struggle to emerge from bankruptcy, Wright could ill afford to scare potential clients with such an opinion.

Behrendt reserved his most serious qualifications for the final three paragraphs, and here Wright edited heavily. Behrendt took issue with the architect on the question of style by explaining,

> Although [Wright] seems to believe, concluding from his own statement, that "any style is offensive now," as an artist he is apparently so much of an individualist as not to see that, when forcing his personal style upon his clients, he is acting against his belief. . . . And for us, today, and particularly in architecture, as correctly stated by Wright himself, any style has become offensive, and most of all the personal one.[141]

Wright saw this statement as a complete distortion of his views. His disagreement with Behrendt, and with most architectural reformers of his day, was that they believed it was imperative to find a style—a modern style—to replace the historical styles of the past. For Barr, Hitchcock, and Johnson the answer had been the International Style; for Behrendt it was a modern vernacular, neither individualistic nor the product of avant-garde aestheticism but easily adaptable in the creation of humane social environments. By the 1930s Behrendt had come to accept the International Style as that anonymous new vernacular. There was, however, an important sense of the term "style" in Wright's use of it that Behrendt's own preconceptions led him to misunderstand. By "style" Wright did not mean a design methodology or set of characteristics that complied with a commonly understood definition; rather, he meant aesthetic expression that rose above the commonplace by the power of imagination. This is why he wrote in "To My Critics," the rebuttal of Behrendt that he sent to McAndrew as his contribution to the catalogue, "Any tyro may emulate any calculated superficial style. While much talk of principle goes with such calculated effort it is definitely a rationalizing after the fact because principles, if involved in this effort at *a* style, do not fructify creation." Then, using capitalization to reinforce his point, he stated, "I say, *a* style is no longer necessary because it cannot be individual and therefore cannot be free. Why let Style die that way again as it has died so many deaths heretofore?"[142]

Behrendt closed his essay by reprising his theme from *Modern Building*, calling Wright "one of the most imposing figures from the past period of individualism who has lived on into our time." Because Wright was "an emotionalist," "the younger generation is inclined to distrust him"; and yet, Behrendt concluded, the principle on which his work was based would last even if his forms did not. Infuriated by the last few sentences, Wright crossed out the entire paragraph, and where Behrendt had written "But even if the form in which he presented his ideas should prove to be evanescent," the architect inserted the phrase "and the individual and democratic state be replaced by the totalitarian or communistic or socialistic ideal of architecture." Wright was increasingly of the opinion that the disagreements between himself and the proponents of the International Style were fundamentally about politics as much as aesthetics.

Behrendt's closing paragraphs went to the heart of the argument Wright had had with European modernism for almost a decade, so it is no wonder that on the same day he read the essay he edited his own manuscript "To My Critics in the Land of the Danube and the Rhine," eliminating references to the 1931 Berlin dispute, otherwise refining the language, and retitling the piece "To My Critics." Wright's use of this text as his rebuttal to Behrendt is both revealing and ironic. First, it suggests that he had internally been propelled back to 1931, so that he associated Behrendt with the *Neue Sachlichkeit* critics of his Berlin show. Second, it had been Behrendt who had primarily defended him in that instance, using some of the very same arguments and even the exact language he would use in his essay for the Modern.

With Wright's letter the confrontation ended; Behrendt bowed out gracefully. On October 5 Wright composed a reply that was both blunt and warm at the same time; although clearly angry, he also conveyed his appreciation for Behrendt's longstanding support. "What you wrote was no doubt written in good faith even if mistaken as I believe," he admitted. "In self defense I have taken the unusual—perhaps unwarranted liberty of trying to rectify what I know to be mistaken. But, if you are not convinced, and are of the same opinion still—I shall be your friend just the same as before and hope someday we may understand each other better."[143] To this Behrendt graciously replied: "I regret that until now I did not have any opportunity to talk to you at length and to discuss with you the problems of our mutual interest. I know the loss is all on my side." He signed this letter, "In unchanged admiration I am, as ever, Sincerely yours."[144]

In private, though, Behrendt confided to Mumford his frank reaction: "It is a typical outburst of his exalted temperament. You should see the changes in the manuscript which he suggested: pure megalomania."[145] Mumford, who had already begun to sour on Wright over the war in Europe—Mumford was an uncompromising interventionist, Wright an equally ardent pacifist—had read Behrendt's essay in draft. "It is a wise and penetrating and beautifully balanced appreciation," Mumford had told his friend, "and it does honor and justice to its subject, as no other essay that I know has done."[146] "What depths of uncertainty must lie under that shell of success, for Wright to take such steps to protect himself against criticism," Mumford now surmised. "He must have more serious weaknesses than one suspected!"[147]

Exhibition Usonian House

The cancellation of the catalogue in September was an irretrievable loss, although several of the essays eventually appeared in journals. Nor was the publication the only disappointment: in early December, McAndrew learned that the Exhibition House, the most inventive aspect of the show, had also to be aborted.

Wright had intended the Exhibition House (fig. 32, plates 5–7) to be a full-scale Usonian House similar to the Herbert Jacobs House in Madison, Wisconsin (1936–37; fig. 33).

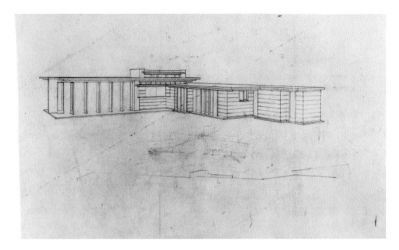

32. Frank Lloyd Wright. Exhibition Usonian House.
Project for The Museum of Modern Art, New York. 1940.
Perspective and elevation. Pencil on tracing paper, 13 x 22 ⅜" (33 x 56.8 cm)
The Frank Lloyd Wright Foundation

33. Frank Lloyd Wright.
Herbert Jacobs House, Madison. 1936–37

It was to be fully furnished and connected to New York City utilities for radiant heat and functioning plumbing.[148] Because the Usonian House was intended as an affordable housing solution for the middle class American family, numerous innovations in plan, materials, construction, and mechanical systems were introduced to lower costs. An L-shaped plan divided the house into public and private zones; one large room with fireplace combined the functions of living room, dining room, and study (plate 7). The bedrooms were small but were outfitted with generous storage. To reduce construction costs, kitchen and bathroom were built back to back. Materials were traditional and industrial—brick, machine-milled boards (usually cypress or redwood), and glass—and were left in their unfinished states and natural colors both inside and out. Wright's real originality, however, lay not in the modernity of the materials but in the radical concept of the building system. The house sat directly on a concrete mat, which served as both foundation and floor; after the brick fireplaces were erected, the prefabricated wood-sandwich walls were put in place. The opposition between the board-and-batten walls and the floor-to-ceiling glass French doors was a response to the typical setting imagined for the Usonian House, in suburbia: on the street side the house was closed for privacy but on the garden side it opened to light and the view.

Modern model houses had been built in Europe since the early 1920s, and the demonstration houses constructed at the Bauhaus. The tradition had continued with Le Corbusier's Pavillon de l'Esprit Nouveau, constructed for an exposition in Paris in 1925, and had reached a peak in 1927 with the Weissenhof Housing Colony, Stuttgart, designed by a range of modern architects headed by Mies and sponsored by the Deutsche Werkbund. Probably the project Wright envied most was Mies's Exhibition House of 1931 (fig. 34), a component of a show called *Die Wohnung unserer Zeit* (The dwelling of our time) that was part of the German Building Exhibition in Berlin.[149] Later the Museum would build two modern houses in the Sculpture Garden (Marcel Breuer, 1949; Gregory Ain, 1950), but when Wright suggested the idea, no American museum had incorporated a feature of such popular appeal in an architectural exhibition.[150] As novel as its construction in the Garden would have been, even more daring was the agreement to disassemble the house, crate the parts, and send it on tour.

34. Ludwig Mies van der Rohe. Exhibition House, *Die Wohnung unserer Zeit* (The dwelling in our time) exhibition, Berlin, 1931

Throughout 1940 the Exhibition House suffered numerous delays and setbacks that McAndrew and Wright, working together, overcame one by one. First were the issues of the construction estimate and McAndrew's fund-raising campaign; then, in order to obtain a building permit and hire a contractor, Wright's studio had to produce eleven sheets of working drawings (plates 10–20). The Exhibition House was logistically separate from the show—it had its own schedule, which called for it to open later but to remain on display much longer—but Wright grew impatient as the months passed, bombarding McAndrew with letters and cables: "When can we go to work? We are ready now. The mat should go down at once so the house can go up."[151] The permit process was long and difficult but the office of Philip L. Goodwin (a Museum Trustee and one of the architects of the Museum's new build-ing, completed the previous year) acted as the architect of record, obtaining, with some dif-ficulty, the required variances and approvals from the City of New York.

In trying to reassure Wright during the confrontation over the publication, McAndrew had inadvertently caused a problem by informing the architect he had "the whole garden for the house." Wright naturally took advantage of this opportunity to site the Exhibition House exactly where he wanted it: directly behind the Museum, so that it would be visible and directly accessible from the glass doors at the rear of the lobby. In response to McAndrew's suggestion of a different placement, he argued that in any other location "ALL PERSPECTIVES BECOME BAD, UNITY OF SHOW DISRUPTED." "HOUSE CAN GO WHERE YOU WISH BUT IT WILL THEN HAVE TO BE DEMOLISHED JANUARY 15," McAndrew responded, "IF IT CAN GO TWENTY-FIVE FEET OR MORE TO THE WEST IT CAN REMAIN UNTIL NEXT SEPTEMBER." Wright immediately retorted, "WOULD RATHER HAVE THE HOUSE RIGHT FOR A FORTNIGHT THAN WRONG FOR A YEAR. WHEN MAY WE START WE ARE READY."[152] In the end, however, neither the city building code nor the house's placement was the stumbling block that prevented its construction. The problem lay in the legalities of the land ownership behind the Museum, a situation of which neither Barr nor McAndrew, although they had collaborated together on the design of the Sculpture Garden (fig. 35) for the opening of the Museum's new building in May 1939, seems to have been fully cognizant.

The 100-by-400-foot plot (fig. 36) actually comprised three distinct areas, all pro-vided to the Museum by John D. Rockefeller, Jr. The lot immediately behind the Museum (fig. 37), 75 feet wide and 100 feet deep, was deeded to MoMA, but the lots to the west and east of it were at that time leased (fig. 38). Whether the land was owned or leased, how-ever, was not the issue: restrictions imposed by Rockefeller precluded the erection of *any* structures behind the Museum, except within a confined area too small for the Wright house no matter where it stood. McAndrew had thought of the house as an exhibit, not a building; Rockefeller disagreed. The deed and lease restrictions were clear, and Rockefeller rendered his final decision on the day the show opened. While the issue was strictly legal, he also raised aesthetic issues—"In my judgment," he wrote, "were such a house as contemplated built even temporarily, it would materially detract from rather than add to the appearance of the general area"[153]—and expressed his disapproval of Wright's low-cost housing: "I have myself been much interested in inexpensive, conveniently arranged, well built, modern homes and have spent some time and money in studying and experimenting with the problem," Rockefeller told John E. Abbott, the Museum's executive vice-president. "From what little I know of the subject," he went on, "it does not seem to me that the proposed building is economical either to build, to maintain or to operate."[154] At Abbott's request, McAndrew had argued the case to Rockefeller in a four-page memorandum, but both Rockefeller and the Chairman of the Board, Stephen C. Clark, were in accord. "I heartily concur in your criticism of the plan of this house," Clark wrote to Rockefeller. "As an attempt to solve the cheap housing problem, it is ridiculous and I am glad that it is not going to be erected in the garden."[155] On December 2, then, McAndrew informed the architect, "We shall have to give up the whole project. This comes hard, as it has been one of my pet schemes for about two years."[156] At this point the show was scheduled to close in a month, and Wright put up no fight. In the years ahead, however, he held tenaciously to the idea of building an Exhibition House in Manhattan despite all realistic obstacles, and in 1953 he was finally successful with his exhibition *Sixty Years of Living Architecture*, at the Fifth Avenue site of the future Solomon R. Guggenheim Museum.[157]

The Exhibition

Plans for the exhibition progressed through the fall in parallel with those for the Exhibition House. McAndrew, following standard procedure, composed a program, drew up a work schedule, and issued requests for the delivery of drawings and models; but once the Museum conceded to most of Wright's demands, the architect quickly took over all remaining aspects of the show, virtually ignoring the curator's careful preparations. Indeed, except for the outline he and McAndrew had worked out together, he reverted to the methods he had employed in his touring show of 1930, choosing all the material and designing and installing the exhibition. Aside from his experience in Boston earlier in the year, he had never previously worked with a museum (actually, before the founding of the Modern, in 1929, the opportunities to do so were rare indeed), and at the Chicago Architectural Club between 1893 and 1914 he had been accustomed to hanging his own work. In any case, Wright's dominating personality could never have been harnessed long enough to submit to a curator's program. Indeed, in a rare occurrence, the exhibition even opened with two titles, the Museum's—*Two Great Americans: Frank Lloyd Wright, American Architect, and D. W. Griffith, American Film Master*—and Wright's: *The Work of Frank Lloyd Wright: In the Nature of Materials*.[158]

As Wright's enthusiasm built up during the fall, he assigned apprentices to the fabrication of more and more models. "As the date for the exhibition grew nearer, . . . " Besinger would recall, "much more of everyone's time was required, and the pressure and tempo of work increased."[159] As a result, at Wright's instigation, the opening was postponed from

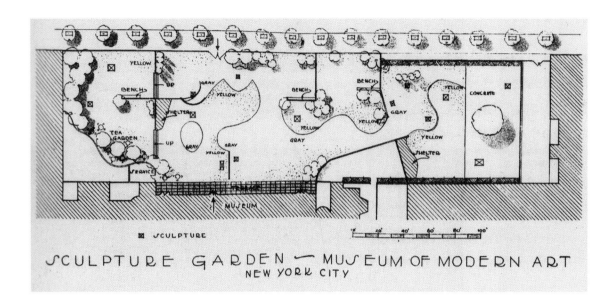

35. John McAndrew and Alfred H. Barr, Jr. Sculpture Garden
for The Museum of Modern Art, New York. 1939. Plan

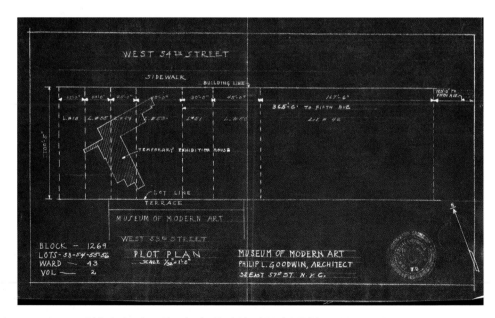

36. Philip L. Goodwin. Plot plan for Frank Lloyd Wright's Exhibition Usonian House. 1940.
Department of Architecture and Design Study Collection, The Museum of Modern Art, New York.
At the time, the Museum owned lots 51 and 53 and leased the lots to either side.
Only a small part of the Exhibition House site was on Museum-owned land

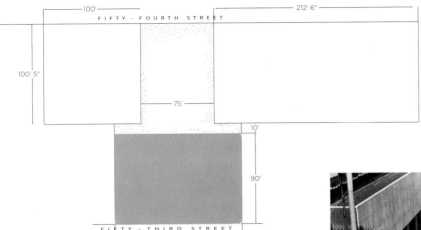

37. Site plan of the Museum, the rear lot it owned, and the two adjoining lots it leased from John D. Rockefeller, Jr., at the time of the Wright exhibition

38. McAndrew's and Barr's Sculpture Garden for the Museum in 1939, looking west toward the proposed site of Wright's Exhibition House

October 28 to November 12.[160] (The closing was scheduled for January 5, 1941.) Despite McAndrew's gentle pleadings, Wright respected neither the Museum's schedule nor its requests to receive materials in advance; setting his own timetable, he arranged to have all the materials in New York just three days before the opening.

"We emptied all the drawings out of the vault in rather strange disarray and put them on a truck," apprentice Victor Cusack would recall.

> And I went to New York, but The Museum of Modern Art was not at all prepared, because they wanted to know completely in advance exactly what was going to be shown, how was it going to be mounted and everything else. Mr. Wright wanted to, in his inimitable way, design the exhibition himself. But he felt he could only do that on the site when he had the drawings and he could pick and choose and decide what he wanted to show and what he didn't want to show.[161]

Wright had decided to use a truck to transport the material because it was a safer method than crating the models and model bases for shipping by rail. "Five apprentices—Gene Masselink, John Hill, Davy Davison, Marcus Weston, and Victor Cusack—were sent to New York . . . to help with the installation of the exhibit," Besinger reports.[162] The truck arrived at 53rd Street at the same moment as a caravan carrying First Lady Eleanor Roosevelt, who was paying a visit to the Museum during National Art Week. We "got in the way of her entourage," Masselink would recall, "and made her fifteen minutes late for her next appointment."[163] When Wright and his wife, Olgivanna, arrived, three intense days commenced of working around the clock. "The first thing that happened was that the entire staff of The Museum of Modern Art was required to turn to and mount all these drawings," according to Cusack.[164] At least one journalist noticed that the exhibition bore "the marks of a hurried completion."[165]

With the exception of a few views of Wright posed with models, or of models alone (figs. 39–43), no installation photographs of the exhibition have survived. One can only speculate on its design and layout from preliminary sketches (plates 1, 2), Wright's correspondence with the Museum, and newspaper accounts. The final outline, written by McAndrew but closely following Wright's ideas, laid out four sections on two floors (see the Appendix in the present volume).[166] On the ground floor the visitor was to move through a gallery titled "Reforming the House," which would explicate Wright's design philosophy and principles of organic architecture. Here models, drawings, and photographs would illustrate the topics "The Human Approach," "Simplification," "The Open Plan," "New Forms," and "Relation to Nature." A sketch (plate 1) for the installation also indicates a small gallery set aside for the projection of a color film, narrated by Wright, documenting the Taliesin Fellowship.[167] From the ground floor the visitor was originally to exit into the garden for a tour through the Exhibition House, first visible through the glass wall and doors at the rear of the Museum's lobby (fig. 44). For Wright this visual relationship was central to the installation: "The actual house in the court seen through the windows in connection with the plans and models inside the museum was my idea of the show."[168] On the second floor the

39. Wright viewing the model of the Frederick C. Robie House at *Frank Lloyd Wright: American Architect*, 1940. *Newsweek*, November 25, 1940, p. 28

40. Wright with the model of Wingspread, and with, behind him, the display racks he designed, at *Frank Lloyd Wright: American Architect*, 1940. From the *New York Times*, November 11, 1940

visitor would find two sections: "In the Nature of Materials," which focused on the use of both industrial and organic materials, and the twelve-by-twelve-foot model of Broadacre City (fig. 45).

From the sheer number of drawings and photographs on display it is evident that Wright preferred an encyclopedic survey to a more narrow scope emphasizing a distinct ideological point of view. "I wanted rather to give the 'folks' a comprehensive amble through the work of the years for a kind of 'birds eye view,'" he would explain.[169] There was also an emphasis on the projects and topics that European critics considered "modern." Of the twenty models probably displayed, for instance, only two dated to before 1925: the Robie House, favored by Dutch, German, and Russian critics as Wright's finest and most characteristic work of the Oak Park years (figs. 13, 39), and the San Francisco Call Building (1913), one of his relatively rare essays in that most modern of typologies, the skyscraper. The enormous new wood model (fig. 46) he had had made of the latter (replacing the much smaller original plaster one) extended from a base to within eight inches of the gallery ceiling, towering over the visitor. In addition to presenting a quantity of material, Wright wanted the show to be a vivid visual experience. It was rich in color—the models realistic, the perspectives rendered in delicate colored pencil. A most important innovation was the use of oversize color transparencies to record the architect's latest structures, such as Taliesin West (Scottsdale, Arizona, 1937–59).

Although all of McAndrew's letters indicate his belief that the Museum would supervise the design and installation of the exhibition, Wright gradually took over those functions. First, he asserted that he wanted the drawings and photographs unmatted, and they were to be shown separately because of the "danger of killing the drawings by photographs."[170] The show was to be organized around a series of freestanding screens supporting drawings (figs. 47, 48; plate 3), with hinged boards on the ends to mount photographs—a system almost identical to the one Wright had used in his show of 1930–31. The Taliesin Fellowship made the bases for the models (plate 4) in Wisconsin, although Wright asked the Museum to build fifty small plywood stools "so anyone so minded can sit down to the lower perspectives which are invariably enchanting."[171] The finishes and color scheme—unfinished walnut

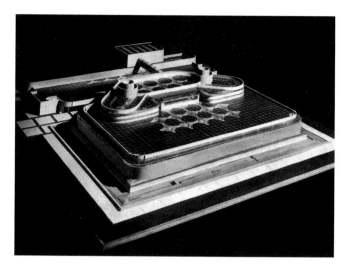

41. Frank Lloyd Wright. Usonia I, Lansing, Mich. Project, 1939.
Model with text panel at *Frank Lloyd Wright: American Architect*, 1940

42. Frank Lloyd Wright. S. C. Johnson & Son, Inc.
Administration Building, Racine, Wisc. 1936–1939. Model

43. Frank Lloyd Wright. Ralph Jester House, Palos Verdes, Calif.
Project, 1938. Model

plywood for the screens and model bases and "general wrapping paper tan" paint for the walls—were intended to keep "the show fresh and delicate."[172] One newspaper reported that Masselink had "designed two alphabets, one of two-inch letters and one of one-inch . . . making eight thousand letters of wood and fine veneer cut by members of the fellowship and used in setting up the titles and other legends."[173] Much of the text was to be glued to the bottom edges of the freestanding screens, leading McAndrew to warn Wright that if the public "bend down to read titles four inches from the floor they may get bumped often and intimately";[174] Wright responded with slight modifications.

Text panels presented Wright's ideas on a variety of subjects, including his scathing critique of the Federal Housing Authority. Although visual documentation of these panels is missing, an important one was quoted as saying,

> No building in the collection shown here is designed by way of taste. All are founded upon or rooted in principle. What romance and individuality each possesses is by way of principle at work. These buildings are what they are solely because principles understood are comprehensively and conscientiously practiced in conceiving and building them. These buildings have resemblances to each other not because of personal idiosyncrasy but because all have the countenance of principle.[175]

Masselink, clearly proud of the results of many days of intense labor, would recall, "We had about twenty beautifully made models and the effect of the softly lit walnut paneled walls and screens covered with drawings and photographs and then suddenly a model brilliantly lit like a solo dancer poised in the center of a carefully arranged space was dramatic and really breath-taking. The last room was devoted only to Broadacre City . . . which was brilliantly lighted with 'sun' of many lights and the walls were left dark."[176]

With these well-thought-out methods—the separation of the drawings and photographs, the delicate color scheme, the dramatic lighting, the descriptive text panels—Wright intended to create the "show to end all shows." But when the show opened (fig. 49), reviewers and critics generally saw it as a failure. The problem was not the work but the installation, which, as in the Museum's *Bauhaus: 1919–1928* exhibition of only two years earlier, was perceived as unintelligible.[177] Writing in the *New York Times*, Edward Alden Jewell, while conceding that "the installation . . . might be worse," also complained that "the whole oeuvre is virtually flung at you" with "no simple, systematically marshaled verbal exposition."[178] His colleague Geoffrey Baker concluded that the Broadacre City model "was unintelligible without a guide book."[179] Isabel Cooper in *New Masses* admitted that Wright was "a great American" but thought the exhibition consisted of "hundreds of uncatalogued items, labeled badly or not at all, with discrepancies of date and exaggerated claims, notably 'firsts' credited to the atelier Wright"; in fact the designer "simply plumps down contents of files, drafting-table drawers, etc.," and asks the visitor to take "your pick."[180]

The most damning critiques appeared in the art press. Milton Brown wrote in *Parnassus*, "We can only marvel at the scope of his genius, the amazing richness of his inven-

44. View from the Museum lobby into the Sculpture Garden, 1939

45. Wright's Broadacre City model, installed in the living room at the Taliesin Fellowship Complex. Wright included the same model in *Frank Lloyd Wright: American Architect*, but no photographs of its installation there have been found

46. Model of Wright's San Francisco Call Building under construction for *Frank Lloyd Wright: American Architect*, Taliesin, summer 1940. Left to right: Hans Koch with Wright apprentices Marcus Weston and Blaine Drake

47. Display racks designed by Wright at Taliesin, c. 1934

48. Display racks designed by Wright in the drafting studio at
Taliesin West, Scottsdale, Ariz. These racks are identical
to those used at the Museum in 1940

49. Invitation to the exhibition *Frank Lloyd Wright: American Architect*, The Museum of Modern Art, November 12, 1940–January 5, 1941. Pamphlet file, exh. 114, MoMA Archives

tion, and the revolutionary effect of his experiments," but he found the show "a bewildering mélange."[181] Dimitri Tselos in *Art in America* considered "the fragmentary and rather confused exhibition" "a real disappointment" and wished for "drawings and plans touched up, matted, and clearly labeled."[182] Even sympathetic reviewers directly or indirectly connected to the Museum offered qualified praise or outright criticism. Frederick Gutheim, who had provided citations for the bibliography, found it refreshing after years of viewing "slick drawings and presentations" to encounter "ink stains, dog-eared corners, and thumb prints," giving Wright's drawings "a frank

and refreshing authenticity and lack of pretense."[183] Talbot Hamlin, who sat on the Museum's Architecture Committee and had written an essay for the canceled Festschrift, said in *The Nation*, "Of the exhibition itself as a display it is charitable to say little." Nevertheless he said a lot, chiding Wright "as strangely lacking . . . in any conception of what ordinary museum-going Americans need in the way of explanation and guidance."[184] A consistent complaint, echoed by Brown, was that "surprisingly enough there is no catalogue."[185] This last criticism was

a particular sore point for the Museum, even motivating Barr to make a public statement: "Mr. Wright, insisting upon 'no prejudgments in advance of the show,' refused to permit the publication of the catalog as planned, although it had been intended as a tribute to him."[186]

Almost no one mentioned the meaning behind the pairing of Wright and Griffith (fig. 50); the reviewers simply failed to notice it. But the Museum issued a press release that was quoted in the *New York Times*:

> Actually a curious parallel exists. America's greatest film director and America's greatest architect . . . had an immense influence on European motion pictures and architecture. After the first World War this influence was felt in the country of its origin in the guise of new European trends, even though European architects and motion picture directors openly acknowledged their debt to Wright and Griffith.[187]

The criticisms proliferated despite the best efforts of the Museum, which had issued a press release titled "Greatest Living Architect Comes to Museum of Modern Art" before the opening.[188] Surely in an effort to secure a favorable review, Sarah Newmeyer, the director of the Museum's publicity department, forwarded this document to Mumford along with a personal note.[189] She was obviously unaware of his thoughts on the show, at least as he wrote on them to Behrendt; the letter itself is lost, but Behrendt replied, "I went to the exhibition . . . which convinced me that my last article was much too tame in its criticism. I heartily agree with everything you say in your last letter about your own experience in the show: badly arranged and bare of all instinct in the selection of material. And his latest work is full of the same formalism and doctrinism which he so loudly and frequently criticized in Le Corbusier's work."[190] Mumford did in fact write a review, but did not publish it. There is no way to determine for certain what transpired, but Wright's behavior during the exhibition's press preview would certainly have incurred his ire: playing off a story that had dominated the headlines for months—of the Blitz, the massive German air raids on London—Wright chose to present Broadacre City as bombproof. Under the subtitle "Says an Optimist Could Find a Blessing in the Destruction of European Cities," the *New York Times* quoted the architect proclaiming, "I would not say that the bombing of Europe is not a blessing because at least it will give the architects there a chance to start all over again." Making a case for his decentralized model community, he added, "Concentration of population is murder—whether in peace time or in war."[191] When reminded of the destruction of London buildings designed by Christopher Wren, Wright retorted, "I don't think anyone will miss Wren's work very much."[192] Although these sentiments won Wright space in the newspapers, to many they must have appeared insensitive or worse.

By May 1941 Wright's isolationist political views had become so vociferous that Mumford broke off contact with him. They did not speak for ten years.[193] Mumford's silence was one of the great losses of Wright's entire career, given the writer's profound insight into Wright's enduring value—a unique perception for its time, and quite clear in his unpublished review of the MoMA show. Although Mumford briefly mentions the exhibition's inadequacy, he directs most of his remarks to a critique of Wright as an architect and engineer. Taking into account the work of the 1930s, he concedes that Wright is not the leader of a movement for a modern vernacular; instead, he is a formalist. "The human being whose needs he would satisfy," Mumford concludes, "is one who like himself puts architectural logic and esthetic design above every other need in a dwelling place." Yet Mumford rises above polemics to capture one of Wright's unique characteristics: a universality far greater than the International Style.

> He was to bring together, by a complete act of spiritual assimilation, the East and the West; he was to create new forms in which the native talents of the West, with its rationality, its skillful engineering, its mechanized energy would be united to the patient handicraft and love of nature that had flowered in the Japanese dwelling. . . . this union of the orient and occident, which took place long before anyone dreamed of calling the work of Le Corbusier and his imitators the international style, will probably remain one of Wright's outstanding contributions to forms.[194]

In the Nature of Materials

As the reviews appeared in the weeks after the opening, Wright's opinion of the show changed markedly. He was obviously stunned by the criticism that the exhibition was unintelligible, which made him sensitive to the Museum's sign reading "Arranged by the architect himself." He also picked up on the comment that the absence of a publication added to the show's confusion. As a result he took action in two ways. First, in several letters to

50. Exhibition announcement for the simultaneous Wright and D. W. Griffith retrospectives. Pamphlet file, exh. 114, MoMA Archives

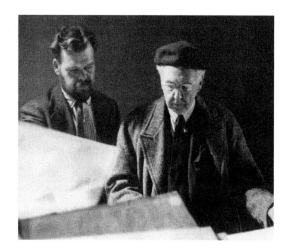

51. Hitchcock and Wright reviewing drawings for
In the Nature of Materials, 1941

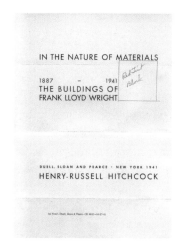

52. Frank Lloyd Wright. Title page for
Henry-Russell Hitchcock, *In the
Nature of Materials: 1887–1941,
The Buildings of Frank Lloyd Wright*
(New York: Duell, Sloan and Pearce,
1942). Proof, 10 x 9"

McAndrew, he expressed his displeasure, requested that the sign be removed, and refused to allow the exhibition material to continue on as a traveling show.[195] Second, less than two weeks after the opening he wrote to Henry-Russell Hitchcock with a tantalizing offer. To make sure the show "could be truly memorialized, properly on record instead of passing out forlornly misunderstood as it is now likely to do," Wright proposed hiring Hitchcock to put photographs "in serial order perhaps under the classification I attempted which was 'in the nature of materials' (grouping buildings under structural headings with some heed paid to chronology) but with not so much critical reviewing as interpretation of the ideas explaining facts with proper significance." At the same time that Wright was making his intentions for the book clear, he recognized the need to allow the historian latitude: "The work would be entirely yours and would be as you would have it of course. My function or the relation of any one else in relation to it would be purely as you needed or could use it." As further inducement, Wright provided a financial arrangement: he would secure publication and pay "all your expenses and $250.00 besides, guaranteeing you another advance of $250.00 from the publisher—the royalties above that to go 2/3rds to you and 1/3rd to me. The money is not much for your pains but more might come thru later."[196]

Hitchcock must have foreseen the need for such a publication, since he agreed immediately in an eighteen-page handwritten letter.[197] Several months earlier, in fact, he had described his ideal Wright book to McAndrew as

> a continuous and coherent critical study . . . so that for once . . . his work could be all seen and all studied in one volume. There have, I think, been too many tributes to the man and too few serious objective studies. . . . However, I imagine that the chances of giving offense are rather great and while he is alive such a study might be dangerous to make. If you can get the ingredients together, . . . that will alone be worthwhile. As I have gathered together the Wright books . . . I am again amazed how useless most of them are, how confused, uncritical, and generally dominated by some of the more personal aspects of the man.[198]

Wright with display racks, drafting room,
Taliesin West, c. 1942

As the show came to a close, Wright's attention shifted to his publishing venture with Hitchcock (fig. 51),[199] who, because of his close ties with the Museum, had open access to the catalogue raisonné of executed buildings and projects previously compiled by Henrietta Callaway, a researcher in the Museum's Department of Architecture, and to drawings and photographs exhibited in New York. Hitchcock was well placed to execute Wright's desire to "memorialize" the exhibition, then, but as the book took shape through 1941, conflict inevitably arose. Hitchcock approached his task by conducting research, composing his text, and determining the size, shape, and graphic layout of the material to be illustrated. As a result, he wanted the book to have an oblong format. Wright, however, had made arrangements with his publisher—Duell, Sloan and Pearce—to bring out the volume as part of a "triptych" along with *On Architecture* (an anthology of his writings edited by Gutheim) and a revised edition of *An Autobiography*. As a result, he took considerable offense at Hitchcock's desire for an oblong format, since the other two books were square. Disagreement also arose over the buildings illustrated, the photographs, and the page layouts (fig. 52).[200] Wright won on some points, such as the square format, but conceded on others. In the end, when the book appeared, in the spring of 1942, the reviews were excellent, and he seemed to take his cue from them when he wrote Hitchcock a brief, uncharacteristically lukewarm note—neither searing in criticism nor effusive in praise: "I am wondering how you like the new book and your role of expositor instead of critic? It seems becoming to you. I agree with your critics—you have 'done a good job.'"[201] In light of their recent encounter, the most gracious review came from Behrendt in *The Yale Review*. He pointed out the text was "subsidiary to the illustrations," making the book more "a *catalogue raisonné* rather than a critical analysis of Wright's art"; but he termed it "long overdue and much wanted in view of the high rank this architect holds." Salvaging one line from his unpublished essay, he closed by reiterating yet again, "In our midst there is living a great genius, one of the greatest architects of all history."[202]

Even in its truncated form, the Wright retrospective was a landmark architectural exhibition in the Museum's history, ranking with the 1932 "International Style" show and the historic Mies exhibition of 1947. The book, had it been published, would have been the first comprehensive publication on the architect's career ever undertaken in his native land. Even as it turned out, the meticulous research applied to the catalogue raisonné, once appended to *In the Nature of Materials*, served as the definitive source on Wright's work for almost fifty years. And despite the bitter disappointments of 1940, Wright's architecture continued to be exhibited at the Museum until his death, in 1959, and well beyond.

NOTES

This study could not have been completed without the cooperation, assistance, and support of three institutions. First, the author is grateful to the staff of The Museum of Modern Art, especially John Elderfield, Peter Reed, Michelle Elligott, and William Kaizen; of the Frank Lloyd Wright Archives, especially Bruce Brooks Pfeiffer, Oscar Muñoz, and Margo Stipe; and of the Getty Research Institute, especially Wim de Wit and Mark Henderson. Robert Wojtowicz, Kai Gutschow, and Thomas S. Hines provided invaluable assistance. On innumerable occasions, Randall H. Kennon and Thomas M. Hartmann gave timely suggestions and encouragement. This essay is part of my forthcoming book, *Wright on Exhibit, 1894–1959.*

The designation "MoMA Archives" refers to The Museum of Modern Art Archives, New York. "FLWA" indicates the Frank Lloyd Wright Archives, Taliesin West, Scottsdale, Arizona. Since both Wright and the Museum kept copies of much of their correspondence with each other, many documents appear in both places; I have noted the archive in which I found each document cited here, but its presence in one archive does not preclude the presence of an identical or similar document in the other.

1. Geoffrey Baker, "Wright as Iconoclast," *New York Times*, November 24, 1940. Public Information Scrapbooks, MoMA Archives, reel 12, frame 623.

2. Milton Brown, "Frank Lloyd Wright's First Fifty Years," *Parnassus* 12, no. 8 (December 1940): 37, and Dimitri Tselos, "Frank Lloyd Wright," *Art in America* 29 (January 1941): 42.

3. Frank Lloyd Wright, telegram to John McAndrew, September 14, 1940. FLWA.

4. McAndrew explained to Wright, "There is no longer time to see an adequate catalogue through the press—and after all the exhibition need not be incomplete without a catalogue." McAndrew, letter to Wright, September 18, 1940. FLWA.

5. Department stores such as Macy's had sponsored model houses. Alfred Frey and A. Lawrence Kocher had built their Aluminaire House at a New York exhibition of the Architectural League in 1931, and thirteen houses, including George Keck's "House of Tomorrow," had been shown in 1933 at the Century of Progress Exposition in Chicago.

6. Wright, letter to E. Baldwin Smith, February 8, 1930. FLWA.

7. Smith, letter to Wright, February 10, 1930. FLWA.

8. Wright appears to have been interested in promoting a major exhibition of his work as early as 1927. He apparently broached the subject with the Dutchman Alphons Siebers who, in turn, wrote to H. P. Berlage. Berlage demurred and suggested J. J. P. Oud as a better contact. Oud was ill and the matter was dropped. See Donald Langmead and Donald Leslie Johnson,

Architectural Excursions: Frank Lloyd Wright, Holland and Europe (Westport, Conn., and London: Greenwood Press, 2000), p. 109.

9. Wright, letter to W. R. B. Willcox, October 17, 1930. FLWA. Although Wright mentions four models in this letter, eventually there were five, all representing work of the preceding five years: the Blue Sky Mausoleum project (1928), the San Marcos Water Gardens project (1929), the Richard Lloyd Jones House (Tulsa, 1928–31), the Gas Filling Station project (1927–30), and, the image most often reproduced in press coverage, the St. Mark's-in-the-Bouwerie Towers project (1927–31).

10. The draftsmen who worked on these drawings were Heinrich (Henry) Klumb from Germany, Takehiro Okami from Japan, and Rudolph Mock from Switzerland. As Klumb remembered later, "I suggested that we might try to reduce his delicate renderings of his best known buildings to two-dimensional black on white graphic presentations that modern architects were addicted to. His answer: 'do it.' Okami and I went to work and produced several, including the Robie House (drawn by myself), the Winslow House, Yahara Boat Club, Bock Atelier, Unity Temple, and the Larkin Building. All were drawn in ink on roll-up window shades." In Edgar Tafel, ed., *About Wright: An Album of Recollections by Those Who Knew Frank Lloyd Wright* (New York: John Wiley & Sons, 1993), pp. 101–2.

11. The published literature on this traveling exhibition contains many disagreements on its venues and dates. The sequence in the United States was as follows: Princeton University (May 6–14, 1930); Architectural League, New York (May 29–June 12, 1930); Art Institute of Chicago (September 25–October 12, 1930); State Historical Library, Madison (October 15–25, 1930); Layton Art Gallery, Milwaukee (November 20–December 8, 1930); Art Museum, University of Oregon, Eugene (March 6–10, 1931); and Henry Gallery, University of Washington, Seattle (March 11–15, 1931). Wright also tried to line up stops at Yale University, Cornell University, Harvard University, and in Los Angeles, San Francisco, and Ann Arbor, but these attempts failed. The European tour was as follows: Stedelijk Museum, Amsterdam (May 9–31, 1931); Preussische Akademie der Künste, Berlin (June 17–July 12, 1931); Staatl Beratungsstelle für das Baugewerbe, Stuttgart (July 22–August 16, 1931); Kunst van Heden, Koninklijke Maatschappij der Bouwmeesters, Antwerp (September 12–28, 1931); and Palais des Beaux-Arts, Brussels (October 3–11, 1931).

12. Donald Walker accompanied the exhibition to several venues in the United States. Klumb arrived in Germany in December 1930 to secure venues in Europe. Contrary to some published accounts, it was Klumb rather than H. Th. Wijdeveld who initiated this work, approaching supporters of Wright, especially Wijdeveld, Heinrich de Fries, and Erich Mendelsohn, to whom Wright had written in advance. After a conflict arose among these three, Klumb deferred to Wijdeveld, who took the leading role. Although Paris was suggested as a

venue, that did not materialize; Klumb's passport was expiring and Wright could no longer afford his salary after the Brussels show. Klumb, letters to Wright, January 12, February 13, March 5, March 12 (with marginal note from Wijdeveld), May 28, and July 16, 1931, and telegrams to Wright, July 25 and August 25, 1931; Wright, letter to Klumb, January 26, 1931, and telegrams to Klumb, January 26, March 20, May 12, July 3, July 20, July 28, and August 26, 1931; and Michael (Kostanecki), George (Cronin), and Karl (Jensen), letter to Klumb, n.d. FLWA.

13. The arrangements for the European tour began in conflict. Friction arose when de Fries insisted that the show open in Berlin rather than Amsterdam, requiring Klumb to negotiate the dispute. De Fries finally withdrew, allowing Wijdeveld to gain a more dominant role. The Dutch and German venues were secured, but Klumb's ambitions for the tour included France, England, Austria, Switzerland, and Sweden. These plans failed for a variety of reasons, especially Klumb's personal situation: his passport was expiring on September 26; he was engaged to be married and intended to bring his wife back to Taliesin, but the American government refused him permission to enter the country without a written statement from Wright detailing his employment and providing an exact declaration of his salary. In addition, Wright's finances were desperate and he could no longer afford to send Klumb a stipend to support him in Europe. De Fries, letters to Wright, December 14, 1930, and January 20 and 24, 1931; Wijdeveld and Klumb, telegram to Wright, March 28, 1931; Wright, letters to Wijdeveld, April 6 and May 12, 1931, and telegrams to Wijdeveld, March 30 and April 29, 1931; Wijdeveld, telegrams to Wright, April 14, April 16, April 22, and May 10, 1931. FLWA.

14. The German Building Exhibition was held in Berlin from May 9 to August 2, 1931. See Wallis Miller, "Mies and Exhibitions," in Terence Riley and Barry Bergdoll, *Mies in Berlin,* exh. cat. (New York: The Museum of Modern Art, 2001), pp. 338–49.

15. Klumb, letter to Wright, May 28, 1931. FLWA.

16. Philip Johnson, letter to Alfred H. Barr, Jr., July 11, 1931. Department of Registration exhibition files, Exh. #15, Johnson-Barr/Blackburn Correspondence, MoMA Archives. Also quoted in Riley, "Portrait of the Curator as a Young Man," *Studies in Modern Art no. 6: Philip Johnson and The Museum of Modern Art* (New York: The Museum of Modern Art, 1998), pp. 41–42.

17. See Riley, *The International Style: Exhibition 15 and The Museum of Modern Art* (New York: Rizzoli International, 1992), p. 74.

18. Wijdeveld, ed., *The Life-Work of the American Architect Frank Lloyd Wright* (Santpoort, the Netherlands: C. A. Mees, 1925).

19. Wright, telegram to Wijdeveld, April 6, 1931, and Wijdeveld, telegram to Wright,

April 22, 1931. FLWA. See Wright, *In the Cause of Architecture: Essays by Frank Lloyd Wright for Architectural Record, 1908–1952,* ed. Frederick Gutheim (New York: Architectural Record Books, 1975), pp. 131–230. The publication that served as a catalogue in Amsterdam was a section of an issue of a Dutch architectural magazine, *Bouwkundig Weekblad Architectura* 52 (April 4, 1931): 117–28. This periodical comprised comments by Wijdeveld and text from three of Wright's lectures—"The Architect and the Machine," "Technique and Imagination," and "The New World"—translated into Dutch and extensively illustrated with drawings and models dated between 1927 and 1930. On Wijdeveld's motives see Langmead and Donald Leslie Johnson, *Architectural Excursions,* pp. 113 ff.

20. See Penny Fowler, *Frank Lloyd Wright: Graphic Artist* (San Francisco: Pomegranate, 2002), pp. 114–15.

21. Henry-Russell Hitchcock, *In the Nature of Materials: 1887–1941, The Buildings of Frank Lloyd Wright* (New York: Duell, Sloan and Pearce, 1942).

22. In 1927, although *Neue Sachlichkeit* was in the ascendancy, it was still possible for Ernst May, editor of the polemical organ *Das neue Frankfurt,* to ask Wright to contribute to a special issue on the topic of concrete construction and flat roofs. Wright's short text, three elevations, and a ground-floor plan appeared alongside contributions from Oud, Le Corbusier, André Lurçat, Heinrich Tessenow, and others in "Das Flache Dach," *Das neue Frankfurt* 1, no. 7 (October–December 1927): 186–88. May, telegram to Wright, August 26, 1927. FLWA. May had seen Wright's work in Oak Park on a trip to America in 1925. See Robert Wojtowicz, *Lewis Mumford and American Modernism: European Theories for Architecture and Urban Planning* (Cambridge and New York: Cambridge University Press, 1996), p. 86.

23. These articles appear in a scrapbook of newspaper clippings and photographs of the 1931 tour compiled by Wijdeveld. The scrapbook gives the erroneous impression that Wijdeveld was the organizer and designer of the traveling exhibition; in fact Wright, and possibly members of his studio, chose the material and designed the panels. Adjustments were made in Europe, but principally by Klumb. Wijdeveld did design graphics that accompanied the exhibit in Amsterdam. Wijdeveld, ed., "Frank Lloyd Wright Scrapbook, 1931," archival #950024, 2 microfiche, Getty Research Institute. The original is in the FLWA.

24. One reviewer, whose essay was subtitled "Greatness and Decline of a Pioneer" of Modern Architecture," clearly stated that Wright had been highly regarded in Europe before 1910 yet had suffered a "fall from grace": "One has to say that America and her Babbitts completely took over this man, who was for us a great hope and paragon." (Babbitt, of course, is the eponymous businessman hero of Sinclair Lewis's bourgeois-debunking novel of 1922.) The article is quoted in Wilhelm Lotz, "Frank Lloyd Wright und die Kritik," *Die Form* 6

(September 1931): 357. Although Lotz describes the piece as anonymous, the full citation is Paul F. Schmidt, "Grösse und Niedergang eines Bahnbrechers der modernen Architektur," *Baukunst* 7 (August 1931): 278–79.

25. Of Ernst Wasmuth's two smaller books, one, *Frank Lloyd Wright, Chicago*, was rejected by Wright and consequently reserved for European distribution only. The book available in the United States was *Frank Lloyd Wright: Ausgeführte Bauten und Entwürfe*. See Anthony Alofsin, *Frank Lloyd Wright: The Lost Years, 1910–22. A Study in Influence* (Chicago and London: The University of Chicago Press, 1993), p. 76.

26. Walter Curt Behrendt, "Frank Lloyd Wright, Chicago. Achtes Sonderheft der Architektur des zwanzigsten Jahrhunderts. Ernst Wasmuth, A.-G. Berlin 1911," in *Kunst und Künstler* 2, no. 9 (September 1913): 487.

27. See Alan Crawford, "Ten Letters from Frank Lloyd Wright to Charles Robert Ashbee," *Architectural History* XIII (1970): 68–69.

28. Quoted in ibid., p. 70. For Ashbee's complete English text with the excised passages printed in italics see Alofsin, *Frank Lloyd Wright: The Lost Years*, Appendix B, pp. 313–16.

29. Behrendt visited Chicago, New York, and Pittsburgh. See Detlef Mertins, "Introduction," in Behrendt, *The Victory of the New Building Style*, 1927, Eng. trans. Harry Francis Mallgrave (Los Angeles: Getty Research Institute, 2000), p. 18.

30. See M. David Samson, "'Unser Newyorker Mitarbeiter': Lewis Mumford, Walter Curt Behrendt, and the Modern Movement in Germany," *Journal of the Society of Architectural Historians* 55, no. 2 (June 1996): 126–39. On Behrendt before his move to America see ibid., pp. 1–84.

31. Lewis Mumford, *Sticks and Stones: A Study of American Architecture and Civilization* (New York: Boni & Liveright, 1924); "The Social Background of Frank Lloyd Wright," in *Wendingen* (1925); *The Brown Decades, A Study of the Arts in America, 1865–1895* (New York: Harcourt, Brace and Company, 1931).

32. Mumford, *The Brown Decades*, p. 165.

33. Le Corbusier, *Towards a New Architecture*, 1923, Eng. trans. Frederick Etchells (New York: Payson & Clarke, 1927).

34. Mumford, "Frank Lloyd Wright and the New Pioneers," Appendix A in Donald Leslie Johnson, *Frank Lloyd Wright versus America: The 1930s* (Cambridge, Mass.: The MIT Press, 1990), p. 349. Originally published in *Architectural Record* 65 (April 1929): 414–16.

35. Ibid., p. 350.

36. Behrendt's argument, which seems remarkably similar to Mumford's, caught the attention of many critics. Lotz, Behrendt's

successor as editor of *Die Form*, wrote an editorial in response to the question posed by the title; his unique answer was: both. Lotz, "Frank Lloyd Wright und die Kritik," pp. 357–58.

37. Behrendt, "Frank Lloyd Wright: Zur Ausstellung in der Akademie der Künste in Berlin," *Frankfurter Zeitung und Handelsblatt*, June 30, 1931. After reading Behrendt's article, Mumford told Wright, "So acute on the whole, and so appreciative and honest." Mumford, letter to Wright, August 14, 1931. FLWA.

38. There is no surviving correspondence from Klumb for this period, but it can be assumed that either he or Wijdeveld mailed the clippings to Wright at Taliesin.

39. I have been unable to verify whether or not Wright's text was published in the *Frankfurter Zeitung*. It was published in full, however, in *De 8 en Opbouw* 3, no. 18 (September 2, 1932): 177–84, with a rebuttal by Sigfried Giedion, "Die architektonische Front," and comments by the editor, Johannes Duiker. The text is reprinted as "Frank Lloyd Wright's Manifesto" in *Forum* 22, no. 6 (January 1972): 136–37. See also *Frank Lloyd Wright: Collected Writings, 1931–39*, ed. Bruce Brooks Pfeiffer (New York: Rizzoli International, in association with The Frank Lloyd Wright Foundation, 1993), 2:18–20.

40. Wright was using the term "International Style" far in advance of the opening of The Museum of Modern Art's "International Style" exhibition (actually titled *Modern Architecture: International Exhibition*), in February 1932. Philip Johnson had used the term in print the year before, however, in "The Architecture of the New School," *Arts* 17 (March 1931): 393–98. Even from the distance of Wisconsin, Wright was following events in New York carefully. For the definitive account see Riley, *The International Style*, pp. 89–93, and also Richard Guy Wilson, "International Style: The MoMA Exhibition," *Progressive Architecture* no. 2 (February 1982): 97.

41. Johnson, letter to Mumford, January 3, 1931, as quoted in Riley, *The International Style*, p. 26 and note 26.

42. Barr, "Notes on Russian Architecture," *The Arts* 15 (February 1929): 106.

43. Mumford, letter to Wright, January 10, 1932, in Pfeiffer and Wojtowicz, eds., *Frank Lloyd Wright and Lewis Mumford: Thirty Years of Correspondence* (New York: Princeton Architectural Press, 2001), p. 121.

44. Hitchcock, "Frank Lloyd Wright," in Hitchcock, Johnson, and Mumford, *Modern Architecture: International Exhibition*, exh. cat. (New York: The Museum of Modern Art, 1932), pp. 30–31.

45. Ibid., p. 38.

46. Johnson, letter to Oud, April 16, 1932, quoted in Riley, *The International Style*, p. 41.

47. Johnson sent Wright a copy of his pamphlet *Built to Live In*, published by the

Museum in 1931. Riley explains, "Slightly coy, it does not identify publicly the architects chosen for the exhibition, although a certain amount of reading between the lines gives a clue as to the names of the world's 'most prominent architects.'" Ibid., p. 44. Later, in a letter to Wright dated February 28, 1933, discussing details of the continuing traveling exhibition, Alan R. Blackburn, Jr., executive director of the Museum, verified that the pamphlet had been sent. FLWA. The text of the pamphlet is reprinted in *Philip Johnson: Writings*, foreword by Vincent Scully, introduction by Peter Eisenman, commentary by Robert A. M. Stern (New York: Oxford University Press, 1979), pp. 28–31. Stern dates the publication to March 1931.

48. Wright, telegram to Johnson, January 18, 1932. FLWA.

49. Mumford, telegram to Wright, January 21, 1932. FLWA.

50. See Riley, "Portrait of the Curator as a Young Man," p. 37; Stern, Gregory Gilmartin, and Thomas Mellins, assisted by David Fishman and Raymond W. Gastil, *New York 1930: Architecture and Urbanism between the Two World Wars* (New York: Rizzoli International, 1987), p. 343; and Riley, *The International Style*, p. 40.

51. The traveling show of 1930–31 had of course appeared in New York, but Wright was intent on a larger show there. He told Johnson, "We should have an exhibition after yours is over in New York to use [the models] in connection with the material just returned from Europe. Perhaps you could help me arrange it." Wright, letter to Johnson, February 2, 1932. FLWA. Johnson replied that he would be happy to help, and suggested further discussion. Johnson, letter to Wright, February 4, 1932. FLWA.

52. The exhibition ran at the Modern from February 9 to March 23, 1932. In a letter to Johnson dated April 19, 1932 (FLWA), Wright mentions a recent visit to New York, but by that time the show had moved on to the Pennsylvania Art Museum, Philadelphia, and Johnson was preparing to go on to the next stop, in Hartford, Connecticut.

53. Wright, letter to Johnson, February 11, 1932. FLWA.

54. In ibid., dated two days after the private preview of the exhibition, Wright refused to participate in the traveling version of the "International Style" exhibition because he disagreed with the show's principles. In a later comment indicating how closely he was following Johnson's interest in Mies, he suggested, "Some day let's persuade Mies to get rid of those damned little steel posts that look so dangerous and interfering in his lovely designs. He really doesn't need them as much as he thinks he does." Wright, letter to Johnson, February 26, 1932. FLWA. Johnson hoped that the Museum's readiness to distribute "Of Thee I Sing" would help to convince Wright to stay in the traveling show. The Wright material was still in the show when it opened at the Sears Roebuck Building, Chicago, on June 8, 1932.

55. Wright, letter to Hitchcock, February 26, 1932. FLWA.

56. Riley, "Portrait of the Curator as a Young Man," pp. 43–44; Riley, *The International Style*, p. 83 and note 34; Franz Schulze, *Philip Johnson: Life and Work* (New York: Alfred A. Knopf, 1994), pp. 81–83. Riley points out that Johnson "had recently invested in the magazine and was briefly on its editorial board." Riley, *The International Style*, p. 209, note 34.

57. Wright, letter to Johnson, April 19, 1932. FLWA.

58. Hitchcock, letter to Wright, April 22, 1932, quoted in Schulze, *Philip Johnson: Life and Work*, p. 84. The original of the letter does not appear in the Wright Archives, suggesting that it may not have been sent. The author is grateful to Robert Wojtowicz for pointing this out.

59. Johnson, letter to Wright, April 25, 1932. FLWA.

60. Wright, letter to Johnson, May 24, 1932. FLWA. Johnson and Hitchcock did in fact take an extended trip to Chicago and its environs during the course of their research, and spent a weekend at Taliesin in the summer of 1932. Johnson, letter to Wright, n.d. FLWA.

61. Barr, "Letter to the Editor," *Parnassus* 13 (January 1941): 3.

62. Johnson also arranged for Wright's inclusion in the Triennale di Milano, May–September 1933.

63. Riley, "Portrait of the Curator as a Young Man," pp. 44–45.

64. Architecture Committee Minutes, January 21, 1936, MoMA Archives. Notes on these minutes were provided to me by Peter Reed, February 28, 2003, to whom I am grateful. The H. H. Richardson show ran from January 14 to February 16, 1936.

65. In 1937 Barr announced that the Department of Architecture would probably want to hold a Wright exhibition in two years, in honor of the architect's seventieth birthday. Architecture Committee Minutes, November 19, 1937, MoMA Archives. Notes provided by Peter Reed. Wright was born on June 8, 1867; however, beginning sometime in the 1920s, the architect had begun to use 1869 as his birth year. Assuming that the Museum had originally planned the retrospective for 1939, the staff would have justifiably assumed he would be seventy.

66. See A. Conger Goodyear, *The Museum of Modern Art: The First Ten Years* (New York: The Museum of Modern Art, 1943), p. 115.

67. See Russell Lynes, *Good Old Modern: An Intimate Portrait of The Museum of Modern Art* (New York: Atheneum, 1973), p. 178.

68. McAndrew said that he heard about the house from Aline Bernstein, a former student of his who was related by marriage to the Kaufmann family. See Donald Hoffmann,

Frank Lloyd Wright's Fallingwater: The House and Its History (New York: Dover, 1978), pp. 69–70. Franklin Toker maintains that the Museum's growing recognition of Wright after 1935—and thus the interest in mounting Wright exhibitions—was due to a number of factors: the departure of Johnson, who was known to be a supporter of Mies and unfavorable to Wright, but also the general shift in world politics as Adolf Hitler gained power in Germany. Toker writes, "In the summer of 1937, [Nelson] Rockefeller wrote Hitchcock that MoMA's leadership was tiring of German modernism, and he asked Hitchcock to support more home-grown American architects. This meant that in the fall of 1937, Hitchcock and the MoMA curators were scrambling to mount a show by an American architect." The source of this information was a Russian architect, Berthold Lubetkin, who was traveling with Hitchcock when he received the letter. Toker, *Fallingwater Rising: Frank Lloyd Wright, E. J. Kaufmann, and America's Most Extraordinary House* (New York: Alfred A. Knopf, 2003), p. 264 and unnumbered note on p. 445. The anecdote was previously published in Meryle Secrest, *Frank Lloyd Wright* (New York: Alfred A. Knopf, 1992), p. 463 and unnumbered note on p. 597. Neither author seems to have seen the letter and neither provides a citation for it; the Hitchcock papers are closed to researchers until 2008.

69. *The Architectural Forum* 68, no. 1 (January 1938).

70. McAndrew, telegram to Wright, December 31, 1937. FLWA. Wright, telegram to McAndrew, January 5, 1938. Registrar Exhibition Files, Exh. #70, MoMA Archives.

71. *A New House by Frank Lloyd Wright on Bear Run, Pennsylvania*, exh. cat. (New York: The Museum of Modern Art, 1938), n.p.

72. *Time* 31, no. 3 (January 17, 1938).

73. Goodyear, "Appendix F: Circulating Exhibitions from 1932 through June 30, 1939," and "Appendix H: Exhibitions, 1937 to 1938," in *The First Ten Years*, n.p.

74. Elizabeth Bauer Mock was the first former Taliesin apprentice to join the staff of the Modern. Her husband, Rudolph, was a draftsman in Wright's studio from January 1931 until April 1933; Betty Mock was in residence at Taliesin from September 1932 until her husband's departure. Her sister, Catherine Bauer, was a well-known writer on architecture and housing.

75. McAndrew, "Architecture in the United States," *The Bulletin of The Museum of Modern Art* 6, nos. 1–2 (February 1939): 9.

76. The architecture section was in any case reorganized for a showing in New York, under the title *Three Centuries of American Architecture*, after which it was sent on tour. See Goodyear, *The First Ten Years*, Appendix H.

77. Barr, memo to Dorothy C. Miller, October 10, 1940. Alfred H. Barr, Jr., Papers (AAA:3262;405), MoMA Archives.

78. Trustee Minutes, vol. 5, October 19, 1939, p. 4, MoMA Archives. Notes provided by Peter Reed.

79. In 1937, Barr had announced the intention of holding a Wright exhibition in 1939 (see note 65). By February 9, 1939, the Wright show had been approved for the 1939–40 season; Trustee Minutes, February 9, 1939, vol. 5, p. 5, MoMA Archives. Notes provided by Peter Reed. In November of 1939 McAndrew informed Wright that the exhibit was being rescheduled from summer to fall 1940. McAndrew, letter to Wright, November 6, 1939. Registrar Exhibition Files, Exh. #114, MoMA Archives.

80. James S. Plaut, letter to Wright, May 3, 1939. FLWA. See also "The Boston Museum of Modern Art," *The Bulletin of The Museum of Modern Art* 5, no. 3 (March 1938): 3, and Lynes, *Good Old Modern*, pp. 166–67, 292–93.

81. Plaut, letter to McAndrew, December 23, 1939. Registrar Exhibition Files, Exh. #114, MoMA Archives. The two institutions shared the costs of new photography, two new models (of the Charles Ross House [Lake Delavan, Wisconsin, 1902] and the Herbert Jacobs House [Madison, 1936–37]), and the repair of two existing models (for the unbuilt Stanley Marcus House [Dallas, 1935] and the Suntop Homes [Ardmore, Pennsylvania, 1938–39]). The agreement stipulated that the Modern would own the Ross and Jacobs models at the close of the exhibitions.

82. Plaut, letter to Wright, July 14, 1939. FLWA. The final exhibition dates were January 24 to March 3, 1940.

83. Plaut, letter to McAndrew, September 26, 1939. FLWA.

84. Edgar Tafel, *Apprentice to Genius: Years with Frank Lloyd Wright* (New York: McGraw-Hill, 1979), pp. 66, 68.

85. McAndrew, letter to Mumford, January 31, 1940. Registrar Exhibition Files, Exh. #114, MoMA Archives.

86. Walter Gropius, *Apollo in the Democracy* (New York: McGraw-Hill, 1968), pp. 167–68.

87. Plaut, letter to McAndrew, December 23, 1939. Registrar Exhibition Files, Exh. #114, MoMA Archives. Plaut was sensitive to the fact that McAndrew too planned to ask Mumford to write; he notes in this letter, "I do not want to step on your toes." Not only did McAndrew not view this as a conflict, he sent Plaut Mumford's address. McAndrew, letter to Plaut, December 26, 1939. Boston Correspondence, MoMA Archives.

88. Plaut, letter to Wright, January 8, 1940. FLWA.

89. *Frank Lloyd Wright: A Pictorial Record of Architectural Progress*, exh. cat. (Boston: The Institute of Modern Art, 1940), n.p.

90. The quotations came from Wright, *Modern Architecture: Being the Kahn Lectures for 1930* (Princeton: at the University Press, 1931); Wright, *An Autobiography* (London and New York: Longmans, Green, 1932); and the *Architectural Forum* special issue on Wright of January 1938.

91. Wright inscribed a copy to Frederick Langhorst, a former apprentice, "Fred!--the worst introduction I ever had. F. L. L. W." Copy in the collection of the Getty Research Institute.

92. Joseph Hudnut, "Foreword," in *Frank Lloyd Wright: A Pictorial Record of Architectural Progress*, n.p.

93. Wright, letter to McAndrew, November 19, 1940. FLWA.

94. Trustee Minutes, vol. 5, October 19, 1939, p. 4, MoMA Archives. Notes provided by Peter Reed.

95. See "Prospectus for Frank Lloyd Wright Show," October 20, 1939. Registrar Exhibition Files, Exh. #114, MoMA Archives.

96. McAndrew, letter to Wright, November 6, 1939. Registrar Exhibition Files, Exh. #114, MoMA Archives.

97. Expense List, n.d. Registrar Exhibition Files, Exh. #114, MoMA Archives.

98. For a description of the preliminary proposals and contents of the final publication, see pp. 106–15.

99. "We had thought of having two main essays of between four and six thousand words each and had wanted to ask you and Behrendt to write them." McAndrew, letter to Mumford, January 31, 1940. Registrar Exhibition Files, Exh. #114, MoMA Archives. McAndrew wrote to Mumford again on June 14 and reminded him "you would know later whether you would have time to write a short piece on Wright's American Background." The preparations for the Wright show were being played out against the backdrop of World War II, however, and the day McAndrew wrote his letter was the day Paris fell to the Germans. As a result, Mumford declined again because he "was using every waking moment in writing a short book . . . on the background of the present situation." McAndrew, letter to Mumford, June 14, 1940. Registrar Exhibition Files, Exh. #114, MoMA Archives. Sophia Mumford, letter to McAndrew, June 18, 1940. Registrar Exhibition Files, Exh. #114, MoMA Archives. Mumford's participation was still undecided in August, when McAndrew wrote to the architect Harwell Hamilton Harris, "After refusing because of other work, Mumford has suddenly decided that he can do something." McAndrew, letter to Harris, August 13, 1940. Registrar Exhibition Files, Exh. #114, MoMA Archives. By August 21 Barr had informed McAndrew's assistant, Janet Henrich, "[Mumford] can't, pressure of 'X.'" "X" was an exhibition that the Museum was developing with Mumford and Leslie Cheek, director of The Baltimore Museum of Art, addressing the crisis of the war in Europe. Henrich, memo to Barr, August 21, 1940, with Barr's handwritten response in margin. Registrar Exhibition Files, Exh. #114, MoMA Archives.

100. McAndrew, letter to Behrendt, January 19, 1940; McAndrew, letter to Mumford, January 31, 1940; Henrich, letter to Behrendt, March 11, 1940. Registrar Exhibition Files, Exh. #114, MoMA Archives.

101. Mumford, letter to McAndrew, March 10, 1940. Registrar Exhibition Files, Exh. #114, MoMA Archives.

102. The buildings Behrendt illustrated were the Isabel Roberts House (River Forest, Illinois, 1908), the Avery Coonley House (Riverside, Illinois, 1906–8), and Wright's own Taliesin, Spring Green, Wisconsin, 1911–59). Behrendt, *Modern Building: Its Nature, Problems, and Forms* (New York: Harcourt, Brace and Company, 1937), pp. 126–39, 143.

103. Ibid., p. 139.

104. Ibid., p. 130.

105. Ibid., pp. 132–33.

106. Oud's statement actually read, "Whereas Wright proved to be an artist rather than a prophet, cubism paved the way for the more actual execution of that which was his theory too." The manuscript, which is in English, is typed on Oud's letterhead: "The Influence of Frank Lloyd Wright on the Architecture of Europe," c. 1922, manuscript, Accession #840055, Getty Research Institute. It was first published in Wijdeveld, ed., *The Life-Work of the American Architect Frank Lloyd Wright*.

107. Behrendt, *Modern Building*, p. 143.

108. "A. B. M." for Harcourt, Brace and Company, letter to Wright's apprentice Gene Masselink, April 29, 1937; Masselink, letter to Harcourt, Brace and Company, May 4, 1937; Masselink, letter to Charles A. Pearce of Duell, Sloane and Pearce, May 6, 1937. FLWA.

109. Architecture Committee Minutes, April 11, 1940, p. 6, MoMA Archives. Notes provided by Peter Reed.

110. Behrendt, letter to Wright, May 27, 1940; Wright, letter to Behrendt, June 6, 1940. FLWA.

111. Wright, letter to McAndrew, May 30, 1940. Registrar Exhibition Files, Exh. #114, MoMA Archives.

112. Wright, letter to Behrendt, June 6, 1940. FLWA. In calling Boston's Institute of Modern Art the Museum of Modern Art, Wright is confusing the old and new names of the institution.

113. One of Alfred Stieglitz's biographers writes, "Alfred Barr precipitated a crisis. . . . Stieglitz had loaned a 1911 proto-cubist sculpture by Picasso to the museum for its Picasso retrospective. Stieglitz said it was shown at '291' in the first Picasso show in America; Barr had his art historian's doubts and wrote in the catalogue, 'probably.' Furious, Stieglitz broke off relations with the museum and cancelled the show." Nancy Newhall, *From Adams to Stieglitz: Pioneers of Modern Photography*, introduction by Beaumont Newhall, foreword by Michael

Hoffman (New York: Aperture Foundation, 1989), p. 155. *Picasso: 40 Years of His Art* was shown from November 15, 1939, until January 7, 1940.

114. Stieglitz, letter to Beaumont Newhall, July 17, 1940. Beaumont and Nancy Newhall papers and photographs, #9200060, Box 113, Folder 14, Getty Research Institute. See also Richard Whelan, *Alfred Stieglitz: A Biography* (Boston: Little, Brown, 1995), p. 565.

115. Wright, letter to McAndrew, September 16, 1940. Registrar Exhibition Files, Exh. #114, MoMA Archives.

116. Curtis Besinger, *Working with Mr. Wright: What It Was Like* (Cambridge: at the University Press, 1995), p. 97.

117. Wright, telegram to McAndrew, December 17, 1939; Wright, telegram to McAndrew, December 21, 1939; Wright, telegram to McAndrew, January 5, 1940. Registrar Exhibition Files, Exh. #114, MoMA Archives. McAndrew, telegram to Wright, January 10, 1940; Wright, letter to McAndrew, January 12, 1940. FLWA.

118. Besinger, *Working with Mr. Wright*, pp. 97–100.

119. Barr, memo to McAndrew, July 30, 1940; "Schedule for Catalogue and Exhibition," September 5, 1940. Registrar Exhibition Files, Exh. #114, MoMA Archives.

120. Wright, telegram to McAndrew, September 10, 1940; Wright, telegram to McAndrew, September 10, 1940. FLWA.

121. Lesley Cheek, Jr., Papers and Alfred H. Barr, Jr., Papers, 6.B.13. a–e, MoMA Archives.

122. In the early stages, when three exhibits were still planned, Barr had informed the Museum's executive vice-president, John E. Abbott, that the "three one man shows would occupy less than the ground and second floors." Barr, memo to Abbott, March 3, 1940. Registrar Exhibition Files, Exh. #106, MoMA Archives. McAndrew, telegram to Barr, September 13, 1940. Registrar Exhibition Files, Exh. #114, MoMA Archives.

123. The other essay was Talbot Hamlin's "Frank Lloyd Wright: His Influence in America." See pp. 137–42 in this volume.

124. McAndrew, telegram to Wright, September 14, 1940. FLWA.

125. Wright, telegram to McAndrew, September 16, 1940. Registrar Exhibition Files, Exh. #114, MoMA Archives.

126. As the confrontation between Wright and the Museum was developing, significant changes were taking place within the Museum itself. The President of the Board of Trustees, Nelson Rockefeller, was spending time in Washington, D.C., where he was about to assume a post in government. He would shortly resign his position at the Museum to become Coordinator of the Office of Inter-American Affairs. Barr, meanwhile, was increasingly losing influence, in the buildup to his eventual dismissal in

1943. As a result, these two important figures were less in evidence. The chairman of the board, Stephen C. Clark, and the executive vice-president, Abbott (a former stockbroker), were making more of the administrative decisions, and their major concern was to stabilize the Museum financially. Barr "barred his door to the problems of the men and women who had their own battles for recognition, for budgets, and for trustee approval and sympathy. It became more and more difficult for his colleagues to get him to make decisions, to answer urgent questions. . . . In this atmosphere Abbott collected more and more administrative power to himself." Lynes, *Good Old Modern*, p. 226. Clark later stated that due to his preoccupation with "a number of problems which have arisen in Nelson [Rockefeller]'s absence, I have paid little attention to this exhibition." Clark, letter to Rockefeller, November 16, 1940. Rockefeller Archive Center of the Rockefeller University.

127. Wright, letter to McAndrew, September 16, 1940. FLWA.

128. Barr, postcard to McAndrew, n.d. (postmarked September 17, 1940). Registrar Exhibition Files, Exh. #114, MoMA Archives.

129. Wright, letter to McAndrew, November 19, 1940. Registrar Exhibition Files, Exh. #114, MoMA Archives.

130. The only surviving MoMA correspondence concerning both the catalogue raisonné and the bibliography is from a Museum researcher, Henrietta Callaway, Department of Architecture. However, Grant Carpenter Manson, a student at Harvard University who was completing his Ph.D. dissertation on Wright's work between 1889 and 1910, shared his research with McAndrew. He provided facts concerning addresses and dates, which were incorporated into the catalogue raisonné. Manson later published his dissertation as *Frank Lloyd Wright to 1910: The First Golden Age* (New York: Reinhold, 1958). Frederick Gutheim, who was editing an authorized anthology of Wright's writings, *Frank Lloyd Wright on Architecture: Selected Writings, 1894–1940* (New York: Duell, Sloan and Pearce, 1941), was providing citations for the bibliography. Beaumont Newhall and Bernard Karpel had some involvement in the compilation of these sections. Newhall was the Museum's librarian between 1939 and 1940, and Karpel was his assistant. After Karpel succeeded Newhall as librarian, he was responsible for updating the bibliography as *What Men Have Written about Frank Lloyd Wright: A Bibliography Arranged by Decades from 1900 to 1955*, which accompanied a special issue of *House Beautiful* in November 1955. The catalogue raisonné was revised and published in Hitchcock, *In the Nature of Materials*.

131. Abby Aldrich Rockefeller, Nelson Rockefeller, Archibald MacLeish, Philip Goodwin, Beardsley Ruml, and Barr reviewed "Exhibition X." The Executive Committee of the Board of Trustees rejected the exhibition on October 4, 1940. Lesley Cheek, Jr., Papers and Alfred H. Barr, Jr., Papers, 6.B.13. a–e, MoMA Archives.

132. McAndrew, letter to Wright, September 18, 1940. FLWA.

133. Wright, telegram to McAndrew, September 19, 1940. Registrar Exhibition Files, Exh. #114, MoMA Archives.

134. Wright, letter to McAndrew, September 19, 1940. FLWA.

135. McAndrew, telegram to Wright, September 19, 1940. Registrar Exhibition Files, Exh. #114, MoMA Archives.

136. Wright, telegram to McAndrew, September 20, 1940. FLWA.

137. One building was conspicuous by its absence: Fallingwater. Despite the worldwide publicity it had recently received, in part through its exhibition at the Modern, Behrendt never mentioned it—perhaps because the client was a wealthy merchant and the building a luxurious weekend retreat, so that it did not conform to his social program.

138. See Behrendt's essay on pp. 116–24 in the present volume, as well as Wright's emended version of it on pp. 125–33.

139. Wright, letter to Behrendt, September 19, 1940. FLWA.

140. Behrendt, "Frank Lloyd Wright," manuscript, Version 2B. FLWA, p. 14.

141. Ibid., pp. 20–21.

142. Wright, "To My Critics," September 14, 1940, a revision of "To My Critics in the Land of the Danube and the Rhine," July 23, 1931. FLWA.

143. Wright, letter to Behrendt, October 5, 1940. FLWA.

144. Behrendt, letter to Wright, October 17, 1940. FLWA.

145. Behrendt, letter to Mumford, n.d. (c. September 19–22, 1940). Lewis Mumford Papers, Special Collections, University of Pennsylvania. I am grateful to Robert Wojtowicz for providing me with material from the Mumford archive.

146. Mumford, letter to Behrendt, July 9, 1940. Lewis Mumford Papers, Special Collections, University of Pennsylvania.

147. Mumford, letter to Behrendt, September 23, 1940. Lewis Mumford Papers, Special Collections, University of Pennsylvania.

148. In a meeting with Barr, Abbott, and McAndrew, Wright stated, "The house would be completely equipped—furnished, with radio, practical kitchen, etc. as well as heating and sewerage." Meeting notes, September 25, 1940. Registrar Exhibition Files, Exh. #114, MoMA Archives. The sewer connection was refused by the city; the heat was changed from radiant heat to steam heat as a practicality.

149. See Miller, "Mies and Exhibitions."

150. See Mary Anne Staniszewski, "Houses in the Museum's Garden," *The Power of Display: A History of Exhibition Installations at the Museum of Modern Art* (Cambridge, Mass.: The MIT Press, 1998), pp. 199–202.

151. Wright, letter to McAndrew, October 10, 1940. Registrar Exhibition Files, Exh. #114, MoMA Archives.

152. Wright, telegram to McAndrew, October 9, 1940; Wright, letter to McAndrew, October 10, 1940; Wright, telegram to McAndrew, October 10, 1940; McAndrew, telegram to Wright, October 11, 1940. FLWA. Wright, telegram to McAndrew, October 11, 1940. Registrar Exhibition Files, Exh. #114, MoMA Archives. It is unclear what McAndrew had in mind in saying that if placed as Wright wanted it the house would have to be demolished on January 15, but could elsewhere stay up until September.

153. John D. Rockefeller, Jr., letter to Clark, November 12, 1940. Rockefeller Archive Center of the Rockefeller University.

154. John D. Rockefeller, Jr., letter to Abbott, October 29, 1940. Rockefeller Archive Center of the Rockefeller University.

155. Clark, letter to John D. Rockefeller, November 16, 1940. Rockefeller Archive Center of the Rockefeller University.

156. McAndrew, letter to Wright, December 2, 1940. FLWA. It is unclear from the correspondence whether McAndrew's earlier suggestion to move the site of the house was a response to the deed restrictions imposed by John D. Rockefeller, Jr. This is unlikely, however, because Rockefeller's restrictions applied to the entire 400-foot length of the property. There is no mention in the correspondence of the fact that Wright did move the house as requested. However, a comparison of Wright plot plans reveals the shift. Taliesin drawing 4000.009 (plate 9) clearly shows the original placement on axis with the Museum rear entrance. Taliesin drawing 4010.001 (plate 10) reveals that the original placement had been erased and redrawn, shifting the building to the west, as McAndrew had suggested. Drawing 4010.001 clearly shows how the shift has made the entrance to the Exhibition House very awkward. Even after Wright moved the site, the project was still canceled.

157. Wright designed and built a temporary pavilion to house his exhibition, in addition to the Usonian House. [Frank Lloyd Wright], *The Usonian House, Souvenir of the Exhibition: 60 Years of Living Architecture, the Work of Frank Lloyd Wright*. N.p.: The Solomon R. Guggenheim Museum, n.d.

158. See "Greatest Living Architect Exhibits Mass of Work," *Alameda Times-Star*, MoMA, reel 607; *New York Motion Picture Herald*, August 24, 1940, reel 614; and Tselos, "Frank Lloyd Wright," p. 42.

159. Besinger, *Working with Mr. Wright*, p. 100.

160. McAndrew, letter to Wright, October 24, 1940. FLWA.

161. Victor Cusack, in an interview with Cusack, William Wesley Peters, and Robert Mosher by Indira Berndtson and Greg Williams, Taliesin West, April 7, 1991. Transcription, p. 22. FLWA.

162. Besinger, *Working with Mr. Wright*, p. 100.

163. Masselink, quoted in "Local Man Had Charge of N.Y. Architecture Show," *Grand Rapids Herald*, December 1, 1940. Public Information Scrapbooks, MoMA Archives, reel 12, frame 647.

164. Cusack, interview with Berndtson and Williams, p. 23.

165. Alan Mather, "The Perennial Trailblazer," *Pencil Points* 21 (December 1940): sup., 16.

166. "Exhibition Outline," October 1, 1940. FLWA. This document is not on Museum letterhead and is not signed. I have concluded that McAndrew is the author from internal evidence.

167. The film arrived in poor condition, prohibiting regular screenings. Neither the film nor documentation of its contents survives in the Wright Archives in Scottsdale. I am grateful to Oscar Muñoz for providing this information.

168. Wright, letter to McAndrew, December 9, 1940. Registrar Exhibition Files, Exh. 114, MoMA Archives.

169. Wright, letter to McAndrew, November 19, 1940. Registrar Exhibition Files, Exh. #114, MoMA Archives.

170. Meeting notes, September 25, 1940, The Museum of Modern Art. Registrar Exhibition Files, exh. 114, MoMA Archives.

171. Wright, letter to McAndrew, November 1, 1940. Registrar Exhibition Files, Exh. #114, MoMA Archives.

172. Wright, in meeting notes, September 25, 1940, 2. Registrar Exhibition Files, Exh. #114, MoMA Archives.

173. "Local Man Had Charge of N.Y. Architecture Show," *Grand Rapids Herald*.

174. McAndrew, letter to Wright, October 14, 1940. Registrar Exhibition Files, Exh. #114, MoMA Archives.

175. Wright, quoted in Tselos, "Frank Lloyd Wright," p. 43.

176. Masselink, quoted in "Local Man Had Charge of N.Y. Architecture Show," *Grand Rapids Herald*.

177. "Bauhaus art, design, and architecture were respected by many of the critics who hated the show, but the way the . . . elements were put together . . . was indecipherable and somehow beyond the ability of American audiences to assimilate." Staniszewski, "The Bauhaus Debacle," in *The*

Power of Display, p. 145. The critical outrage against *Bauhaus: 1919–1928* certainly made an impact on Barr and McAndrew: "The attacks in the press on the Bauhaus show . . . were so disturbing to the trustees of the Museum that Barr and McAndrew prepared 'notes on the reception of the Bauhaus Exhibition' in which they analyzed the criticisms." Lynes, *Good Old Modern*, p. 182. This may have affected their treatment of Wright: beginning with the invitation and continuing with signs affixed to the walls of the galleries, the Museum designated the exhibition "arranged by the architect himself." Although the phrase was perfectly accurate, Wright seems to have sensed that the Museum was disowning the exhibition and took umbrage, stating, "I was surprised when you dumped the show on me as 'arranged by himself.'" Wright, letter to McAndrew, November 19, 1940. Registrar Exhibition Files, exh. 114, MoMA Archives. Wright continually pressed to have the signs removed and eventually the Museum complied.

178. E. A. J. [Edward Alden Jewell], "Museum of Modern Art: Two New Exhibitions Present the Careers of Frank Lloyd Wright, D. W. Griffith," *New York Times*, November 17, 1940. Public Information Scrapbooks, MoMA Archives, reel 12, frame 625.

179. Baker, "Wright as Iconoclast."

180. Isabel Cooper, "The Art of a Master Builder," *New Masses*, December 17, 1940. MoMA Archives, reel 12, frame 649.

181. Brown, "Frank Lloyd Wright's First Fifty Years," p. 37.

182. Tselos, "Frank Lloyd Wright," p. 42.

183. Gutheim, "First Reckon with His Future: Frank Lloyd Wright's Exhibit at the Modern Museum," *Magazine of Art* 34 (January 1941): 32.

184. Hamlin, "Frank Lloyd Wright," *The Nation* 151, no. 22 (November 30, 1940): 541–42.

185. Brown, "Frank Lloyd Wright's First Fifty Years," p. 38. In place of a catalogue, and by arrangement with Wright, the Museum sold copies of and subscriptions to a magazine produced by Wright and the Taliesin Fellowship, *Taliesin* 1, no. 1 (October 1940), titled "Broadacre City, The New Frontier." According to Alofsin, "The issue was planned as early as 1935 but appeared five years later, partly in anticipation of Wright's forthcoming exhibition in 1941 at the Museum of Modern Art." Alofsin, "Broadacre City: The Reception of a Modernist Vision, 1932–1988," *Center: A Journal for Architecture in America* 5 (1989): 28. *Taliesin* 1, no. 1 is listed in Robert Sweeney, *Frank Lloyd Wright: An Annotated Bibliography* (Los Angeles: Hennessey & Ingalls, 1978), #2040.

186. Barr, "Letter to the Editor," *Parnassus* 13 (January 1941): 3.

187. Jewell, "Modern Museum Opens Two Shows," *New York Times*, November 13, 1940. Public Information Scrapbooks, MoMA Archives, reel 12, frame 622.

188. The press release, of c. November 10–11, 1940, stated, "Generally considered the world's greatest living architect, Wright has certainly been its most influential one." The phrase may have been borrowed from Mumford, who had written at the time of the Museum's Fallingwater exhibition, "Wright [is] at the top of his powers, undoubtedly the world's greatest living architect, a man who can dance circles around any of his contemporaries." Mumford, "At Home, Indoors and Out," *The New Yorker* 13 (February 12, 1938): 31.

189. S. N. [Sarah Newmeyer], letter to Mumford, November 22, 1940. Registrar Exhibition Files, Exh. #114, MoMA Archives.

190. Behrendt, letter to Mumford, January 5, 1941. Lewis Mumford Papers, University of Pennsylvania.

191. "'Bomb-proof City' Shown as Model," *New York Times*, November 11, 1940. Public Information Scrapbooks, MoMA Archives, reel 12, frame 622.

192. "Frank Wright Here, Believes Cities Doomed," *New York Herald Tribune*, November 11, 1940. Public Information Scrapbooks, MoMA Archives, reel 12, frame 616.

193. See Pfeiffer and Wojtowicz, eds., *Frank Lloyd Wright and Lewis Mumford*, p. 23.

194. Mumford, untitled ms. Lewis Mumford Papers, University of Pennsylvania, folder 7343. Since the first page of the typed manuscript is missing, its association with the Museum's retrospective, or the intended publisher, cannot ultimately be determined. Internal evidence suggests, however, that the text was a review of the exhibition. I am extremely grateful to Robert Wojtowicz for calling it to my attention and for providing a copy. Quotation from this unpublished manuscript is courtesy of the Estate of Lewis and Sophia Mumford.

195. Critical reaction seems to have been the deciding factor in Wright's refusal to permit a traveling show. "If editors of House and Garden (N.Y. Sunday Times) Magazines, etc., etc., are so flat dumb," Wright told McAndrew, "where these [models] are concerned why expect the dear people to understand them no matter how well presented? . . . Drawings may be easier if they are in color. But I am beginning to doubt somewhat, that too." Wright, letter to McAndrew, December 1, 1940. Registrar Exhibition Files, Exh. #114, MoMA Archives.

196. Wright, letter to Hitchcock, November 23, 1940. FLWA. In advertising copy Wright composed at the request of his publisher, Duell, Sloan and Pearce, he stated, "The show at the Museum of Modern Art contained the best I've built from 1893 to 1940 and at last it is here put in order by able . . . Hitchcock. His opinions on architecture I have distrusted as far too academic but since it is safer to trust the enemies to one's point of view rather than one's friends I asked him to record the show in its entirety." Unpublished manuscript, December 28, 1940. FLWA.

197. Hitchcock, letter to Wright, November 27, 1940. FLWA. The history of *In the Nature of Materials* must remain tentative until the twenty-five feet of Henry-Russell Hitchcock Papers on deposit at the Archives of American Art, Smithsonian Institution, Washington, D.C., become open to researchers on July 22, 2008.

198. Hitchcock, letter to McAndrew, n.d. (c. June 15–30, 1940). Registrar Exhibition Files, Exh. 114, MoMA Archives. A month later, Hitchcock told McAndrew that he hoped a book by Manson—based on his doctoral dissertation—could be used as the publication accompanying the exhibition. He also expressed the need for a second volume by Manson to complete a comprehensive study of Wright's career. Hitchcock, letter to McAndrew, July 14, 1940. Registrar Exhibition Files, Exh. 114, MoMA Archives. When Manson finally published his book, in 1958 (as *Frank Lloyd Wright to 1910: The First Golden Age*, New York: Reinhold Publishing Corporation), he announced that two volumes would follow to bring the study up-to-date; they never appeared.

199. In the first sentence of the Preface to *In the Nature of Materials*, Hitchcock stated, "This book is intended to be a sort of *ex post facto* catalogue of the exhibition . . . at the Museum of Modern Art . . . in 1940." With this vague language the historian left a lasting impression that the Museum had planned the publication to record the exhibition. Hitchcock, *In the Nature of Materials*, p. xxvii. In his "Foreword to the Reprint Edition" of *In the Nature of Materials*, Hitchcock admitted that he acted "to a degree" as a "ghost" for Wright, noting that the copyright was in both their names. He explained, "Mr. Wright personally oversaw the selection and preparation of all the visual material, passed the wording of even the shortest captions, and established all the details of the exceptional design." Following *An Autobiography*, he declared the book could stand as "a second 'classic' production of the Master." Hitchcock, *In the Nature of Materials* (reprint ed. New York: Da Capo Press, 1973), p. xxxiii.

200. On December 22, 1941, Wright protested to his publisher, Charles Duell, that Hitchcock "has chosen the dullest photographs and . . . has no very clear idea of how to preserve a format in face of natural difficulty. The way the thing looks now—a hash has been made of perfectly splendid material." Wright, letter to Charles Duell, December 22, 1941. FLWA.

201. Duell sent Wright two reviews: on May 4, 1942, *Time* called the book "thorough," and Mumford in *The New Yorker* wrote of "a superb job." Wright, letter to Hitchcock, May 28, 1942. FLWA.

202. Behrendt, "The Record of Frank Lloyd Wright," *The Yale Review* 32, no 1 (Autumn 1942): 180. Despite his disagreement with Behrendt over the essay of 1940, Wright never forgot this writer's importance to his career. In 1953 he dedicated his traveling retrospective *Sixty Years of Living Architecture* to several key supporters living and dead, including Behrendt.

Santa Fe

The Chief

Dear John — On the way far west
I hear the prominent description of the
arrangement of the show by myself
is still flaunted at the entrance —
please take it down. If for no other
reason because it is a misleading
half truth.

I think, from you, should come the
statement that the actual house in
the court seen through the windows
in connection with the plans and models
inside the museum was my idea of
the show. When that promise fell it
is unfair to boast of a show arranged
by me.

I did the best I damn could from
Sat evening to Tuesday evening to
get the drawings together while painters
electricians and carpenters were still
mixed up with them and none by
an eleventh hour idea of how to do it

LETTERS & TELEGRAMS
Introduction

The letters, telegrams, and memos among the participants in *Frank Lloyd Wright: American Architect* are extremely lively. What follows is a selection from this correspondence, telling the story of the fraught collaboration between Wright and The Museum of Modern Art. These writings are drawn largely from archives at the Museum, the Frank Lloyd Wright Foundation in Scottsdale, Arizona, and the Rockefeller Archive Center in Sleepy Hollow, New York. Capturing the event as it unfolded, they offer a behind-the-scenes look at the production of a major retrospective exhibition of America's foremost living architect, with all its give-and-take, and in all its immediacy.

Three main issues emerge as the correspondence progresses: the book accompanying the exhibition, the design of the installation, and an "Exhibition Usonian House," based on the Herbert Jacobs House in Madison, Wisconsin, to be built in the Museum's garden in order to demonstrate Wright's ideas about efficient and affordable housing. One of the first orders of business in the letters is the book, whose publication came to a grinding halt when Wright objected so vehemently to one of its essays that he threatened to cancel the entire show. After a heated exchange of letters and telegrams, however, the book alone was jettisoned and exhibition planning continued apace. With growing excitement, Wright and curator John McAndrew roughed out the installation. Wright sent plans for the exhibition house to McAndrew, but no other materials for the show. McAndrew worked diligently to get the house built but had difficulty doing so, for a variety of bureaucratic reasons. Only three days before the show was to open, Wright arrived in New York with a cargo of drawings, photographs, and models. He installed the show himself, with the help of his own assistants and the Museum's staff, and the exhibition had its private opening on November 12, 1940. (It opened to the public on November 13.) That same day, John D. Rockefeller, Jr., who owned some of the land in the garden and had effective control over what the Museum could do with the rest, denied permission for the house, which was never constructed.

What comes through in these letters is the differences among Wright's, McAndrew's, and the Museum's agendas, and the difficulties to which they led. Wright wanted a thematic overview of his career, focusing on concerns that were essential to his continuing architectural practice. He and McAndrew were in general agreement about the organization of the exhibition around his formal development and the theme of "the nature of materials." It was the book, whose essays McAndrew hoped would make clear Wright's influence on other architects and on the field in general, that caused the architect distress. Having read an essay to which he objected, he recognized what kind of weight the book would possess in forming the view that the public, and prospective clients especially, would have of his accomplishments. He was still, after all, a working architect.

Behind the scenes, and largely outside the purview of the correspondence, another battle was being fought: both Wright and the Museum were seeking, in different ways, to promote his work as particularly American architecture. The Museum wanted to incorporate him into a pantheon of American modernists, initially intending to present his work in one of three simultaneous exhibitions along with the photographer Alfred Stieglitz and the film director D. W. Griffith. (Wright's show ended up running alongside Griffith's alone.) At one point in the planning of the show, the Museum's interest in foreign affairs was ignited and a patriotic anti-Nazi exhibition, *For Us, the Living* (or the "mystery show," as it is called in the correspondence), was designed; had this show been realized, it would have run concurrently with Wright's. But Wright, who was strongly opposed to American involvement in World War II, saw his vision for America as unique and tied to no agenda but his own. The show as he conceived it was to feature his vision for the Americas: Broadacre City and the Usonian House. With the cancellation of the house in the garden, however, the experience of an actual Usonian House was withheld from visitors, and Wright's own stake in a nationalist agenda— inexpensive and well-designed housing—was considerably lessened.

The correspondence can be read as disagreement in action. Today the struggle matters more than the end result, and through its progressive unfolding it demonstrates the divergent priorities of Wright and the Museum circa 1940.

—WK

These letters are variously located in the Avery Architectural and Fine Arts Library, Columbia University, New York; The Museum of Modern Art Archives, New York; the Rockefeller Archive Center of the Rockefeller University, Sleepy Hollow, New York; and the Frank Lloyd Wright Foundation Archives, Scottsdale, Arizona. The annotations are those of the present editors.

Dear Mr. Wright:

Thank you so much for two wonderful and stimulating days at Taliesin.[1] It was fine to be there at last—after several unlucky attempts. The visit was one which I shall always remember with great pleasure and, I hope, profit.

The date for the exhibition has finally been set for next October. This seems an advantage for many reasons. In the first place there certainly will be a far greater attendance in the fall than in summer. I don't know why this is, but it has always been true for the ten years that the Museum has been running. Also, the fall may be a better date in relation to the exhibition in Boston.[2] There will be more time to work peacefully on it and less rush for you. The principal advantage for us is that perhaps by that time more of your newest work may be far enough along to be shown in photographs. We want to show this very much.

Plans of the exhibition space are being sent to you under separate cover with the relevant information written on them.

The general scheme of the exhibition which we discussed has been received here with enthusiasm. I described it as in three main parts, plus a separate section for Broadacre City.[3] In the first part would be shown your early work up to the War. It could begin with a series of houses, in showing which it was intended to make as vivid as possible the *human approach*, *open plan* and *organic* character. After these could be a group with Unity Temple,[4] the 1894 office front,[5] San Francisco skyscraper[6] and Larkin Building.[7] It might be a very good idea in the explanatory labels for these to use quite a few quotations from your writings of the period. It would be quite dramatic to quote some of the prophetic things which you have said with the actual early dates when you said them.

The second part I said would cover in general the period of 1915 to 1935 to begin with a continuation of the ideas of the first part, with quite full representation of Taliesin. (I know this is hard to photograph and probably hard to exhibit, but since it has never been properly done I think we ought to try very hard to do the best we can, as it surely has to be an important item in the show.) This second section would principally be devoted to developing your many new ideas and construction and use of materials in this period.

The third large section will show as much of your recent work as we can get. Broadacre City would go in the room which we looked at treated as a complete idea in itself separate from the first three divisions. The film would also have to be somewhat separate.

I think this ought to make a good show, one which will be clear and vivid to our very mixed public. When they have seen the show indoors, they go out to the house in our garden. I am now working on the financing of this.

I will write Eugene Masselink about the different models—repairing old ones and making new ones, etc.

Everyone had settled in the Ardmore houses when I saw them last week.[8] They certainly are a fine idea. I wish there was one near here for me to rent.

Again thank you for two such rewarding days. I shall never forget them.

Sincerely,

John McAndrew

■ ■ ■ ■

Letter from McAndrew to Walter Curt Behrendt, January 19, 1940

Dear Dr. Behrendt:

. . .There is another favor I should like to ask you. The Museum is planning a fairly large exhibition of the work of Frank Lloyd Wright for next fall. We have already done preliminary work on this with Mr. Wright; he is enthusiastic about it and we hope to make an important and handsome show of it.

The catalog will contain a full chronological list of his works, a bibliography, about fifty pictures, and a number of articles. We had thought of having two essays of between four thousand and six thousand words each and had thought of asking you and Lewis Mumford to write them; there would also be articles of about three thousand words, perhaps, by Fiske Kimball, Russell Hitchcock and myself.

In addition, there would be a number of shorter pieces of only one or two pages each about special aspects of Wright–his influence on different countries at different times, etc., or tributes to him on the occasion of his seventieth year. To write these we had thought of asking [Alvar] Aalto, [Erik Gunnar] Asplund, [Willem Marinus] Dudok, Tony-Garnier [sic], George Howe, Mies [van der Rohe], [Richard] Neutra, [J. J. P.] Oud, [Auguste] Perret, [Henry] van de Velde, etc. The whole book would, as you see, be a sort of Wright omnibus somewhat in the nature of a Festschrift.

This is just the general outline of the book. The different nature of the different articles contributed will, of course, have to be worked out so that the book will have coherence as a whole. But, as we are particularly anxious to have both you and Mr. Mumford discuss Wright for us because we feel that you two have written on his work with more intelligence and sympathy than anyone else I am writing to you now to beg you to help us. Unfortunately, we would be able to pay only $125 each for the long articles. We would not need the text until July.

I am going to Mexico on the first of February and hope very much that you will write back and say "yes" before then.

I was in Buffalo for a few hours in the middle of October with John Yeon; we tried all morning to reach you and were very much disappointed at our failure.

Sincerely,

[unsigned carbon copy]

■ ■ ■ ■

My dear John: I suppose it is time preparation for the September show be put on in earnest. And I sincerely hope we can avoid the fate that befell the show in Boston.[10] Many felt that show was put on with "tongue in cheek" owing to the scandalous introduction by [Walter] Gropius mouthpiece–[Joseph] Hudnut–the big bad photo of the old granny at the entrance–me– and the examples of bad influence–chosen for exhibit instead of Gropius, [Le] Corbusier, [Erich] Mendelsohn, Mies Van der Rohe, and Oud themselves et al. Well, I don't think any-thing of the sort was intended–I respect [James] Plaut more than that. But it was all they really knew about it–I fear.

      The chronology was all wet, too.

      We have had only a stray copy of the catalogue for that show accidentally turning up at Taliesin, because we could take no pride in it.

      Let's veer away from that sort of thing if we are heading into it. Once is enough. I haven't heard from you about the house in the court either. Are we going to have money to build and furnish it as we like?

      And what plans have you to placate the profession by letting them show how far they have "caught up" and give them the equality of "credit" they like to have? If any. They call it "going the old man one or so better" or "beating him to it." Museum strategy must have some-thing up its sleeve for that, if not in mind. Or am I wrong again?

      Curt Behrendt writes that he is to write something. He asks for enlightenment on a point and I am sending him a copy of the *Architectural Record* of 1908 from which he can get what he wants.[11] May I ask who sits in judgement? And whether the also-rans get another chance to pull down the show to their level? They seem unfairly active. Anyhow, let's hear from you. No I am not getting a persecution complex–we, the people–are like that–that's all.

      We–(I especially)–need encouragement. We are so busy that we don't have much heart to concentrate on "shows" of any kind unless we are pressed a little now and then. As a matter of fact we've been able to do little more than keep it in mind–to date.
Faithfully yours,
Frank Lloyd Wright

■ ■ ■ ■

Dear John McAndrew: Mr. Wright will be in New York at the Lafayette Hotel next Tuesday, June 18th–he expects to see you while there.

      I'm enclosing a copy of the Institute of Modern Art's catalogue with notations written in by Mr. Wright which he thought you might find entertaining at least.
Sincerely yours,
Eugene Masselink

■ ■ ■ ■

Letter from Behrendt to McAndrew, July 20, 1940

Dear Mr. McAndrew:

Here is the essay on Frank Lloyd Wright which you asked me to write for your "Festschrift." I finished it before I left Buffalo for my vacation and left it with Lewis Mumford when I drove up to Amenia to see him.

On his suggestion I added the little insert on page 3.

Now it is up to you to say what you think of it: I hope you will be perfectly frank in your criticism.

Here I am spending half of my day, in the morning, in the library reading up on books which I wanted to study for years. The rest of the time is given over to all sorts of outdoor recreation, and this is the right place for it!

Greetings.

Sincerely yours,

W. C. Behrendt

■ ■ ■ ■

Letter from McAndrew to Behrendt, August 10, 1940

Dear Dr. Behrendt,

So sorry that your manuscript was not acknowledged when it arrived so promptly. The different members of the architecture department have been coming and going on fragmentary vacations, and some correspondence has been badly delayed.

Thank you for the article; it is exactly what we wanted. I have read through it twice already, and am delighted with it.

The treasurer will send you a check in the next few days.

I hope you will stop in New York on your way back, and that we will see you here for lunch or a drink or something.

Sincerely,

[unsigned carbon copy]

■ ■ ■ ■

Letter from Wright to McAndrew, August 27, 1940

Dear John: Herewith snaps of the Alabama House: "The Rosetree." [12] Plenty of Swish? We'll get some good photos.

I suggest as caption for your catalogue:

IN THE NATURE OF MATERIALS: THE WORK OF FRANK LLOYD WRIGHT.

Sincerely,

FLLW

■ ■ ■ ■

Dear Dr. Behrendt:

Not being sure where you are, I am sending you two copies of this letter, one to Hanover and one to Buffalo, hoping that one of them will reach you promptly.

We have been rereading all the articles for the catalogue very carefully, thinking of their relation to each other, of illustrations and possible footnotes. The following questions have come up:

Page 3–We do not see quite what you mean by the influence of Art Nouveau on Wright. Is there any specific illustration of this which we could have in order to prevent confusion. We have not been able to find one. Also is not the advanced part of McIntosh's Glasgow Art School [Charles Rennie Mackintosh's Glasgow School of Art] later than Wright's developed style? We doubt whether any developed McIntosh [sic] designs were published early enough for Wright to see them before he had already developed his own style independently.

Page 12–The collapse of the vaults of the Cathedral of Beauvais occurred in the later part of the 13th century, (if I remember rightly. I have not looked it up.) By that time Gothic construction was already completely developed; in fact the decline had already set in by 1260. The collapse of the Beauvais vaults was due according to Pol Abraham to the settling of the foundations rather than to any flaw in the construction itself.[13] Would it be agreeable to you if we reworded your sentence thus: "In the development of Gothic construction the occasional collapse of vaults of daring new construction was, as an experience, an important stimulus to further exploration."

Page 12, next paragraph–Would you be willing to have us add Edgar Kaufmann and Herbert Johnson to your list of loyal Wright clients?

Everyone who has read your article has been very much pleased with it. We are very happy to have it as the chief contribution to our catalogue. We have made occasional very slight changes in phraseology and have added a few footnotes giving the sources of important quotations. We will send you a copy including these in a few days.

Sincerely,

[unsigned carbon copy]

■ ■ ■ ■

Dear Mr. McAndrew:

Your letter was received just an hour before our departure. But I will answer it right away.

Page 3: you may be right about McIntosh [sic] Glasgow. However–I feel very strongly that in Wright's–even in [Louis] Sullivan's–ornament there *is* an Art Nouveau note. It may be difficult to trace the influence down to certain European artists. But the influence is there–perhaps you call it of the "Zeitgeist."

Page 12: *you* are right: the collapse of Beauvais occurred 1275.[14] So I accept the proposed rewording.

Page 12: yes: you may add any name you prefer to the list of Wright's clients.

I am glad to know that you and your friends are pleased with the article. I for myself wish to add one or two sentences in the last paragraph and I will do so when I have the proofs.

The check which you announced about 5 weeks ago has not yet been received. It would be fine if I could have it soon—the more so as I am about to move!
With best wishes,
Sincerely and hastily,
W. C. Behrendt

▪▪▪▪

Telegram from Wright to McAndrew, September 5, 1940

DEAR JOHN. NEED BOTH FLOORS DON'T WANT TO GIVE UP MAIN
FLOOR RELATING TO GARDEN NOR THE BUILDING OF THE HOUSE.
FORWARDING PLANS FOR PERMIT. WHAT THE DEVIL IS THE MATTER.
CANNOT BE THAT WE ARE ALL IMPOTENT. GIVE ME NAMES OF
THOSE YOU HAVE ASKED FOR HELP. ALSO SENDING DRAWINGS FOR
CATALOGUE AND FOR WOODEN HOUSE SHOW.
FRANK LLOYD WRIGHT

▪▪▪▪

Telegram from McAndrew to Alfred H. Barr, Jr., Director of The Museum of Modern Art, September 13, 1940

MR WRIGHT PREPARING 16 GOOD LARGE MODELS. HAS UNEARTHED
WEALTH OF ORIGINAL DRAWINGS. MANY IMPORTANT UNPUBLISHED
MAY WE HAVE ADDITIONAL SPACE GROUND FLOOR. CAN YOU TELEPHONE
ME PERSON TO PERSON SPRING GREEN 110
JOHN

▪▪▪▪

Telegram from Wright to McAndrew, September 14, 1940

BEHRENDT HAS EITHER IGNORANTLY OR DELIBERATELY TWISTED MY
MEANING AND IMPLIED UNTRUTHS CONCERNING MYSELF AND MY WORK.
IF THE MUSEUM VALUES HIS OPINION ENOUGH TO PASTE IT ACROSS
THE FACE OF MY EXHIBITION THERE IS GOING TO BE NO EXHIBITION. I

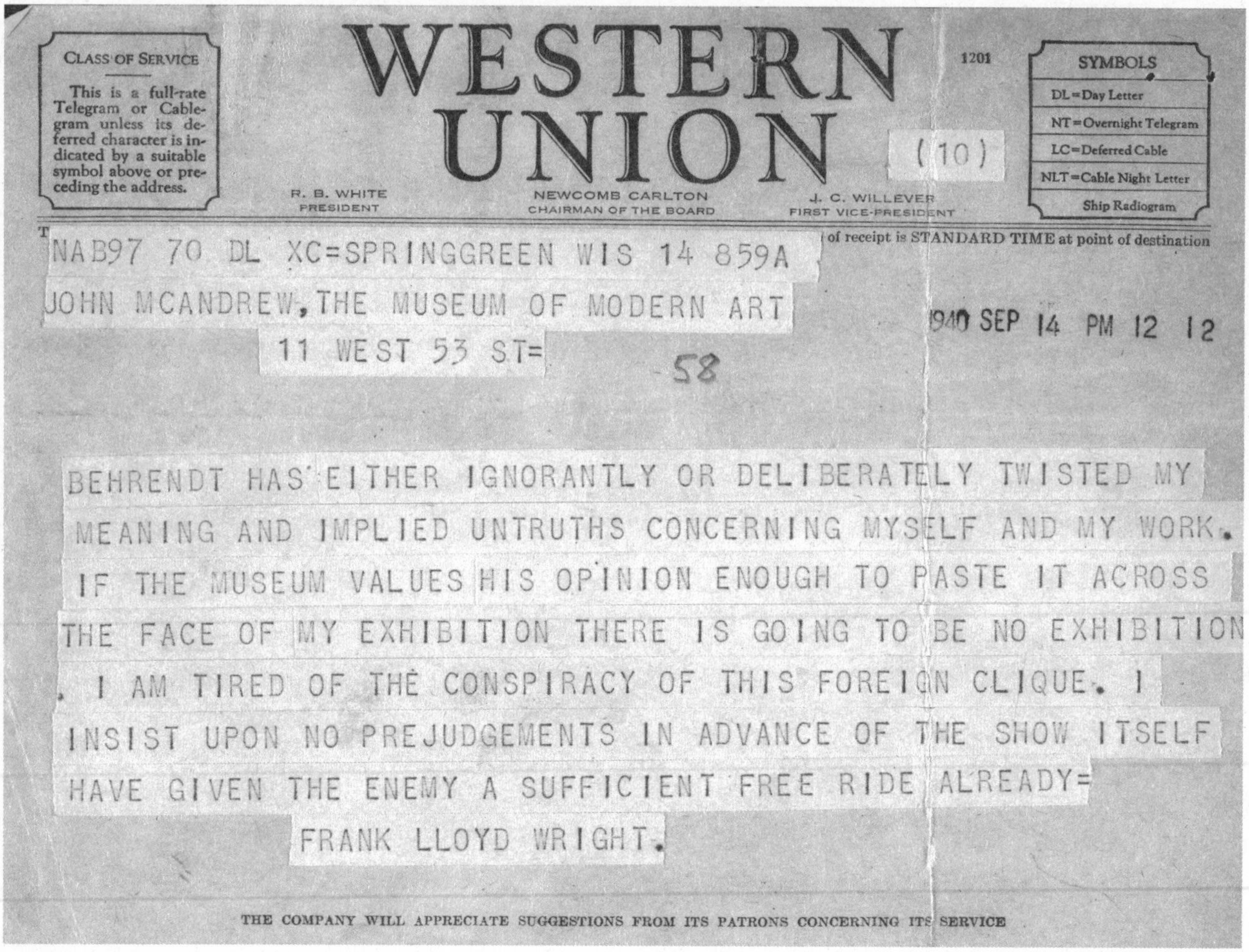

CLASS OF SERVICE

This is a full-rate Telegram or Cablegram unless its deferred character is indicated by a suitable symbol above or preceding the address.

WESTERN UNION

1201

(10)

SYMBOLS
DL=Day Letter
NT=Overnight Telegram
LC=Deferred Cable
NLT=Cable Night Letter
Ship Radiogram

R. B. WHITE PRESIDENT — NEWCOMB CARLTON CHAIRMAN OF THE BOARD — J. C. WILLEVER FIRST VICE-PRESIDENT

NAB97 70 DL XC=SPRINGGREEN WIS 14 859A

of receipt is STANDARD TIME at point of destination

JOHN MCANDREW,THE MUSEUM OF MODERN ART
11 WEST 53 ST=

1940 SEP 14 PM 12 12

58

BEHRENDT HAS EITHER IGNORANTLY OR DELIBERATELY TWISTED MY MEANING AND IMPLIED UNTRUTHS CONCERNING MYSELF AND MY WORK. IF THE MUSEUM VALUES HIS OPINION ENOUGH TO PASTE IT ACROSS THE FACE OF MY EXHIBITION THERE IS GOING TO BE NO EXHIBITION. I AM TIRED OF THE CONSPIRACY OF THIS FOREIGN CLIQUE. I INSIST UPON NO PREJUDGEMENTS IN ADVANCE OF THE SHOW ITSELF HAVE GIVEN THE ENEMY A SUFFICIENT FREE RIDE ALREADY=
FRANK LLOYD WRIGHT.

THE COMPANY WILL APPRECIATE SUGGESTIONS FROM ITS PATRONS CONCERNING ITS SERVICE

AM TIRED OF THE CONSPIRACY OF THIS FOREIGN CLIQUE. I INSIST UPON NO PREJUDGEMENTS IN ADVANCE OF THE SHOW ITSELF. HAVE GIVEN THE ENEMY A SUFFICIENT FREE RIDE ALREADY.
FRANK LLOYD WRIGHT

■■■■

Telegram from McAndrew to Wright, September 14, 1940

MUSEUM WANTS TO CONTINUE WITH EXHIBITION AND CATALOGUE AS SCHEDULED, WE HOPE WITH YOUR COOPERATION AND ADVICE. BEHRENDT ADMIRES YOU PROFOUNDLY AND CERTAINLY INTENDED NO DISTORTIONS OR UNTRUTHS. IF YOU WILL WIRE US WHAT PARTS

OF ARTICLE YOU TAKE EXCEPTION TO, WE WILL TRY TO STRAIGHTEN
MATTERS OUT. PLEASE HELP US, FOR WE NEED YOUR HELP.
JOHN

■■■■

Letter from Wright to McAndrew, September 15, 1940

My dear John: The more I think over the situation at the Museum of Modern Art with the
three ring circus we are getting into there, moreover (as it now appears to me) getting in as
"also Americana" with obituaries pasted on our show in advance . . . well, it isn't good enough.
That's all.

There seems to be money to build a building, for exhibition purposes, by Leslie
Cheek[15] but not enough to build the one by Frank Lloyd Wright. This packing of the little
museum beyond its capacity, as well as the Behrendt piece, opens my eyes to what I failed to
see clearly before:

I am now back with Leonardo and Time has marched on. Time doesn't have much to
show at the moment but no doubt the foreign boys, et al., will attend to that.

So all things considered—no single one of them final—add up to biding our own
good time. We will go on leisurely with the preparations we have begun for a show of our
own somewhere sometime under circumstances less feverish and under auspices not quite
so advanced.

You may therefore definitely count us out. For the time being at least. Anyhow, John,
you have been swell and I thank you—just the same.
As always,
Frank Lloyd Wright

■■■■

Telegram from Wright to McAndrew, September 16, 1940

KINDLY RETURN IMMEDIATELY ALL MATERIAL WE LOANED YOU
FOR PURPOSES OF CATALOGUE.
FRANK LLOYD WRIGHT

■■■■

Telegram from Wright to McAndrew, September 16, 1940

BEHRENDTS PERVERSION A STRAW IN THE WIND. MUSEUM TOO SMALL
AND SINCE SO CROWDED WHY NOT TAKE MY SPACE FOR MYSTERY
SHOW.[16] WE CAN WAIT FOR MORE QUIET TIME. AM I TO UNDERSTAND
FROM YOUR TELEGRAM THAT MUSEUM INTENDS TO CONTINUE WITH
OR WITHOUT MY COOPERATION.
FRANK LLOYD WRIGHT

■■■■

Letter from Wright to McAndrew, September 16, 1940

My dear John: I am sorry to have put you in such a tough spot. When you were here I thought I could go through with it, though greatly disappointed to find that what was to be a concentration of the Museum's resources on a complete showing of my work was to be really several shows, encroaching on the space we needed to give a show in keeping with our powers and resources. I intended to make it the show to end all other shows of my work.

Then just after you left I read Behrendt's article to find not only the same subtle subversion of my real usefulness as an architect to my own and this coming generation that got itself on record in the Boston catalogue, but also actual twistings of my own meaning in order to prove me false to my own principles and prove his case. Then I read [Talbot] Hamlin's article–inoffensive and ineffectual and I began to see the whole set-up as a post mortem–a kind of "Americana" extra, illustrated by a Griffith's bygone–etc. Both of us associated with a "mystery show" of more Americana set up in a building built beside the one we intended to build in the court.

Putting it all together it made a dismal picture. I had looked forward to a real honor and a real opportunity to get things on straight for a time at least with real ammunition all around only to find the museum had no money for us. Its real interest was elsewhere (no money in architectural shows)–space already inadequate made more inadequate.

Why should I invest thousands of my own money and concentrate my own time to do something epochal under those conditions when by biding my time the whole matter might be greatly improved? We had not seen any catalogue material or format either and were not to see any it seems. Not an auspicious circumstance either. So finally I decided to hold off.

My only regret is–at the moment–that I seem to desert you at the last moment when you had evidently been having an uphill pull all the way. It is that "uphill pull" that I am resenting now. That there should still be (at this time) such back drag is quite too much when all is added together. But I hope we shall continue friends, John, just the same. I've never had much faith or respect for what the museum has come to represent so there is little lost there.
Yours with regret but relief–
Frank Lloyd Wright

■ ■ ■ ■

Postcard from Barr to McAndrew, September 16, 1940

Dear John,
I suggest this policy on Wright–most tentatively for, since you've not phoned today I suppose all's well for the moment.

Explain to him that we have asked only those writers who admire him greatly–but having asked them we cannot censor their remarks–therefore if Wright does not want a Festschrift on this basis we have no other alternative than to abandon it–but the decision is *immediate*. This is just a suggestion–but let's not let the matter drag on. We can publish some of the essays later perhaps. A.

■ ■ ■ ■

Dear Mr. Wright,

As you will, of course, appreciate, it is very difficult for me to write to you. We are still desperately anxious to have your exhibition, and want to urge you to reconsider your decision. We will make every effort to eliminate the causes of your present dissatisfaction.

Two of them eliminate themselves: (1) There is no longer time to see an adequate catalogue through the press—and after all the exhibition need not be incomplete without a catalogue. (2) The large "mystery" exhibition has been shelved because money could not be raised. This exhibition was always separate from the regular activities of the Museum and was in no way a competitor of yours. The hoped-for money was to have been from separate sources; it was not using funds normally available to the Museum, which might therefore have been used for your exhibition instead.

As to the space—we will give you the ground floor as originally planned (including the whole garden for the house) and in addition the five bays on the second floor facing the garden.

I have raised $1000 more on the house (from Philip Goodwin and a friend). The Museum can put in $2500, Philip Johnson $500, an anonymous donor $1000,[17] and Pittsburgh Plate Glass probably about $500. Total: $5500. We have found a contractor who will build it at cost (the cost may be higher in New York than in Madison).

We have about $1800 left in our budget for the exhibition itself. Of this about half will be needed for installation costs (carpenters, painters, electricians, etc.).

The Museum wants to have the exhibition very much, and certainly does not want to make "Americana" of your work, nor to bury you alive as an "Old Master." With greatness on your side and real appreciation on ours, what we want and what you want are really the same—an adequate presentation of your work which will leave the spectator with some vivid understanding of your true importance.

May I beg you one last time to reconsider, and let us work out something good together. Not just because I am in hot water, but because I and the whole Museum staff really want to see the exhibition and the house right here in New York. I hope you will wire "yes."

Anxiously,

[unsigned carbon copy]

. . . .

Letter from Wright to McAndrew, September 19, 1940[18]

My dear John: No answer to my question leads me to believe the Museum people would proceed with its show over my head. So it is only fair to warn them that I shall enjoin the museum from doing anything of the kind. A man must have some protection against the circulation of matter prejudicial to his practice of his profession and an exploitation of his work objectionable to him because presented in equivocal manner also objectionable.

The conclusions of the Behrendt piece are distinctly objectionable. I am not an adventurer in experiment to gratify a passion for experiment at my clients' expense. Youth in America does not distrust me. I am not a hangover from a bygone era. I did not say that we no longer wanted any style; I said the exact opposite.

Anyone reading the Behrendt piece as a preface to a voluntary showing of my work would consider these statements endorsed by me and would be foolish to ever employ me under any circumstances whatsoever.

So unless the Museum wants to be involved in a serious suit which will add nothing to their credit and give me a lot of undesirable action myself–this is fair warning to lay off. I am writing this to find out if it is going to be necessary. I think you can tell me if you want to.
Sincerely, as always
Frank Lloyd Wright

■ ■ ■ ■

Letter from Wright to Behrendt, September 19, 1940

Dear Curt Behrendt: I have objected to your foreword (or preface) to the proposed show of my work at the Museum of Modern Art because you represent me as a reckless experimenter at the expense of my clients to gratify my own passion for mere experiment, and you misquote me and misunderstand my reference to the undesirability of *a* style (as any style whatever)–and finally you assume that I am a hangover from a past distrusted by youth today because of my personal style as a romanticist and therefore destined to disappear in the larger view of art which is impending.

Now I submit that these are not the facts and I have taken the liberty of putting some few of the objectionable points in order with what I believe I can show to be the truth.

I should like your reaction to my presumptuous editorial amendments–see copy of your manuscript herewith.[19]
Sincerely yours,
Frank Lloyd Wright

■ ■ ■ ■

Telegram from Wright to McAndrew, September 19, 1940

IF SILENCE ASSENTS THAT MUSEUM INTENDS SHOW OVER MY HEAD
WOULD LIKE INTERVIEW WITH MUSEUM AUTHORITIES WHEN I REACH
NEW YORK NEXT WEEK WEDNESDAY.
FRANK LLOYD WRIGHT

■■■■

Telegram from McAndrew to Wright, September 19, 1940

NO SHOW HERE WITHOUT YOUR CONSENT AND HELP. SORRY TO
HAVE BEEN SLOW IN ANSWERING. LETTER WAS MAILED YESTERDAY.
JOHN

■■■■

Telegram from Wright to McAndrew, September 20, 1940

THAT EQUIVOCAL CATALOGUE GONE AGONY ABATED. AT WORK AGAIN
ON EXHIBIT. WILL FIND OTHER CONTRIBUTIONS TOWARD HOUSE.
WILL BE IN NEW YORK NEXT WEDNESDAY.[20]
FRANK LLOYD WRIGHT

■■■■

Telegram from Janet Henrich, McAndrew's assistant, to McAndrew, September 21, 1940

BEHRENDT RECEIVED FANTASTIC LETTER AND REVISED VERSION OF
ARTICLE FROM WRIGHT TODAY. BRINGING COPIES FOR YOUR AMAZEMENT
AND AMUSEMENT. LETTER IMPLIED, AT LEAST, THAT SHOW IS STILL ON.
THOUGHT YOU MIGHT LIKE TO KNOW. BEHRENDT'S CHECK NEVER CAME
HOPE YOU CAN DO SOMETHING ABOUT IT MONDAY. HAPPY WEEKEND CHUM
JANET

■■■■

Letter from Behrendt to Wright, September 30, 1940

Dear Frank Lloyd Wright:
I have your letter of September 19. As you did not like my article, I withdrew the manuscript
from the Museum of Modern Art.
Sincerely yours,
Walter Curt Behrendt

■■■■

Dear Mr. McAndrew:

In reply to a letter from Frank Lloyd Wright, telling me that he has protested against the publication of my essay as an introduction to the book which you plan to publish, I wrote him that I withdrew the manuscript from the Museum of Modern Art. I am sorry that this project, which was started under such promising auspices, had to end in a mess caused by bad temper of a "genius."

I would like you to send me, at once, my check, for which I have already asked several times, so that I can get this whole thing out of my system.

Sincerely yours,

W. C. Behrendt

■■■■

Letter from Wright to Behrendt, October 5, 1940

Mr dear Curt Behrendt:

I am sorry anything should interfere with our mutual admiration. You have been very kind, even generous, to me and I took exception to your piece for the Museum Catalogue in the event of the show which I intend to end all shows of my work because of certain errors I felt you would not have made had we known each other better or had you known our people better. We have really seen very little of each other as you know. Having had the Boston show subjected to a foolish offensive prejudgment on its face, I was unwilling that another should follow it.

This time I asked to see what the museum intended to put as a label on the show. Well–to be candid, I found that if the first two thirds of your piece were true the subsequent third could not possibly be or vice versa. Certain errors of fact also I could not overlook–like the reference on the construction of the Imperial Hotel, wrong implication from my statement concerning style, and the danger to my clients of my chronic experimental habit comparing it to that of the middle ages which made the vaulting eventually fall down, the mistrust of American youth, etc., etc. These mistakes given authority as the preface to the show would have been damaging to my practice to the degree that anyone had faith in Behrendt and the Museum. Perhaps I am wrong to consider either important. But I well know the misconceptions current concerning myself and my work and I did not wish to increase the confusion of mind. I did not know you shared the confusion until I read your preface, hence my protest direct.

Furthermore I object on principle to the habit of having some critic issue prejudgments for an exhibition that is intended to speak to intelligent people for itself. So the catalogue was withdrawn. There will be none. I, for one, do not regret the fact in this case.

I do not, and hope you do not, feel this to be a sufficient basis for any sort of ill feeling between us. I certainly do not. What you wrote was no doubt written in good faith even if mistaken as I believe. In self defense I have taken the unusual–perhaps unwarranted liberty of trying to rectify what I know to be mistaken. But, if you are not convinced, and are of the same opinion still–I shall be your friend just the same as before and hope someday we may understand each other better.

Sincerely yours as always,

Frank Lloyd Wright

■ ■ ■ ■

PLEASE SEND AIRMAIL NEW LOCATION FOR HOUSE AND I WILL
SEE WHAT I CAN DO. ANXIOUS ALSO FOR OTHER MATERIAL AS SOON
AS POSSIBLE SO THAT WE CAN GET AHEAD WITH WORK HERE AND
PREVENT DISASTROUS LAST MINUTE RUSHING. REGARDS
JOHN

■ ■ ■ ■

Letter from Wright to McAndrew, October 10, 1940

Dear John: We agreed to the position of the house and indicated it in red pencil on a drawing in your treasurer's office.[21] If you have lost it, herewith is the original placement I showed you at Taliesin. This is better all around I think than the red pencil placement because I allowed you at that meeting to push the house off the axis I had fixed so that access from the Museum would be easy (a natural approach from the corridor). Seems to me the back-yard as a whole is going to be better with the house well situated than with the house pushed to one side. I think you would think so could you see the house built and in proper place.

When can we go to work? We are ready now. The mat should go down at once so the house can go up. The coils and boiler complete are a contribution and in work already.

As to dates: John, we can't be ready by your opening date. We intend to charter an express car if we can. At any rate a freight car, perhaps attached to a slow passenger train and bring everything down in it. We are making all the pedestals for models ourselves–so all we will have to do is to place the sixteen or seventeen models in the place marked on the plans.

A drawing of the natural walnut plywood screens we will require for showing our drawings is herewith–I offer it as a good way to show plans with perspectives above. The photographs will perhaps be placed on the walls but I hate to spoil the background for the screens with them. But we have 20 color enlargements 11x14 for the window wall, etc., etc.

We are working on something, now, to show you–disposing of the black and white photographs. So why can't the opening event be postponed one week (ten days would be better)–to make it a success instead of a promise? Your invitations could be sent out for the later date or notice given of postponement–attributing all the blame to me.

Here's hoping–because the work we have been doing night and day (all hands) for two months is wonderful and you will have seen nothing to compare with it in your life-time–I promise you.

This is the show to end all F.LL.W. shows–
Faithfully,
F.LL.W

■ ■ ■ ■

Telegram from McAndrew to Wright, October 11, 1940

HOUSE CAN GO WHERE YOU WISH BUT IT WILL THEN HAVE TO BE
DEMOLISHED JANUARY 15. IF IT CAN GO TWENTY-FIVE FEET OR MORE
TO THE WEST IT CAN REMAIN UNTIL NEXT SEPTEMBER. IT DOES NOT
LOOK POSSIBLE NOW TO POSTPONE OPENING. REGARDS,
JOHN

■ ■ ■ ■

Telegram from Wright to McAndrew, October 11, 1940

WOULD RATHER HAVE THE HOUSE RIGHT FOR A FORTNIGHT THAN
WRONG FOR A YEAR WHEN MAY WE START WE ARE READY.
FLW.

■ ■ ■ ■

Letter from Behrendt to Wright, October 17, 1940

Dear Frank Lloyd Wright:

If there would have been any ill feeling on my part about your disliking my piece written for the Museum of Modern Art, your most cordial letter would have removed it.

I can see your points although I cannot agree with your arguments, of course. My essay was written as another attempt to interpret your work and its significance for the movement towards an organic architecture.

Even in view of the few statements in my article to which you took exception, my readers, I believe, must feel the deep admiration which I have for your work, and have had ever since, many years ago, I saw the first piece of it. If some of this admiration could be conferred upon my readers, my article, I believe, would have served its purpose.

I regret that until now I did not have any opportunity to talk to you at length and to discuss with you the problems of our mutual interest. I know the loss is all on my side.
In unchanged admiration I am, as ever,
Sincerely yours,
Walter Curt Behrendt

■ ■ ■ ■

Dear Mr. Wright:

The red-tape on the building permit seems endless; it now looks as though we ought to have it by Tuesday or Wednesday. The Fire Commissioner is going over the prints now; we expect no trouble from him though there may be a little delay. It will be necessary to have all our draperies flame-proofed. After the Fire Commissioner, the City engineers have to go over the prints and that too will take a little time.

Is it your intention to let a number of small separate contractors rather than to hand the whole job over to one contractor? This procedure makes things much more difficult in the city. Each contractor has to be all Union and each has to file liability insurance papers with the Building Department. The Northeastern Construction Company which is now figuring on the concrete and brickwork is an excellent firm and willing to do the whole job at cost. I would urge that we make them contractor for the whole thing–millwork, roofing, everything. It will simplify and speed things up here, I am sure.

It was good to hear that you had obtained a gift of the boiler and pipes. I hope the donors will not mind that the boiler is not used, for we shall have to use City Steam for the heating in the pipes.

Will you let me know the name of the nursery which will give shrubs and trees and ask them to get in touch with me, for we must do some moving before frost.

The exact location of the house cannot yet be fixed. It may still have to be shifted a few feet one way or the other because of property lines and other red-tape.

Finally: the Building Department will need a set of cloth prints of the building and on these prints must be noted all the points, exceptions, etc. They are allowing us certain minor violations which will have to be noted on the prints. If you could send us a set of tracings air mail, we would make these notations on them and have the cloth prints made for the Building Department. None of the notes or other requirements will affect the prints or construction of the building in any way.

Enclosed is a print of the two floors of the exhibition based on the drawing you sent to us [plate 2]. We would like to keep as close to the outline-program of the show (which we sent you)[22] as is possible for our public is not well informed on architectural matters and seems always to get more out of an exhibition that has some definite and clear program. This is partic-ularly important in the beginning. Might it not be wise, therefore, to give the ground floor over to domestic work, bringing the house models down from the second floor and even sacrificing the handsome effect of the skyscraper model on the first floor for the sake of consistency (we could send that model to the second floor to be shown near St. Marks.)[23] You will notice that I suggest exchanging the positions of the Johnson and Robie houses in order that the program could be followed more clearly at the beginning.[24] This seemed a good idea also for the reason that the Robie model is so inferior to the models you are making that it really ought to be seen before them in order not to make it look the miserable step-child it would appear after the handsome new ones.

The long row of stands facing the long east wall are shoved back between the columns as I was afraid that there would not be comfortable room for people to look at the drawings and to have others pass by them if it encroached into that space at all. The Willey or some other model might be placed at the end of this wall in a dramatic position at the end of a long sweeping vista.[25]

Will it be necessary to have seats in the little projection room, or is it your intention to have people watch the films while standing? I am not sure how long the films are.

I am sorry that the exit arrangements were not indicated clearly on my drawing; the exit from the first floor exhibition area to the stairway has to be through the same broad hall that is used as entrance.

On the second floor we were afraid that the long unbroken row of pictures on the south wall might discourage our often timid and easily fatigued public, therefore I suggest interrupting with foliage and a bench as shown and letting the visitor alternate from side to side in looking at the pictures. A long line of plants would make him continue to the easternmost bay (where the Johnson model is shown) and then work back in a westerly direction to the dramatic climax of Broadacre City. I have suggested that the long free-standing drawing racks be cut up a little to leave a wider passage for crowds between the end and the window.

We are finding out about the possibility of a freight car and our Registrar, Miss Dudley, will write you what arrangement is possible within the next few days.

And now at last some very good news which I hope will please you: it has been decided to postpone the opening until November 12th. This extra time ought to relieve pressure and make it possible for us to have the first-rate show we all want so much.
Sincerely,
John McAndrew

■ ■ ■ ■

Letter from Wright to McAndrew, October 28, 1940

Dear John: The changes you suggest upset, somewhat, the general effect of the model grouping as I see it and diminishes the effect I wanted to get. The tall models should by no means be seen together–each should be isolated and accented seen as features of the whole. One good reason–the 1911 skyscraper is 3/8" scale.[26] St. Marks is only 1/4" scale. The Johnson House should be seen all around. We have yet two most interesting houses–Spivey and Jester yet to place.[27] Also we have comparatively little space for drawings.

Don't you allow too much for plants and crowd? We will have to leave out much needed material. If essential we can do this but how essential is it?

Nothing for photographs has been left. What shall we do with them? I do not like them mixed up with the drawings–as you know.

The "toot and scramble" of the altered plans is much weaker as a whole than as I hoped it would be. Can't we compromise, or something?

Another thing. The model of the Jacobs House is interesting seen in connection with the actual house—as I had it, etc.[28] The long screen surfaces you have seen fit to break up were really in keeping with the style we know how to use best—and had intended to use for continuity in showing progressions. Why must benches break them up? And the screens of course don't have to go between the posts unless you have reasons.

The strategic views (closures of the vistas) you have given over to benches which seems a sad waste. I think there should be benches but not as primal features of the show (have suggested bench features). But no doubt we can work all this out together except that we won't have screens enough to get the space I wanted. Was perhaps economy in this direction a motive in the rearrangement? If so we could arrange to fix that.

Faithfully,

F.LL.W.

N.B. Original drawings [of the Exhibition House] are in this afternoon's air-express. Kindly return them to us *immediately* after you have made your necessary cloth prints.

Herewith the first and second floor layouts. I have marked on these prints myself and wish to have you make photostats of the drawings and return the originals to me.

We can take over the sub-bids from Lyman on wood fabrication, do the masonry and be responsible for the whole thing but bid on masonry is double what it ought to be.

I have written Will Harris concerning shrubs and trees and will let you know outcome.

■■■■

Letter from John D. Rockefeller, Jr., to John E. Abbott, Executive Vice-President of The Museum of Modern Art, October 29, 1940

Dear Mr. Abbott:

Mrs. Rockefeller has given me your letter of October 22nd with the plans and photographs which accompanied it. The plans and photographs have been returned to you this morning as requested.

As I have explained to Mrs. Rockefeller, the deed transferring the property which I gave the Museum of Modern Art in the rear of its present building restricts construction on the property to a certain area adjacent to the building, covering in a small, semi-circular shape less than half of the property, and to a height not to exceed 16'6" above the curb.[29] It also restricts any such building to the corporate purposes for which the museum was incorporated.

I take it from the blueprints that if the building under consideration were to be constructed as laid out, it would not be confined within the area described in the deed. If this assumption is correct, it would appear that the trustees of the Museum of Modern Art are asking me to waive the conditions and to grant consent to the erection of the proposed building. Is this assumption correct? If so, will you kindly give me the following information:

What is the cost at which such a building can be produced for general use? How large a lot is required to accommodate and to give it adequate setting? Has the building ever been built? Is it a prefabricated building and, if so, by whom made? What relation has the designer of the building to its present exploitation? Would he be a party to its manufacture and general use and would he derive profit therefrom?

I have myself been much interested in inexpensive, conveniently arranged, well built, modern homes and have spent some time and money in studying and experimenting with the problem. From what little I know of the subject, it does not seem to me that the proposed building is economical either to build, to maintain or to operate. Moreover, it would seem to require a pretty large tract of land, relatively speaking, and to have various factors which, while attractive, would add considerably to the original cost and the maintenance cost.

Very truly,

John D. Rockefeller, Jr.

■ ■ ■ ■

Letter from McAndrew to Wright, October 30, 1940

Dear Mr. Wright:

Enclosed are prints of layout[30] based on your corrected sketches and also the sketches you sent us. The whole seems to be working out very well. I hope you will like it. And here are a few questions, etc.–numbered thus on plan:

1. Is it necessary for us to build anything in advance for the bench and plywood screen arrangement by the entrance to the exhibition? Perhaps the back of this would be a good place for more photographs.

2. If the Robie model sticks out with a spur wall behind it, it will stop people and make them return to drawings or photographs on the opposite side.

3. Would the Johnson House be all right here? The location of it leaves a little more space for crowds.

4. We could make quite a showing of photographs here.

5. I shoved this back between the columns to leave more room for passage, otherwise uncomfortably tight.

6. This ought to be very attractive at end of vista.

7. Perhaps models of other houses here as well. We all feel very strongly that the single family houses ought to be shown together on the ground floor to bring out some of the important points listed in the outline under "Reforming the House."[31] If we can start people thinking clearly at the beginning of the show by giving them simple, clear and direct exposition in related series of pictures, labels, models, etc., they will continue through the rest of the show with a far more intelligent appreciation of what they see. Most of them will not know anything about architecture when they come in. We want them to when they leave.

End wall in this room white for projection of films.

8. Do you want us to supply the projector? Is the film 16 mm.?

101. (Second floor) Racks arranged this way rather than in opposite rows to keep people moving ahead. We have found that opposite rows really cause circulation trouble if people turn back to look at every picture shown. The result is that when there are even small crowds, people just don't look at all of the material shown.

102. Would this do for the 1911 skyscraper. It could be very dramatic against the tall window with sky for background. Since both it and St. Mark's are skyscrapers, it would seem reasonable to keep them near together but not visible simultaneously (and not mix the 1911 project in with the houses). With them—the two skyscraper models—we could show drawings or photos of the Chicago National Life Insurance skyscraper,[32] Temple Heights,[33] Luxfer Prism,[34] etc. etc.

103. We might paint these walls white or sky blue or a deeper soft brown to make variety and a strong dramatic ending for the exhibition with the presentation of Broadacre City. (Am leaving one or two other walls temporarily white to see how they look.)

I hope you can send me your reactions to these suggestions without delay.

Our carpenters are making up a section of the racks for displaying drawings as a sample. We may be able to get walnut Presdwood[35] for about half the price of walnut plywood, and it will look just the same. (The $588 for the freight car takes up about all the money we had left.)

Could you write me right away, or wire me about the points in this letter. As it is less than two weeks to the afternoon of the twelfth when the critics have to come in for their preview, and to the big private evening opening that night when thousands and thousands will come to see the exhibition, we are desperately anxious to get ahead, as you of course know. Full of excitement and hope,
John

P.S. Perhaps it would expedite matters if you could have the photographs and drawings that are already done sent on ahead now, by parcel post or quick express.

■ ■ ■ ■

Letter from Wright to McAndrew, November 1, 1940

Dear John: Layout now seems O.K. except a fundamental disagreement concerning the tall models. You see, St. Marks belongs with Broadacre City and was ideal as a kind of newel post for the second floor show as well.

The 1911 San Francisco Tall building began and grouped with the early work where it belongs as it was—makes a kind of newel post for the main floor group. On the wall to the side, left as you enter, is a group of black and whites of Larkin, Winslow,[36] Robie, etc., etc.

If it isn't too important to you for some reason not stated, let's leave them where I placed them making the entrance seat part of the walnut pedestal for the 1911—making the ensemble look good to me. The model is not the one you saw. It is new and a beauty and belongs to the scheme as above. *The idea* I have in mind is to characterize strongly at the beginning the early work–and its principal forms–showing the last prairie house–(Johnson) in this group–then proceeding about in order–the Willey house to put abolition of kitchen as objectionable unit, etc., etc., etc.

And too I like very much the perspective of the house in the court seen with the tall white model as a shoulder for the perspective (at the entrance)–rather than have all chicken feed on the main floor with no relief–or am I all wet? If so, why?

Evidently there is something in your mind you don't say or you wouldn't interfere, would you?

I want to start *strong* and end *strong*.

THE HOUSE   (early)   (late)

A brick must be selected [for the Exhibition House] to lay up 9 courses in 26 inches–joints about 5/8" high to be raked 1/2" deep. Bond to be laid out so all vertical joints are very close and stopped with mortar the color of the brick. *You* might pick out a brick harmonious with redwood or send me samples. I am trying here to put six or seven boys in the car with the models so they can do some of the captions at the Museum–will you help at that end?
Faithfully,
F.LL.W.

■■■■

Letter from Wright to McAndrew, November 1, 1940

JOHN: An idea–
Since the models are all placed low so the plan of the building is evident and all roofs come off to show the interiors and this is not one of those exhibitions (I hope) where people walk through as though driven to the W.C. by a cathartic–to enable them to view and study I suggest you have made (for me) 50 small plywood seats to be nested under the models so anyone so minded can sit down to the lower perspectives which are invariably enchanting.

The little plywood seats should be 3/4" x 12 x 14 tops, a 12x12 x 3/4" square piece cut in on the center of the 14" way–thus
[see opposite]

Seat will be 12 3/4" from floor and slip under all models and thus take up no space on the floor. We will take the minor seats after the show.
F.LL.W.

Go on along into debt, John. It will do us all good.
FLW

■■■■

JOHN: An idea --

Since the models are all placed low so the plan of the
building is evident and all roofs come off to show the
interiors and this is not one of those exhibitions (I hope)
where people walk through as though driven to the W.C.
by a cathartic -- to enable them to view and study I suggest
you have made (for me) 50 small plywood seats to be nested
under the models so anyone so minded can sit down to the
lower perspectives which are invariably enchanting.

The little plywood seats should be 3/4" x 12 x 14 tops, a
12x12 x 3/4" square piece cut in on the center of the
14" way - thus

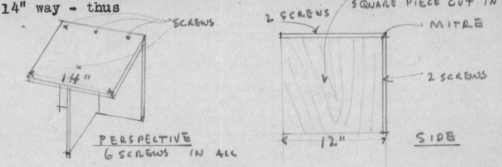

SCREWS

14"

PERSPECTIVE
6 SCREWS IN ALL

2 SCREWS

SQUARE PIECE CUT IN.

MITRE

2 SCREWS

12"   SIDE

Seat will be 12 3/4" from floor and slip under all models
and thus take up no space on the floor. We will take the
minor seats after the show.

F.LL.W.   November 1st, 1940

F.LL.W   Go on along into debt - John - It will do
us all good

Telegram from Wright to McAndrew, November 1, 1940

LET NEWMAN LOEB CONSTRUCTION COMPANY GO AHEAD.[37] CARAWAY
ON WAY TO HELP.[38] EXPRESS CAR LEAVING HERE WITH EVERYTHING
READY TO SET IN PLACE. SEVEN MEN GOING ALONG IN CAR TO CARE
FOR MATERIAL AND HELP WHEN ALL ARRIVES MUSEUM SATURDAY MORNING.
RAILROAD SHOULD ALLOW CARETAKERS TO RIDE ALONG FREE. SOME
DIFFICULTY ABOUT THIS HERE. SEE WHAT YOU CAN DO. EXPECT TO WORK
NIGHTS AND SUNDAY. PREPARING INTEGRAL TITLES HERE SO CONFUSION
AVOIDED. SEVEN HUNDRED DOLLARS FROM YOU NEEDED HERE RIGHT NOW.
FRANK LLOYD WRIGHT

■■■■

Telegram from Wright to McAndrew, November 2, 1940

THIS END OF THE STICK GETTING PRETTY HEAVY AT THE MOMENT. HOPE
YOU WILL DO ALL YOU CAN LETTER CONTAINING PLANS AND SUGGESTIONS
AIR MAILED YESTERDAY. WHY SO SLOW WITH THE HOUSE BEST PART OF THÉ
SHOW. MRS. WRIGHT AND I COMING TO SUPERVISE AND WE HOPE TO DINE.
FRANK LLOYD WRIGHT

■■■■

Telegram from Wright to McAndrew, November 2, 1940

HAVING THIN PLYWOOD ALPHABET MADE FOR ALL TITLES FIXING THEM
TO WALNUT BASES OF MODELS AND TO BE FIXED TO WALNUT SCREENS
WHEN WE ARRIVE. BROADACRE ROOM SHOULD BE SAME SOFT NEUTRAL
COLOR AS SPECIFIED ELSEWHERE. MODELS SO LIVELY NEED QUIET ROOM.
INVESTIGATING VAN TRANSFER TO SAVE DOUBLE HANDLING. ALL EASEL
STANDS SHOULD BE MADE AND IN PLACE BEFORE WE ARRIVE. I WONDER
WHAT STUPIDITY OR FEAR CAN BE HOLDING UP THE HOUSE.
FRANK LLOYD WRIGHT

■■■■

Telegram from McAndrew to Wright, November 2, 1940

GOING AHEAD WITH LAYOUT IN REVISED FORM RECEIVED THIS MORNING.
SKYSCRAPERS OK APART AS YOU SUGGEST. UNDERSTAND REASONS
BETTER NOW. WOULD SOFT SKY BLUE DO FOR BROADACRE ROOM?
HOPEFUL ON HOUSE KEEP YOUR FINDERS CROSSED.
JOHN

■■■■

Dear Mr. Rockefeller:

Thank you very much for your letter of October 29 regarding the Frank Lloyd Wright house which the Museum hopes to build in the garden. It would remain on view throughout the summer of 1941 and would then be circulated to ten other museums throughout the United States for a three-year period.

The building of this house is considered by the Trustees not so much as a building project as an actual architectural exhibition of the work of a man who the Department of Architecture feels is the greatest living architect.

The Trustees of the Museum would like to ask you to waive the conditions covering the garden land and to grant them permission to erect the proposed building as a temporary structure. Since I did not feel qualified to answer the questions set forth in your letter, I have asked John McAndrew, Curator of the Department of Architecture, to do so and I enclose his memorandum to me.

I trust that this will give you the information you desire but should there be anything else that I can provide, I would appreciate hearing from you further or I would be delighted to call upon you at any time.

Very sincerely yours,

John E. Abbott

The following is the "enclosed memorandum" written by McAndrew and mentioned in the letter above.

The principal reason for erecting the proposed house would be to give New Yorkers their first opportunity to see an actual building by America's greatest architect.

The house would be important for many other reasons. The Department of Architecture feels that it would demonstrate vividly several new ideas in architecture which could be applied with advantage to the building of houses for those with relatively limited funds.

Cost. The house would be of a type of plan and construction which Mr. Wright has been developing over the last five years. Several have already been built; several more are in construction. Cost has varied according to size and location. For example:

Jacobs House, Madison, Wis.	$5500
Pope House, Falls Church, Va.	6500
Baird House, Amherst, Mass.	6500
Christie House, Bernardsville, N.J.	
(about 1/3 larger than others)	10000

Construction and heating. The construction is of a simplified new type.

There is no basement. The house stands on a rigid 4" concrete mat which serves also as floor. The heating pipes are embedded in the concrete, eliminating the need (and expense) of radiators.

This type of heating costs less to install than common systems, but costs very slightly more to operate. However, it produces a more even temperature in each room of the house than any regular heating system now in use. Because of this uniformity, the house is kept 10–15° lower in temperature than is usual, and this has been found to be actually more comfortable and more healthy than the results of traditional heating arrangements.

The walls of the house stand on the concrete mat. A few sections are of common brick; the rest are of wood. Redwood clapboards are screwed to each side of a plywood core, resulting in a wall only 2 1/2" thick, but as effective in insulation against the weather as the more elaborate common scheme of a stud frame with wood sheathing and clapboards on the outside and plaster on the inside. The proposed house is finished the same inside and out, that is, redwood and brick. Paint, plaster and interior trim have been eliminated.

The construction is rigid, durable and, for wood, highly fire resistant (no air space).

The flat roof rests on these walls; its ordinary 2 x 4 joists brace the whole construction. It is one flat plane, easy to build and to care for. As far as we can discover, there has been no trouble from leaks in the houses built. There are no gutters; rain drops from the projecting eaves well away from the house.

There is no walled garage. A car is kept under a roof only, in the "car-port." This has proved successful in a climate as cold and snowy as Wisconsin.

Upkeep. This has been found to be below average in the houses already built, despite the slightly more expensive heating. The house is unusually easy to keep clean.

Size. The longest dimensions are about 60' x 80'. The house could be placed comfortably on a lot about 100' x 100'. Those built so far have been on inexpensive land in towns or on the outskirts of small cities rather than on the more expensive land of larger cities or their suburbs.

Prefabrication. Mr. Wright has been studying prefabrication for over forty years. He developed a "ready-cut" wood house around 1910 of which about 40 were built, and a system of pre-cast concrete block construction, developed in a half dozen houses in California in the 1920s.

The type of house under consideration could be semi-prefabricated. That is, the concrete and brickwork would be carried out on the job in the usual manner, but the wooden walls, windows, doors, and all other wood-work would be completed in parts at the mill, trucked to the job and erected there.

Although the houses of this type already executed have been built on a custom basis, and commercial manufacture in quantity has not been seriously envisaged, semi-prefabrication would seem to be successfully applicable (if this were to take place, Mr. Wright would, presumably, be directly concerned, and receive some profit in the nature of royalties. The house the Museum would like to erect would be custom-built, and he would receive no profit.)

The house, planned originally as part of the comprehensive exhibition of Wright's 50 years in American architecture, would be displayed in the garden in much the same way as an important piece of sculpture (or as in the recent Mexican show[39] a temporary structure for the display of pottery and rugs.)

　　　　We believe that, in spite of certain minor defects of planning, the house as a characteristic work of a man whom many consider to be the greatest living architect, would be more interesting to the public than any work of sculpture. We would hope to keep the house on view throughout the coming summer.

■　■■■

Telegram from Wright to McAndrew, November 4, 1940

HAVE ARRANGED WITH TWO LARGE COAST TO COAST LINES VANS
FROM STUDIO DOOR TO MUSEUM DOOR ARRIVING NEW YORK FRIDAY
NIGHT TOTAL COST $525 HOW DO I GET THOSE SEATS
F LL W

■　■■■

Telegram from Dorothy Dudley, Registrar, The Museum of Modern Art, to Wright,
November 4, 1940

DELIGHTED WITH VAN ARRANGEMENTS BUT NEED MATERIAL HERE
THURSDAY NIGHT. PLEASE CONFIRM.
DOROTHY DUDLEY

■　■■■

Telegram from Wright to McAndrew, November 4, 1940

TRUCK ARRANGEMENTS ALL COMPLETED TO ARRIVE FRIDAY
EVENING. TO GO TO WORK SATURDAY MORNING.
FRANK LLOYD WRIGHT

■　■■■

Telegram from Wright to McAndrew, November 5, 1940

DIDN'T I UNDERSTAND YOU WERE SENDING A STIPEND OR IS ABBOTT RECREANT
F LL W

■　■■■

Frank Lloyd Wright, American Architect opens formally on November 12 and to the public on November 13, 1940.

■ ■ ■ ■

Letter from Rockefeller to Stephen C. Clark, Chairman of the Board of The Museum of Modern Art, November 12, 1940

Dear Mr. Clark:

Mrs. Rockefeller told me several weeks ago that the Museum of Modern Art had in mind the erection as a temporary exhibit, of a one-story dwelling house of modern design on its vacant property to the north. A photographic illustration of the house, also plans of it were submitted by Mr. Abbott with his letter of October 22nd to Mrs. Rockefeller. Under date of October 29th I wrote Mr. Abbott a letter, of which I enclose a copy and from which I quote the following paragraphs:

"As I have explained to Mrs. Rockefeller, the deed transferring the property which I gave the Museum of Modern Art in the rear of its present building restricts construction on the property to a certain area adjacent to the building, covering in a small, semi-circular shape less than half of the property, and to a height not to exceed 16'6" above the curb. It also restricts any such building to the corporate purposes for which the museum was incorporated.

"I take it from the blueprints that if the building under consideration were to be constructed as laid out, it would not be confined within the area described in the deed. If this assumption is correct, it would appear that the trustees of the Museum of Modern Art are asking me to waive the conditions and to grant consent to the erection of the proposed building. Is this assumption correct?"

Under date of November 3rd Mr. Abbott wrote me enclosing a memorandum prepared for him by Mr. McAndrew, copies of which I am sending you herewith.

Several years ago I agreed to the use by the Museum for an outdoor sculpture exhibit during the World's Fair, of the unoccupied land on 54th Street to the east and west of the Museum's vacant lot.[40] At that time it was not expected that the Fair would remain open a second year. Although I do not recall that anything has been said to me about the matter, I have let the privilege run on for that further period, which has now ended.

My relations with the Museum of Modern Art, both as an adjacent property holder and as a donor of property to it, have been most pleasant, as I hope they may always be. Perhaps I am wrong but it seems to me that the best assurance of the continuation of such relations is the strict adherence to the terms under which the vacant property was given and the adjacent lands temporarily loaned. Therefore, it would be my hope that the Trustees would not be inclined to press their suggestion of so radical a departure from these agreements.

While it would be inappropriate for me to make suggestions to your Trustees, as an interested property holder in the vicinity I may perhaps be permitted to say that in my judgment, were such a house as contemplated built even temporarily, it would materially detract from rather than add to the appearance of the general area. Furthermore, is it not probable that for a fractional part of what it would cost to build this house, a model of it could be made and exhibited in one of the rooms of the Museum, which model would, to a large degree if not wholly, achieve the desired result?

Feeling sure that you and your associates would want me to speak with the frankness which characterizes this letter and relying upon your acceptance of it in the spirit of sympathetic good will in which it is written, I am,
Very sincerely,
John D. Rockefeller, Jr.

■ ■ ■ ■

Letter from Clark to Rockefeller, November 16, 1940

Dear Mr. Rockefeller:
I have received your letter of November 12, together with copies of correspondence with Mr. Abbott, in reference to the erection of a dwelling-house, designed by Frank Lloyd Wright, as a temporary exhibit in the rear of the Museum.

I cannot tell you how much I regret that this proposal should have caused you so much annoyance and, of course, the trustees will be glad to adhere strictly to the terms of the deed of gift of the property which you so generously gave to the Museum.

The principal reason for suggesting a temporary modification of the restrictions placed on the property was the difficulty which the staff has encountered in dealing with Mr. Frank Lloyd Wright. Mr. Wright is possessed of a highly developed artistic temperament and after the staff had gone to a great deal of trouble and expense in getting together material for this exhibition, he threatened to call it off unless his ideas were strictly complied with. Among other things, he insisted that this dwelling-house should be erected in a particular place in the garden, which involved a slight encroachment on your property and it was for the purpose of trying to placate him that Mr. Abbott made this request of you.

I must confess that, due to my preoccupation with a number of difficult problems which have arisen in Nelson's absence,[41] I have paid very little attention to this exhibition and did not get an opportunity to see it until yesterday. I discovered that there is a model of this dwelling-house in the exhibition and I entirely agree with you that this model will meet all of the requirements of the situation. Moreover, I heartily concur in your criticism of the plan of this house. As an attempt to solve the cheap housing problem, it is ridiculous and I am glad that it is not going to be erected in the garden.

In your letter you say that it is your recollection that our agreement with you in regard to the use by the Museum of your unoccupied property on 54th Street has expired, but I find that a new lease of this property, for one year, was signed on October 15, 1940.

I hope that you will appreciate that we would never want to do anything in connection with the garden of the Museum or with the unoccupied property leased from you which would not meet with your approval. If at any time there is anything in connection with the activities of the Museum which you would like to discuss with me, I would be delighted to come to see you.

Very sincerely,

Stephen C. Clark.

■ ■ ■ ■

Letter from Wright to McAndrew, November 19, 1940

My dear John: Sorry to leave without seeing you. While the show, as a matter of course, leaves much to be desired for clarity, it is the best we can do. The work is there, richly spread but only roughly classified because any really helpful classification would make a show out of one or two or at most three buildings in our space and I wanted rather to give the "folks" a comprehensive amble through the work of the years for a kind of "birds eye view."

But I was surprised when you dumped the show on me as "arranged by himself."[42] I learned it first from the invitation. It was probably wise on your part as the time was so short and the matter so large and various. But, is the show worth something anyway with all its faults—so dumped?

Another surprise (in talking with Barr) was that you thought I had proscribed any catalogue at all. What I really expected (after you said that owing to my objection to gratuitous pre-mortem essays) there was no time to print the literary efforts you had collected with such good intention—to honor me I am sure—was that you would print the catalogue clean as you had already put the work of a real catalogue in upon it.

I saw at the museum the feeling engendered by my objection to the ornamental part of it and suppose the feeling was, "well since he won't have the catalogue we wanted, let's see him get along without any."

Notwithstanding these stresses and strains, John, and the fact that it seemed to me they had you on the spot besides—I want to thank you and your staff for weathering the storm—and thank Miss Herrick [*sic*] especially for "'scullerying' around after us for a week" as she put it apropos of a request for a cup of hot tea one afternoon.[43]

Yes John—I appreciate your effort. But for the suspicion aroused in me by the Boston experience all might have gone well. But for that I should have trusted you fully. Nevertheless as I now see the matter, *I am not yet dead* but working more purposefully and effectively than ever. Your critics took the line of a post mortem. Post mortems are inevitable someday—but are now offensive. Nay—nay. Not now, at least not when I can say "nay." I feel insulted, not honored, by any estimates of the past stultifying the present and cutting off the future. Who knows what is coming? Does the show look as though I had "given my bananas?" Really? If it does that was far from my hope or intention when I put all my resources of the moment in time and money—some several thousand dollars—into doing this thing with you and for you.

Oh well! "'Tis not so deep as a well nor so wide as a church-door" these wounds—I trust.[44] Turnips will not cease their growth—nor the potatoes cease opening and shutting their eyes beneath the ground.

So here's to you, John.

Sincerely,

F.LL.W.

N.B. Can't several "someones" go around and wet-blanket the show for eager visitors because there is no catalogue at all? And could the cinema of our work here be shown?[45] But who could give it the proper lift? I fear no one but you.

I'll be down again before we go west.

F. LL. W.

■ ■ ■ ■

Letter from Wright to Henry-Russell Hitchcock, November 23, 1940

My dear Russell: Thank you for your good letter. As I read your "piece" for the Museum catalogue I considered it both fair to me and valuable, withal well written. The reason the Museum catalogue was dropped was because, being still alive and working at the peak of my career on the up rather than on the down grade, I was impatient of post mortems. I wanted only presentation, explanation, and classification in the catalogue. John McAndrews had prepared a very nice lot of appreciations that, were they true as they began could only be wrong as they ended, even were I dead. But, being more alive than ever, some of the "appreciations" were preposterous. I put too much time and money into this show to end all "Frank Lloyd Wright shows" to see it warped aside from its objective, on its face, by well meant criticisms—but half-baked.

Well—to make the matter complete, not only was the catalogue dropped on the misunderstanding that I wanted no catalogue at all—but I learned from the formal announcement and invitation to [the] reception that *I had designed the installation of the show myself* instead of only trying to help John do it, and the house in the event-yard that was the *culmination* was dropped apparently. There were only a few days for the work left then and we—inexperienced and overburdened, did our best as you may see it. The material is all there for those who can dig for it, and the show is fairly presentable throughout. But with no explanation by way of a pertinent catalogue there is much seeming confusion and more real confusion. Much is likely to be wasted. So what must be, by internal evidence, the greatest thing of its kind in both significance and resources must go half appreciated and very little comprehended.

Now it has occurred to me that your qualifications for taking the thing as it is, getting photographs of the show in serial order, perhaps under the classification I attempted which was "in the nature of materials" (grouping buildings under structural headings with some heed paid to chronology) but with not so much critical reviewing as interpretation of the ideas explaining facts with proper significance . . . well, I believe yours would be about the best ability that could be had anywhere if you were interested to do such a thing at the moment.

I would contribute the money to defray expenses and guarantee to find the publisher to bring out the work on a royalty basis fair to you and I would give you Henry Klumb[46] to work with you to help get the record of inventions, structural schemes, and new building practice behind the show, on straight, without too much effort on your part. Meantime I would give of my own time where and whenever you required it. Thus the exhibit could be truly memorialized, properly on record instead of passing out forlornly misunderstood as it is now likely to do. Something timely and authentic is needed, always has been needed, and lacking where the work has been concerned. Nothing of this sort in any country has happened before because no country ever had anything like it to happen, or could have anything like it unless it would be Italy's Leonardo show–which is relatively less valuable to Italy and the world than this collection of thought-built buildings is to our country–the United States.

The chronology of the works the Museum already has.[47] We could begin with that, authenticate it, and relate it to the show as is: illustrate it with what we have or with fresh material added as you might require it.

The work would be entirely yours and would be as you would have it of course. My function or the relation of any one else in relation to it would be purely as you needed or could use it.

You might get leave of absence for a couple of weeks (or three) (I could put in a plea with your Wesleyan president) and come to the desert for the job, I paying all your expenses and $250.00 besides, guaranteeing you another advance of $250.00 from the publisher–the royalties above that to go 2/3rds to you and 1/3rd to me. The money is not much for your pains but more might come thru later.

I wish you would think of this as seriously, Russell as I am serious in proposing it. Now is the time to do this thing that is needed to be done. And do a catalogue that will take its place as the first really authentic and reliable record and presentation of a fundamental work that might do much more than it has done for the country if the country could really get a look inside this show. As things are it cannot.

Faithfully yours,
Frank Lloyd Wright

■■■■

Letter from Rockefeller to Clark, November 27, 1940

Dear Mr. Clark:

Being without a secretary until today, I have not been able to acknowledge earlier receipt of your letter of November 16th nor to thank you for the gracious spirit which pervades it.

I am interested, although not surprised, to learn that you feel quite as I do about the model house of Mr. Frank Lloyd Wright as well as the inappropriateness of its being erected in the rear of the Museum as was discussed. A model of the house exhibited in the Museum will, on the other hand, be exceedingly interesting and wholly worthwhile as a part of the general exhibit.

Since the receipt of your letter, I have learned through my office that the use by the Museum of my unoccupied property in 54th Street was continued by a renewal of the lease for another year from October 15th although, through an oversight on the part of my office, I was not so advised. Thus this continuing use which I am happy to be a party to, had already been officially agreed to.

If at any time there is anything in connection with the activities of the Museum which I would like to discuss with you, I shall not hesitate to avail of your kind offer to come to see me for that purpose and will be glad to advise you.

It is a source of great satisfaction to all those who know you that you have taken the leadership in the Museum's affairs.[48] I am sure you know what I hear on every side: that you have the complete confidence, respect and esteem of all those related to the Museum.

May I say in closing that I am sorry if anything which I said in my earlier letter gave you the impression that I was annoyed at the suggestion for the temporary use of the Museum's property to the north. After becoming somewhat familiar with the situation, I fully appreciated its embarrassment to you and only regret that anything I said in my letter was capable of being interpreted as indicative of annoyance, which was farthest from my purpose to express.
Very sincerely,
John D. Rockefeller, Jr.

■ ■ ■ ■

Letter from Wright to McAndrew, December 1, 1940

My dear John: I am wondering if anything of value to the museum, myself, or really to the general public can be had by sending out a traveling group of models, etc., to be further misunderstood. If editors of House and Garden (N.Y. Sunday Times) Magazines,[49] etc., etc. are so flat dumb where these are concerned why expect the dear people to understand them no matter how well presented?

It does seem that a proper education in building is the only preparation to really see even the model of a building. Drawings may be easier if they are in color. But I am beginning to doubt somewhat, that too. Our clients must be an astonishingly intelligent and unusual lot. It is easy enough for *them* to see the designs. Only the building itself seems to be "foolproof." And I guess we at Taliesin would better stick to that concrete evidence.

I may be in New York for a day early in the week on the Forum and we will talk it over. The loss of the actual house in the court was a tragedy for the show because that might have given more point to the models than anything else could and have made the whole (as intended) more easily comprehended. Think it over so you will have had some little time on it before I see you.
Faithfully yours,
F.LL.W

■ ■ ■ ■

Dear Mr. Wright,

After pulling all wires, we find that we cannot violate the law to use the property behind the Museum for our house, and that therefore we shall have to give up the whole project. This comes hard, as it has been one of my pet schemes for about two years. But there is nothing that can be done, apparently.

Also, the Film Library has gone over your reels of color film and found them in a dangerous condition. The films are badly dried out and many sprocket holes are broken; the films cannot be shown very often. A couple of weeks of gallery showings would destroy them. Therefore, we are planning to show them informally in our projection room to groups of students, architects, etc.

The attendance at the exhibition has been quite good and people seem to stay quite a long time and study the show seriously. We are gathering copies of the various reviews to send to you, though I suppose you have already seen the more important ones.

There is one gripping mystery! The smaller concrete cast block has vanished. Some admirer with good muscles and plenty of ingenuity made off with it despite our hawk-eyed guards. It is, as you know, insured so we will be able to collect on it.

We have labeled most of the unidentified drawings, put separated pictures of the same building together, and done a little minor tidying that there was not time to do in the opening rush. The show will be photographed soon and we will send you copies.

This letter is going to both Wisconsin and Arizona. In whichever place, I hope it finds you well, busy, and best in spirits.

Sincerely,

[unsigned carbon copy]

■■■■

Letter from Wright to McAndrew, December 9, 1940

Dear John—On the way far west. I hear the prominent ascription of the arrangement of the show by myself is still flaunted at the entrance—please take it down. If for no other reason because it is a misleading half truth.

I think, from you, should come the statement that the actual house in the court seen through the windows in connection with the plans and models inside the museum was my idea of the show. When that promise fell it is unfair to boast of a show arranged by me.

I did the best I damn could from Saturday to Tuesday evening to get the drawings together while painters electricians and carpenters were still mixed up with them and come by an eleventh hour idea of how to do it anyway. I understand why you wouldn't want to be responsible for it but why insist upon my bragging about it?

If anyone is interested to find out they can learn the truth.

I've always trusted my enemies more than my friends when they were honest open enemies–but I can't very well do much with the covert type, the slant and the insignificant ones. They are all pests and they are all I've had to deal with in making this show.

There was one attempt at debunking by a British baby–Baker, I think his name was (N.Y. Times)[50] (I had evidently thrown him a teething ring) but not one thing he said was worth attention because it was evident he didn't know anything of building.

So I've had no benefits of real criticism that could reward me for my pains.

We grow strong by opposition only when opposition is intelligent and well informed.

Evidently what I put into the show was above the heads of those who might be expected to put up a good fight against it.

Especially Broadacre City. The City is predicated on the motor car and traffic problems well solved–children walking to school, mothers walking to market–honestly the whole thing is based upon rapid easy modern transit–and yet "how can people get places" was "in the papers"–etc. etc.

I have yet to hear or see one question raised worth answering.

Which brings me to this question–: why send models and prints and plans of such advanced unusual work as must need patient individual explanation on tour in the country at large?

There would be constant model repairing needed:–and explaining. So–the only way a show should go forth is with an apprentice competent to make repairs and explain to go with it from place to place. If that can be arranged all right. If it can't be then this is final no to any travelling show at all.

In spite of all the tiresome features of the mix-up–John–I still like you and wouldn't hesitate to do anything I could for you because I am sure you meant well.

But I should like some explanation from treasurer Abbott as to why he let me proceed with a detailed set of plans for which I would ordinarily have charged $1000.00 when he had no basis for the encouragement. The matter is on file in the minutes of the conversation between us in his office.

After all has been done and said I do not feel that the museum honored me in this exhibition anymore than I honored the museum. My ideas of such "honors" however may not be conventional. As to expense, I think the time (and money) I spent ($3000.00 wouldn't cover the money from which might be deducted $500.00 received from you) more for me to have contributed besides the work of a lifetime–than the cash expended by the Museum whatever it is–probably much of it overhead that would have gone into some show anyway–

I hope to hear that the sign calling attention to the miscarriage of justice is off–and that Abbott has, at least some compunction of conscience–

To you John–at your 'ome in the Sudan

Frank Lloyd W.

■ ■ ■ ■

Letter from McAndrew to Wright, December 17, 1940

Dear Mr. Wright,

For the last two weeks I have been meaning to write you, but all during the first one I had to be at Vassar haranguing two hundred and fifty girls (which was fine) and during the second one I was felled by miserable grippe germs. Now I am half alive again, and off to Mexico tomorrow for Christmas and New Year's.

The offending sign is being altered: instead of "ARRANGED BY THE ARCHITECT 1 AND 2 FLOORS," it will read "EXHIBITION ON THE 1ST AND 2ND FLOORS." The other half of the sign just reads "FRANK LLOYD WRIGHT."

There have not been any other long reviews, except for a very curious one in the New Masses that finally contrives to get you involved in the class struggle.[51]

We are sending to Russell Hitchcock the drawings and prints he wants, and will forward the rest to Taliesin; I assumed that this would be what you wanted done. We are delighted that Russell is to get to work on an authoritative book, and will put the chronological list and long bibliography we prepared last summer at his disposal.[52]

I hope it is sunny and pleasant where you are,–New York is at its worst, and my grippe and sinus makes me particularly able to gauge just how evil it is.

Yours,

John

NOTES

1. Taliesin, Frank Lloyd Wright House and Studio, Spring Green, Wisconsin (1911–59).

2. John McAndrew is referring to *Frank Lloyd Wright: A Pictorial Record of Architectural Progress*, organized by the Institute of Modern Art, Boston, January 24–March 3, 1940.

3. Broadacre City project (1934–35).

4. Unity Temple, Oak Park, Illinois (1905–8).

5. Luxfer Prism Office Building project, Chicago (c. 1896–97).

6. The San Francisco Call Building project, San Francisco (c. 1913).

7. Larkin Company Administration Building, Buffalo (1902–6, demolished 1950).

8. Suntop Homes, Ardmore, Pennsylvania (1938–39).

9. In writing to McAndrew, Frank Lloyd Wright alternately uses the names "McAndrew" and "McAndrews." This idiosyncrasy is not duplicated in the present volume.

10. *Frank Lloyd Wright: A Pictorial Record of Architectural Progress*.

11. Wright, "In the Cause of Architecture," *Architectural Record* 23 (March 1908): 155–220.

12. Stanley Rosenbaum House, Florence, Alabama (1939).

13. Pol Abraham, *Viollet-Le-Duc et le rationalisme médiéval* (Paris: Vincent, Fréal & cie, 1934).

14. The collapse of Beauvais actually took place in 1284.

15. In the summer of 1940, the Museum began to plan an exhibition presenting "American achievements, emphasizing the rights of liberty and the pursuit of happiness," in opposition to the rise of fascism in Europe. ("Preliminary notes by Mr. Barr and Mr. Abbott, July 2, 1940." Alfred H. Barr, Jr., Papers, 6.B.13.a–e. The Museum of Modern Art Archives.) Leslie Cheek, then the director of the Baltimore Museum of Art, and known for his ambitious and groundbreaking exhibition design, was asked to develop the show. Working throughout the summer and fall, Cheek and Lewis Mumford produced a plan for an exhibition to be titled *For Us, the Living*, to be housed in a special building constructed over most of the Museum's garden. It was to run concurrently with three other American-themed exhibitions: one on Wright, one on D. W. Griffith, and one on Alfred Stieglitz. *For Us, the Living* remained tentatively on the Museum's schedule into the fall, but its existence was kept secret and Wright never knew exactly what was intended. Finally, in early October, the Museum balked at the exhibition's cost and canceled the show.

16. By "mystery show" Wright meant *For Us, the Living*.

17. Edgar Kaufmann, Sr.

18. Wright wrote this letter before he received McAndrew's letter from September 18 above or the telegraph from September 19 that follows. It is not in The Museum of Modern Art Archives so may not have been sent.

19. For Wright's emendations to Behrendt's essay, see pp. 125–33 of the present volume.

20. While in New York on the visit referred to here, Wright met with McAndrew, Alfred H. Barr, Jr., and John E. Abbott, the Museum's executive vice-president, to discuss the exhibition.

21. Wright is probably referring to Abbott, whom he had met on September 25, 1940, and who was then not the Museum's treasurer but its executive vice-president.

22. See the Appendix in the present volume.

23. McAndrew is referring to the models for the San Francisco Call Building and the St. Mark's-in-the-Bouwerie Towers project, New York (1927–31).

24. McAndrew is referring to "Wingspread," the Herbert F. Johnson House, Racine, Wisconsin (1937–39), and the Frederick C. Robie House, Chicago (1908–10).

25. The Malcolm Willey House, Minneapolis (1932–34).

26. The San Francisco Call Building.

27. The Ludd M. Spivey House project, Fort Lauderdale (1939), and the Ralph Jester House project, Palos Verdes, California (1938–39).

28. The Herbert Jacobs House, Madison (1936–37)—the model for the Exhibition House Wright planned in the Sculpture Garden.

29. John D. Rockefeller, Jr., had donated land on 53rd Street to The Museum of Modern Art for the site of its permanent building, designed by Philip L. Goodwin and Edward Durell Stone and constructed in 1939. He also gave the Museum a 75-by-100-foot plot directly behind the new building, designated for use as a sculpture garden to be on display in conjunction with the World's Fair and its concomitant exhibitions a few blocks away in Rockefeller Plaza. As a condition of the gift, restrictions were placed on the use of this land, including a height limitation to prevent the erection of any buildings or additions behind the Museum along 54th Street, where the Rockefellers lived. Although the Museum owned the land, then, it could only build what amounted to a one-story awning abutting the rear of the building without permission from Rockefeller. Just before the new building opened, Rockefeller leased to the Museum an additional pair of lots, to either side of the garden lot he had donated, upon which he had been planning to build apartments. The extended lot, of approximately 400 by 75 feet, constituted the total land used for the garden. In 1946 Rockefeller gave the leased land to the Museum and lifted all restrictions on the entire parcel.

30. These plans of the exhibition design have not been found.

31. For this exhibition outline see the Appendix in the present volume.

32. National Life Insurance Company Building project, Chicago (1924–25).

33. Crystal Heights project, Washington, D.C. (1939).

34. Luxfer Prism Office Building project.

35. A type of Masonite.

36. The William H. Winslow House, River Forest, Illinois (1893–94).

37. Newman Loeb was the company that had bid on the construction of the Exhibition House.

38. Presumably Cary Caraway, an apprentice of Wright's at Taliesin.

39. *Twenty Centuries of Mexican Art*, May 15–September 30, 1940.

40. Rockefeller is referring to the two plots of land he had leased to the Museum on either side of the lot on 54th Street that he had given to the Museum, the three plots together constituting the Sculpture Garden. See p. 49, fig. 37.

41. In 1940, Nelson Rockefeller, the son of John D. Rockefeller, Jr., and the President of The Museum of Modern Art, was appointed to the position of the United States Coordinator of the Office of Inter-American Affairs. In this capacity he spent much of his time traveling in Latin America and so had less time for the Museum.

42. At the last minute, unbeknownst to Wright, materials associated with the exhibition, including signage in the galleries, were printed "as arranged by himself," to indicate that the installation was designed not by the Museum staff but by the architect.

43. By "Miss Herrick" Wright presumably means Janet Henrich, McAndrew's assistant.

44. Wright is quoting the dying words of Mercutio in Shakespeare's *Romeo and Juliet*.

45. Films of Wright's work were to be shown on the first floor of the exhibition. Because of its poor physical condition, it was ultimately dropped from the show.

46. Heinrich (Henry) Klumb was a long-standing apprentice and assistant of Wright's.

47. Wright is referring to the unpublished catalogue raisonné compiled for the exhibition catalogue by Henrietta Callaway (then a member of the Museum's Department of Architecture), Henry-Russell Hitchcock, and others.

48. Clark had been appointed the first chairman of the Museum's board just the previous year, in 1939.

49. Wright is probably referring to an article in the "Living and Leisure" section of the *Times*: Jane Cobb, "Pioneers," *New York Times*, November 17, 1940.

50. Wright is presumably referring to Geoffrey Baker, "Wright as Iconoclast," *New York Times*, November 24, 1940.

51. Isabel Cooper, "The Art of a Master Builder," *New Masses* 37, no. 13 (December 17, 1940): 28–29.

52. The book in question is Henry-Russell Hitchcock, *In the Nature of Materials: 1887–1941, The Buildings of Frank Lloyd Wright* (New York: Duell, Sloan and Pearce, 1942). Though published the year after the exhibition closed, this book became its de facto catalogue.

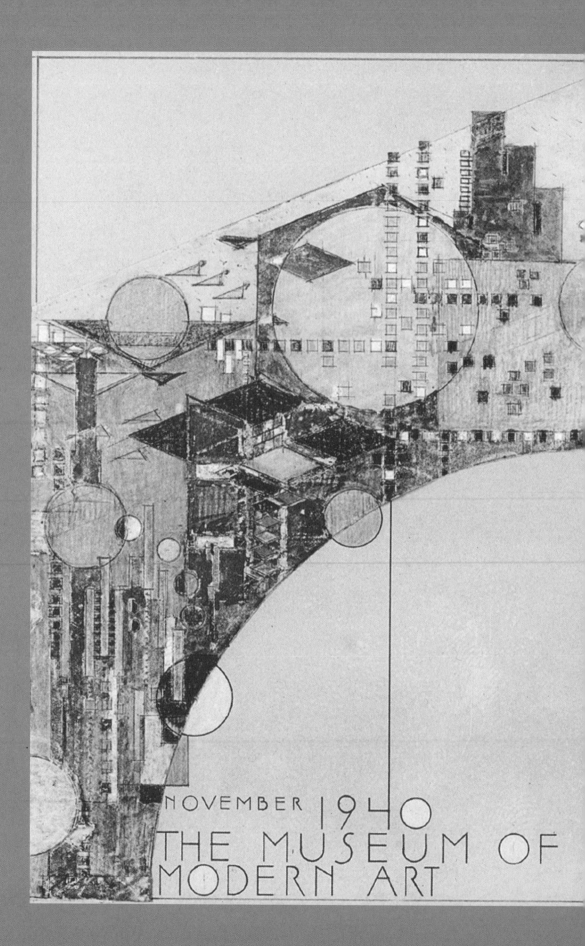

NOVEMBER 1940
THE MUSEUM OF
MODERN ART

ORIGINAL MANUSCRIPTS
Introduction

Less than two months before the exhibition *Frank Lloyd Wright: American Architect* opened at the Museum, curator John McAndrew abandoned the accompanying publication, which had not yet gone to press. The book was planned as a Festschrift—a collection of essays honoring the architect—and was to include an illustrated catalogue raisonné. Wright objected to one of these essays, by Walter Curt Behrendt, and proposed substantial revisions to it. He also threatened to cancel the exhibition if the Museum published the text without taking his objections into account. Reluctantly, the Museum instead canceled the whole book, believing it inappropriate to give the architect the editorial control he demanded.

McAndrew hoped to salvage some parts of the book by including them in the Museum *Bulletin*, but this plan never materialized. As a compromise, the Museum sold subscriptions to *Taliesin*, a quarterly journal published by Wright and his apprentices, during the course of the show. When McAndrew informed the contributing authors of the decision not to publish the catalogue, he advised them that they were free to publish their work elsewhere. Some found venues for their essays (see the Appendix in the present volume); other manuscripts lay dormant in the Museum's files.

The Show to End All Shows contains all of the surviving manuscripts for the planned volume of 1940. Many have never been published; others can now be seen in the context intended for them. The essays were edited by McAndrew and his assistant, Janet Henrich, working with the authors, and are accordingly presented here with these edits intact. Although the book was near completion when the project was canceled, the manuscripts seem never to have been typeset; at any rate no galleys or page proofs have been found.

Where the authors included reference notes, they appear in the essays that follow, which, however, also include additional annotations made as necessary by the present editors. The authors' original notes appear as footnotes numbered with Roman numerals; new annotations appear both as insertions in the text, contained within square brackets, and as endnotes numbered with Arabic numerals. Where the authors cited no sources for quotations, we have indicated the sources wherever we were able to locate them. Plans were made to illustrate some essays in the 1940 book, and we have included a selection of these images when we have located them, or when it is clear what they were to show. The illustration list for the catalogue raisonné appears in the Appendix.

McAndrew's general organizational plan for the Festschrift called for a wide range of essays: longer articles of ten to twelve pages (Behrendt); shorter articles of four to six pages addressing various themes in Wright's work (Talbot Hamlin; Henry-Russell Hitchcock, Jr.; Fiske Kimball; Grant Carpenter Manson; probably McAndrew himself; and Richard Neutra); brief one-to-two-page appreciations of Wright by leading modern architects (Alvar Aalto, Harwell Hamilton Harris, and Mies van der Rohe); and, finally, the voices of Wright's clients (Edgar Kaufmann, Sr.; Liliane Kaufmann; and Edgar Kaufmann, Jr.). McAndrew's exact scheme for the book is unclear, but we have arranged the essays to reflect the general sequence he intended as far as it is known.

As McAndrew's plan for the book developed, he eventually decided to add the voice of Wright himself. His first impulse was to include quotations, presumably from the architect's earlier writings.[1] A document of September 5, 1940, however, sets a deadline of September 9 for a manuscript by Wright to arrive at the Museum, suggesting an amended plan.[2] Then, several days later, when Wright read Behrendt's troublesome essay, he decided to submit his statement "To My Critics" for inclusion in the book. As Kathryn Smith explains in her essay in the present volume (see p. 40), this was an older piece that he revived specifically in response to Behrendt's offending text, quickly editing it for the occasion and dating it "September 14, 1940." Thus it appears here following Behrendt's essay, which appears twice: first, in the form that Behrendt intended and that Wright read; and second, as Wright edited it, even rewriting entire passages. Wright's version of Behrendt's essay is published here in a format that shows Wright's deletions scored through and his insertions in red. As Wright made no changes to Behrendt's notes, they are not repeated a second time.

Wright also designed a cover for the book, which we have adapted for the cover of the present volume and which appears in full on pp. 104–5. It is based on Wright's *City by the Sea* mural for Chicago's Midway Gardens (1913–14, demolished 1929). Finally, he also proposed a title, "In the Nature of Materials," for the Museum's publication. Two years later he would reuse this title for a book he would publish with Hitchcock—"an *ex post facto* catalogue of the exhibition . . . at The Museum of Modern Art . . . in 1940," as the historian would write in his Preface to it.[3] *In the Nature of Materials* appeared a year after the exhibition closed.

Planning the Book

In December 1939, nearly a year before the exhibition opened, McAndrew wrote an outline for the book in the form of a tentative list of contributors. This he submitted to Alfred H. Barr, Jr., director of the Museum, and Monroe Wheeler, director of the Department of Publications, both of whom approved it.[4] As plans developed in the following months, the book was enlarged to include a bibliography, forty illustrations, a complete chronological list of Wright's buildings and projects, and a biographical chronology, making a total count of 128 pages.[5] In size and scope, such a publication would have been comparable to the Museum's other substantial exhibition catalogues of the time—in fact it would have been rather larger than the book published for the simultaneous D. W. Griffith retrospective, recently republished and for many years the standard reference for Griffith's work.[6] Anticipating high demand, the Museum planned to print a first edition of 8,000 copies.

In addition to Behrendt, who was to provide a European perspective on Wright, McAndrew hoped to commission the cultural and architectural historian Lewis Mumford to write a second major essay providing an American view. For the other essays he considered a wide range of possible contributors. For the mid-size articles he anticipated essays from Hitchcock, Kimball, and possibly himself. John Coolidge, a young architectural historian, and Hamlin, both members of the Museum's Architecture Committee, were also considered. For brief tributes of one or two pages, the initial roster was international and ranged from pioneers of modernism to architects of recently established reputation. The prestigious list of proposed writers included Aalto, Gunnar Asplund, Willem Dudok (McAndrew noted that Wright would like this choice), Tony Garnier, Harris, George Howe, Mies, Werner Moser, Neutra, J. J. P. Oud, Gustave Perret, Henry van de Velde, and John Yeon. McAndrew also pondered contributors beyond continental Europe and America: "someone from England; Japan, Russia ([Boris] Iofan?)."[7] And he wanted to include several "non-architects who are Wright enthusiasts," among them the Hollywood actor and director Charlie Chaplin, the novelist and critic Alexander Woollcott, Wright's client Edgar Kaufmann, and the novelist and biographer William Allen White. Barr also suggested that Antonin Raymond—Wright's assistant on the Imperial Hotel and other Japanese projects—could discuss the architect's work in Japan.[8]

In early 1940, McAndrew embarked on an extended research trip to Mexico for the upcoming exhibition *Twenty Centuries of Mexican Art*. Before he left he wrote to Mumford and Behrendt about contributing to the book, but to no one else; and Mumford, unfortunately, was too busy to accept the offer. McAndrew contacted no other authors until June, giving them little more than a month to produce an essay. By then he had modified his outline, reducing the list of short appreciations and making the notable addition of quotations from Montgomery Schuyler and Wright himself.[9]

Not everyone could accept McAndrew's invitation. Woollcott, a friend of Wright's, initially agreed to write but then fell ill. As a fallback, he suggested that the Museum republish his 1930 essay "The Prodigal Father," which had also appeared in his 1934 best seller *While Rome Burns*.[10] McAndrew did not pursue the idea. In that essay Woollcott suspended judgment on Wright's turbulent personal affairs of the 1920s and marveled at the architect's creative genius. He called Wright "This giant. This ingenuous giant," and concluded, "No one in the modern world has brought to architecture so good a mind, so leaping an imagination, or so fresh a sense of beauty."[11] The Philadelphia modernist architect Howe also agreed to write, but had changed his mind by midsummer because he was traveling.[12] He had written no previous essay that could conveniently be dusted off for the occasion, but had shown his admiration in other ways: some years earlier, in a review of Wright's book *An Autobiography*, Howe had claimed that Wright was "without doubt the dominating figure in the architectural world today."[13] Furthermore, Fortune Rock, Howe's recently completed vacation house for Clara Thomas on Mount Desert Island, Maine, can be considered an architectural homage to Wright's Fallingwater.

To write about Wright's influence on American architecture before 1920, McAndrew approached Hamlin, an architect, historian, and librarian. Hamlin taught at Columbia University from 1926 to 1954, lecturing from 1934 to 1944 on the theory of architecture and acting as librarian of the Avery Architectural Library from 1934 to 1945. He was a regular contributor to the journal *Pencil Points*, where he had recently published an article on Wright's recent work, "F.L.W.—An Analysis."[14] When Hamlin submitted his essay to the Museum, in July 1940, he wrote to McAndrew about the renewed appreciation of Wright's work that was beginning to emerge in architectural schools—a perception that would remain relevant for the next decade or more:

> I found working on it most interesting and exciting. Sometimes it seems as though American architecture in 1940 had almost gotten back to where it was in 1915! Certainly, much of the work done in the architectural schools quite independently is developing many of the characteristics of the best Mid-Western architecture of that period. It would be swell if we could illustrate with some of the work of [William Gray] Purcell and [George Grant] Elmslie, [Louis] Guenzel and [William S.] Drummond, and [Walter Burley] Griffin and perhaps show one or two of the most recent California houses as an example of Wright influence today.[15]

McAndrew told Hamlin he was pleased with the essay and thought it fit well with Behrendt's and Hitchcock's.[16]

When McAndrew approached Hitchcock, then the leading American historian of modern architecture and a longtime associate of the Museum, for an essay on Wright's influence abroad,[17] Hitchcock replied, "I do not think I can find very much that is new to say about Wright's foreign influence. But if what is particularly wanted is a sort of tribute, I can certainly provide 1500—2000 words on the subject by July 15th."[18] (In the same letter, Hitchcock warned McAndrew how difficult Wright could be, and how hard it might be to produce an objective study.[19]) The conclusion of Hitchcock's essay is of particular interest: commenting, like Hamlin, on recent changes in contemporary architecture, the author positions Wright perceptively but suspends judgment on his recent architecture, saying it is too early to identify the work's impact. He also observes, however, that the International Style is suffering because of a rigid conformity and because some countries have rejected it for ideological reasons. Wright, he suggests, could "lift modern architecture" out of this dilemma, thus echoing Oud's assessment that Wright escapes the "dogma of theory."

In July of 1940, McAndrew contacted Kimball, architect, prolific author on American architecture, and director of the Philadelphia Museum of Art. McAndrew proposed that Kimball write on Wright's relationship to the architectural profession in America in the last fifty years, but he was open to other suggestions as well. Kimball was traveling and was thus unable to produce a new essay in the time allotted. Instead, he encouraged McAndrew to consider an excerpt of an essay he had written in 1932, for *Architectural Record*, on the occasion of Wright's publication of *An Autobiography*. "I know you would prefer something new," Kimball wrote, "but this is what I have to say about Wright, and I really fear I could not do half so well again. . . . I don't think I ever managed to write anything at all more true and more fundamental. I hope you can and will use it."[20] Perplexed by the topic McAndrew had suggested, Kimball added candidly,

> You speak of Wright's relation to the architectural profession in America. There has really been no relation. Wright is a lone wolf (except for sycophants and disciples). When the profession, which had ignored him, belatedly offered him a love feast in 1932 (I believe it was) he turned on them savagely, as he did again in 1940. There is no love lost today.[21]

Kimball made slight changes and additions to the 1932 manuscript and submitted it for McAndrew's book.

At the beginning of the summer, McAndrew still needed someone to address the theme of Wright and Japan. His problem was resolved in early June, when he was contacted by Manson, a graduate student at Harvard University who had just completed a dissertation on the early years of Wright's career and was hoping that his contacts at the Museum might help him find a New York publisher for it.[22] In the end, Manson's thesis went unpublished until 1958, when it appeared, in revised form, as *Frank Lloyd Wright to 1910: The First Golden Age*, but it was valuable to McAndrew for several reasons: first, it contained a chronology and building list, including some previously "unpublished buildings and complete data on all"—a potentially important contribution to the catalogue raisonné section of McAndrew's book.[23] Second, a chapter from the dissertation—"The Early Impress of Japan on Wright's Work"—usefully complemented the other themes in the Festschrift, and McAndrew and Henrich selected it for inclusion.[24]

Neutra was a logical choice to write about Wright's structural innovations. In 1924, as a member of Wright's Wisconsin studio for several months, this Austrian émigré had worked on some of the architect's most innovative designs, including the National Life Insurance Company Building project of 1924–25. In 1927 he had published the book *Wie Baut Amerika?* (How America builds), a eulogy to American building and construction written for a German audience. Two years later his Lovell House in Los Angeles had firmly established his American reputation as a leading modernist, and in 1932 this building had been featured in the Museum's first architectural show, *Modern Architecture: International Exhibition*. In mid-June, then, McAndrew invited Neutra to write "on technical innovations in Wright's construction, explaining their importance, novelty, how they work, etc."[25] A few weeks later Neutra mailed his essay to McAndrew, noting in his covering letter that since the catalogue was to be honorific, he "felt strongly that well-selected quotations of [Wright's] own early sayings should appear therein and establish his priority wherever possible. I have carefully endeavoured to illustrate the substance rather than indulge in technical detail, which might annoy a broader public."[26] (McAndrew had in fact already decided to include quotations of Wright.) To demonstrate Wright's "structural inspiration in adapting himself to a new regional type," Neutra proposed "showing the enclosed rare picture of early Los Angeles alongside Olive Hill [the Aline Barnsdall House], as reproduced in the Wendingen publication. . . . Both pictures could be brought down to the same smallness as it is only the generic structural character, which is of interesting similarity."[27] The essay vividly conveys the significance and power of structural innovation not as an end in itself but as a means of producing great architecture, and it portrays the struggles Wright faced to create innovative work.

McAndrew's own essay has not been located. The Museum's press release for the exhibition, however, contains a good-sized text by McAndrew on Wright and space—precisely the theme of his contribution to the book, according to his outline and, later, his curriculum vitae. Although certainty is impossible, we feel it is logical to assume that this text is an excerpt from the essay (the practice of adapting the curator's writings in press releases continues today at the Museum), and so we have included it here.

Aalto was an obvious choice for McAndrew: two years earlier the Museum had presented the exhibition *Alvar Aalto: Architecture and Furniture*, and the accompanying publication, with an introduction by McAndrew, had been the first book on the young Finnish architect's work. In 1938 and 1939, too, Aalto had traveled to New York for the World's Fair, for which he had designed the famous Finnish Pavilion—and Wright, on visiting the Pavilion, had proclaimed its architect a genius. In the summer of 1940, when McAndrew contacted him about the Wright catalogue, Aalto was again in the United States, on a visit that would include stops in New York, at Fallingwater in Pennsylvania, with Eliel and Eero Saarinen at the Cranbrook Academy of Art in Michigan, and with Walter Gropius in Massachusetts. Perhaps it was on this visit to Boston that Aalto visited the Harvard Museum of Natural History and saw its famous collection of glass flowers, which he mentions in the short tribute he wrote for the Wright book. The most revealing passages in this essay reflect on the human and emotional qualities that Aalto found in Wright's work— qualities that he himself was striving to bring to modern architecture, which he believed was too rational and bereft of "mystery." He saw Wright's architecture as containing the unknowable, a quality he associated with being human. He does not comment on Wright's use of materials, something he would discuss with interest in later talks, but rather focuses on the overall emotional power of Wright's architecture and its human qualities.

Harris, chosen to write on Wright's relevance for younger architects, was a California modernist who had designed single-family homes in a Wrightian style with "oriental" overtones. Before establishing his own Los Angeles studio, in 1933, he had trained with Neutra and with Rudolf Schindler. Harris's autobiographical essay, written in the third person, recounts his transformation from young sculptor to architect. His epiphany, he says, had occurred upon seeing a Wright house—the Aline Barnsdall House, or Hollyhock House, in Los Angeles, although he never identifies it as such. (He did want to show it in the text's single accompanying illustration, however.) By naming neither the house nor the architect in his essay, Harris attempts to convey a sense of the innocence and discovery in an impromptu encounter with an unknown building. This now-famous autobiographical account was not published until 1952, but the story was sufficiently well-known in 1940 for Hamlin to refer to Harris's epiphany in his own essay. Phrases of Harris's such as "To the young man in architecture [Wright] is the yea-sayer," and "To the youth in architecture," not only refer to his own, personal experience but deliberately recall Wright's lecture in 1930 at the Art Institute of Chicago, "To the Young Man in Architecture," a title that itself is a riff on Louis Sullivan's essay "The Young Man in Architecture" (1900).

McAndrew was skeptical about the personal tone of Harris's essay. In a telegram to the author he wrote, "OTHER ARTICLES COMING IN WHOLE TONE CRITICAL ANALYTICAL FACTUAL. AM WORRIED YOUR ARTICLE MAY SEEM ENTIRELY DIFFERENT KEY. WOULD YOU BE WILLING TO ADD A LITTLE MORE SAYING WHAT YOU THINK WRIGHT'S WORK CAN MEAN IN FAIRLY SPECIFIC INSTANCES TO YOUNGER ARCHITECTS INCLUDING YOURSELF?"[28] Harris promptly wired back, pointing out that his personal experience demonstrated exactly the kind of influence Wright might have on a younger generation of designers: "ARTICLE IS A DESCRIPTION OF THE ACTUAL EXPERIENCE WHICH CAUSED ME TO STUDY ARCHITECTURE STOP IT IS SUCH EXPERIENCES THAT CONSTITUTE WRIGHT'S REAL INFLUENCE UPON THE YOUNGER GENERATION STOP TO TREAT WRIGHT FROM THE CRITICAL ANALYTICAL ANGLE IS I THINK TO MISS HIM ENTIRELY STOP I BELIEVE MY ARTICLE IN KEY WITH SULLIVAN'S AND WRIGHT'S OWN WRITING AND APPROACH STOP I WOULD LIKE VERY MUCH TO HAVE IT STAND STOP."[29] McAndrew reassured him that he and Barr liked the piece, and beyond some minor editing, it stood as Harris intended.[30]

The third short tribute came from the great German modernist architect Mies van der Rohe, whose work had figured prominently in the Museum's *Modern Architecture: International Exhibition* eight years earlier. Since then Mies had emigrated to the United States, becoming Director of Architecture at the Armour Institute of Technology (later the Illinois Institute of Technology), in Chicago. In mid-June of 1940, McAndrew asked him for a short essay.[31] A month later, Mies sent his tribute, acknowledging his early appreciation of Wright's work. It was mailed with a covering letter from Pike Lake Lodge, in Fifield, Wisconsin, where Mies was vacationing.[32]

To represent the client's voice, McAndrew unsurprisingly solicited Edgar and Liliane Kaufmann and their son, Edgar Kaufmann, Jr. The family's country house, Fallingwater, had been the subject of a 1938 exhibition at the Museum and was Wright's most famous building, having appeared on the cover of *Time*. Also, Edgar Kaufmann, Jr., had recently begun what would become a long professional association with the Museum. Edgar Kaufmann's name appeared early on McAndrew's slate of potential authors, and his wife and son were added in the summer of 1940. His essay is his only known memoir about Fallingwater and his relationship with Wright. To tell his story he adopts a diarylike format, as though the piece were compiled from his calendars, correspondence, and notes of the preceding few years.

Of particular interest is Kaufmann's reminiscence of seeing the architect's drawings of Fallingwater for the first time, in September 1935. He describes the excitement of receiving the floor plans and colored elevation on September 15, followed by the arrival of the "Master" on September 21 to review the drawings. Despite its precise-sounding dates, this chronology contradicts the record laid out by correspondence among Kaufmann, Wright, and others. Missing from Kaufmann's account is his visit to Taliesin on September 22 after a business trip to Milwaukee on September 18–21. The trip had been planned since August.[33] This visit figures prominently in the legend surrounding the creation of Fallingwater: according to the extraordinary story told by Edgar Tafel and other Wright apprentices, several hours before Kaufmann's visit that Sunday morning the architect put pencil to paper and produced the plans, sections, and elevations of Fallingwater to show to the client.[34] It is unclear why Kaufmann does not remark on this visit in his essay for McAndrew; perhaps the drawings he saw that day made little impression on him.

Back in Pittsburgh several days later, on September 27, 1935, Kaufmann sent a note to Wright indicating his anticipation of the completed drawings and acknowledging that Wright would bring them to him.[35] That same day, Edgar Jr. also wrote to Wright, telling him that the family was anxious to see what the house would look like: "Father spent quite some time at Bear Run showing just where the various rooms would be and Edgar [Tafel?] sent a rough drawing of the wall masses so that we are all tremendously anxious to see just what the house really will look like. As far as I am concerned, it keeps floating around in a half formed way almost continually asking for a little more information on which to complete itself."[36] The Kaufmanns seem to have had no clear image of their new house, in fact, until after Wright sent drawings to Pittsburgh on October 15, and his subsequent visit several days later to explain them. Despite a confusing chronology, Kaufmann's 1940 essay nevertheless conveys, among other things, the exhilaration of discovering on paper a great work of architecture.

McAndrew also encouraged Liliane Kaufmann to contribute to the catalogue, sending her a telegram on September 5 asking if she had "TIME AND INCLINATION TO WRITE SOMETHING THIS WEEK FOR OUR WRIGHT CATALOG ABOUT LIVING IN THE WRIGHT HOUSE AND RUNNING IT."[37] Liliane promptly produced a short life-style essay, her personal anecdotes suggesting responses to the perennial questions from visitors about what it was like to live in Fallingwater. On September 9 she wrote to McAndrew, "I am glad that you like my very hurried, and somewhat abreviated [sic] article."[38]

Writing on the interior of Fallingwater, Edgar Kaufmann, Jr., structured his essay as extended commentaries on a group of photographs by Luke Swank, a well-known professional photographer based in Pittsburgh. (Kaufmann used five photographs, of which we have located three.) Many years later, when he published the lavish *Fallingwater: A Frank Lloyd Wright Country House*, he provided a similar analysis of the interior in the chapter titled "Inside Fallingwater" and in the book's extended captions.[39] When McAndrew received the Kaufmann family's essays, they were accompanied by a note from Edgar Jr. explaining that his father's manuscript had undergone a "number of typings and retypings," which suggests it had received a good deal of consideration. Edgar Jr. may have worked on it as well, because he explained to McAndrew, "We three authors want you to throw away, cut, rewrite, correct, as you please. I've tried to let E.J.'s keep all its, or his, flavor, so it's long. . . . And we all think it's been great fun, even if you can't use it."[40]

Sadly, McAndrew was unable to use any of the essays. In a letter to the Kaufmanns in early October he succinctly recounted the debacle that had taken place within days of their essays' arrival at the Museum. McAndrew's frustration was palpable:

> The original plans for the book had been discussed with Mr Wright, and he had agreed to them. We thought that it would be possible to publish a book that would be satisfactory to him and to the Museum. As the book was going to press, however, Mr. Wright demanded to see the text. I showed him two articles, and he blew up over the one that praised him more handsomely than any of the others. He demanded complete editorial powers as the only alternative to cancelling the whole exhibition as well as the book. Of course, such editing would have negated the purpose of the book as a critical tribute; also there was not time enough to make changes and still publish the book concurrently with the exhibition.[41]

Even before the exhibition closed, Wright had engaged Hitchcock to collaborate with him on *In the Nature of Materials: The Buildings of Frank Lloyd Wright, 1887–1941*. Images, a list of works compiled for the catalogue raisonné by Henrietta Callaway, and other materials were made available to Hitchcock by McAndrew and Henrich, as he acknowledged in the book.[42] He also recognized Wright's role in shaping the work—"almost as much that of co-author as of subject."[43]

Despite the poor reception given to *Frank Lloyd Wright: American Architect*, Wright's career suffered not at all after the exhibition, and it is unlikely that the book would have buried him prematurely either, as he feared. The catalogue raisonné, in fact, would have been a useful resource, and the essays presented here could only have enhanced the public's understanding and appreciation of America's greatest architect.

—PR

NOTES

1. "Preliminary Outline," June 10, 1940. Registrar Exhibition Files (REG), Exh. #114, The Museum of Modern Art Archives, New York.

2. "Schedule for Catalogue and Exhibition," September 5, 1940. REG, Exh. #114, MoMA Archives.

3. Henry-Russell Hitchcock, *In the Nature of Materials: 1887–1941, The Buildings of Frank Lloyd Wright* (New York: Duell, Sloan and Pearce, 1942), p. xxvii.

4. John McAndrew, memo to Alfred H. Barr, Jr., and Monroe Wheeler, December 1, 1939; Barr, memo to McAndrew, December 2, 1939. REG, Exh. #114, MoMA Archives.

5. "Frank Lloyd Wright: American Architect," undated document. REG, Exh. #114, MoMA Archives.

6. The D. W. Griffith book was only forty pages long. See Iris Barry, *D. W. Griffith: American Film Master*, 1940 (reprint ed. New York: The Museum of Modern Art, 2002).

7. McAndrew, memo to Barr and Wheeler, December 1, 1939. REG, Exh. #114, MoMA Archives.

8. Barr, memo to McAndrew, December 2, 1939. REG, Exh. #114, MoMA Archives.

9. "Preliminary Outline," June 10, 1940. REG, Exh. #114, MoMA Archives.

10. Alexander Woollcott, letters to McAndrew, June 26 and July 14, 1940. REG, Exh. #114, MoMA Archives.

11. Woollcott, *While Rome Burns* (New York: The Viking Press, 1934), pp. 178–79.

12. George Howe, letter to McAndrew, July 16, 1940. REG, Exh. #114, MoMA Archives.

13. Howe, "Creation and Criticism: Two Book Reviews," *Shelter* 2 (April 1932): 27. On Howe's sometimes strained friendship with Wright in the 1930s, see Robert A. M. Stern, *George Howe: Toward a Modern American Architecture* (New Haven and London: Yale University Press, 1975), pp. 141–49.

14. Talbot Hamlin, "F.L.W.—An Analysis," *Pencil Points* XIX (March 1938): 137–44.

15. Hamlin, letter to McAndrew, July 18, 1940. REG, Exh. #114, MoMA Archives.

16. McAndrew, letter to Hamlin, August 14, 1940. REG, Exh. #114, MoMA Archives.

17. McAndrew, letter to Hitchcock, June 14, 1940. REG, Exh. #114, MoMA Archives.

18. Hitchcock, letter to McAndrew, n.d. (mid-June, 1940). REG, Exh. #114, MoMA Archives.

19. Hitchcock wrote that there had been "too few serious objective studies. . . . However, I imagine that the chances of giving offense are rather great and while [Wright] is alive such a study might be dangerous to make." Ibid. See also Kathryn Smith, "The Show to End All Shows: Frank Lloyd Wright and The Museum of Modern Art, 1940," in the present volume, p. 58.

20. Fiske Kimball, letter to McAndrew, August 1, 1940. REG, Exh. #114, MoMA Archives.

21. Ibid. Kimball is presumably referring to a New York dinner, not in 1932 but in 1930, at which Wright was feted on the occasion of his exhibition at the Architectural League. He was also honored during his exhibition in Boston in 1940. On both occasions he may have felt that he was honored as if he were dead rather than as a vital creative force.

22. Manson, letter to McAndrew, June 5, 1940. REG, Exh. #114, MoMA Archives.

23. Ibid.

24. In Manson's book, this became the section subtitled "Influence from Japan" in the chapter "Apprenticeship." See Manson, *Frank Lloyd Wright to 1910: The First Golden Age* (New York: Van Nostrand Reinhold Company, 1958), pp. 34–40.

25. McAndrew, letter to Richard Neutra, June 14, 1940. REG, Exh. #114, MoMA Archives.

26. Neutra, letter to McAndrew, July 5, 1940. REG, Exh. #114, MoMA Archives.

27. Ibid.

28. McAndrew, telegram to Harris, August 27, 1940. REG, Exh. #114, MoMA Archives.

29. Harris, telegram to McAndrew, August 28, 1940. REG, Exh. #114, MoMA Archives.

30. McAndrew, letter to Harris, September 5, 1940. REG, Exh. #114, MoMA Archives.

31. McAndrew, letter to Ludwig Mies van der Rohe, June 14, 1940. REG, Exh. #114, MoMA Archives.

32. Mies, letter to McAndrew, July 20, 1940. REG, Exh. #114, MoMA Archives.

33. See letters in the Frank Lloyd Wright Archives, Scottsdale, Arizona, from Edgar Kaufmann's associate Irwin Wolf to Wright, August 20, 1935; from Wright's apprentice Eugene Masselink to Wolf, August 26, 1935; and from Wright to Kaufmann, September 18, 1935.

34. In his recent book on Fallingwater, Franklin Toker dissects this story in some detail and suggests it may be something of a myth. See Toker, *Fallingwater Rising: Frank Lloyd Wright, E. J. Kaufmann, and America's Most Extraordinary House* (New York: Alfred A. Knopf, 2003), esp. pp. 7, 180–82, and 194–99.

35. Edgar Kaufmann, letter to Wright, September 27, 1935. Frank Lloyd Wright Archives.

36. Edgar Kaufmann, Jr., letter to Wright, September 27, 1935. Frank Lloyd Wright Archives.

37. McAndrew, telegram to Mrs. Edgar Kaufmann, September 5, 1940. REG, Exh. #114, MoMA Archives.

38. Liliane Kaufmann, letter to McAndrew, September 9, 1940. REG, Exh. #114, MoMA Archives.

39. Edgar Kaufmann, Jr., *Fallingwater: A Frank Lloyd Wright Country House* (New York: Abbeville Press, 1986).

40. Edgar Kaufmann, Jr., letter to McAndrew, n.d. REG, Exh. #114, MoMA Archives.

41. McAndrew, letter to the Kaufmann family, October 10, 1940. REG, Exh. #114, MoMA Archives.

42. Hitchcock, *In the Nature of Materials*, p. xlvii.

43. Ibid., p. xlix.

FRANK LLOYD WRIGHT
Walter Curt Behrendt

I.

That Frank Lloyd Wright's architectural work was an individual achievement of national importance that soon would prove to be of international influence, was recognized and announced earlier abroad than in his native country. When, in the early years of this century, his name was known in America to only a few people who found themselves deeply impressed by the bold novelty of his work, his fame had already spread over Europe. Particularly in those countries where the spirit of modern building had already gained a strong foothold he was readily accepted as a leading avant-guardist, and his work was eagerly discussed among the progressive groups as a challenging example to be studied and followed.

Though on the Continent his work and message was received as a revelation, in this country his contemporaries, almost up to the present day, took him for a venturous eccentric who was making a point in being different. Though the Japanese government appointed him as architect for the Imperial Hotel in Tokio, he has never been asked by his own government to design one of the public buildings in the capital. To the man who is reputed and celebrated abroad as the creator of a new architecture, no invitation was extended in his own country to participate in one of those recent fairs which pretended to demonstrate the Century of Progress or the World of Tomorrow. Though documents of his work, drawings, plans, and selected photos had been shown in numerous exhibitions all over Europe, he had to reach the biblical age before he was given in this country the opportunity of a one-man show displaying to the public the results of a lifetime's work, a work overwhelming by its sheer size and its far-reaching scope.

It is about time for the Americans to realize that amidst them there is living a great genius, one of the greatest architects of all history.

II.

The scanty public appreciation, amounting to almost complete neglect, that was given to Wright's work, at least until recent years, throws an illuminating light on the development of architecture in this country.

In their slavish dependence on the standards of taste set by the old countries, standards which were incontestably accepted, American architects as well as art critics were completely unaware of the fresh sprout that was growing in virgin soil of their own country. America was proud of the high level of taste reached in its public buildings. These were designed by the Ecole des Beaux-Arts architects who, imitating in their designs the Classic and

Renaissance pattern, accomplished little more than a pretentious monumentality. These academic standards of taste were already strongly questioned and partly undermined when, in 1910, the early work of Frank Lloyd Wright was first shown in a small monograph published in Berlin.[1] In 1915, however, a publishing house in New York still found enough subscribers for a monumental publication of the complete works of McKim, Mead and White, edited in three large-sized volumes.[2]

This American brand of Beaux-Arts architecture, it must be admitted, was perfect in design and faultless in detail, but how fake in its vaunting idealism, how meaningless as an interpretation of actual life, let alone modern American life. While the conspicuous creations of this academic architecture were widely celebrated, the early beginnings of realistic and indigenous building in this country were hardly noticed.[i]

Frank Lloyd Wright, when he started, had [Louis] Sullivan's shoulders to stand on; and Sullivan, for his part, was in many ways indebted to H. H. Richardson, who had been the first in this country to restore straightforwardness to architecture. Richardson and Sullivan both attended the Ecole des Beaux-Arts, and all through their life remained under the influence of this great academic tradition of Europe. Certain European influences can be traced in Wright's work, too: those of Art Nouveau, for instance, and of the English Arts and Crafts movement. But this applies mainly to some details of interior decoration, and the fact remains that, right from the beginning, the houses designed by Frank Lloyd Wright showed a specific character which, unmistakably and irrefutably, mark them as products of the American soil.

Here was the first indication of a new architecture definitely distinguished from any European style, a genuine expression of American spirit. How was it possible to overlook these striking characteristics in Wright's first houses built around Chicago, in Oak Park and Riverside? How was it possible to miss their novel features? Little critical discernment was needed to perceive the sense of their momentous message. Here was a new type of domestic architecture, and a vernacular one at that. With their low building masses stretching out over the ground and with their far-projecting eaves guarding them from an abundant sun, these houses, in an intimate union with soil and landscape, strike a new regional note belonging to the prairie lands of the Middle West.

Incidentally, some interesting discoveries were to be made in studying the structure of these houses. Unusual, too, were their aesthetic qualities: there was a stunning variety of form, indicating the abundant imagination of the designer; there was the superior manner in which the scale was handled. Compared with their neighbors, haughty imitators of the Georgian or Colonial manner, prettified by a finical detail, Wright's houses look like giants among dwarfs.

i. One remarkable exception: in July 1905 the magazine *Architectural Record* published an article on Frank Lloyd Wright ["The Work of Frank Lloyd Wright: Its Influence," *The Architectural Record* 18, no. 1 (July 1905): 65] which, after a short analysis emphasizing "The striking details, contrasts and episodes" of Wright's design, comes to the following conclusion: "his work . . . is [. . .] legitimate and original; and whatever its influence has been in the past, it will be even more efficacious in the future." The article shows no signature, but we may assume that this prophetic statement came from Mr. Montgomery Schuyler, who, in his various articles written for this magazine, proved again and again his unfailing critical sense for everything that was creative and progressive in contemporary American architecture.

The first test Wright gave of his extraordinary talent revealed him as a great architect. His promising debut, however, was not accompanied by the cheering approval of his confreres, nor was it followed by the encouraging appreciation of art critics. In splendid isolation he started his career, pushed on only by his stolid self-assurance.

III.

When Wright, at the age of twenty-three,[3] had just finished the Winslow house in Oak Park, he was offered the opportunity to go to Paris for several years to attend the Ecole des Beaux-Arts on some sort of private fellowship, sponsored by "Uncle Dan" (Daniel H. Burnham). He refused on the ground that Sullivan had spoiled him for that fountainhead of architectural doctrine. His refusal proves that he was already sure of himself, that he saw his way clear ahead and that nothing could distract him any more from the great aim he had set himself—not even such a splendid and big-hearted offer as would have tempted any other young man.

He was right: the teaching of Louis Sullivan had turned his mind in a direction incompatible with academic doctrine. Wright had no use for academic architecture and its modern species of eclecticism. For him it was a meaningless elaboration, nothing but "a rubbish heap of styles."[4] Conscious of his own creative power, he was out to "formulate, not to reformulate."

The idea of architecture, born dormant within him and awakened by his "lieber Meister,"[5] had already germinated and taken shape so that he was now able to define it. His was a concept of organic architecture—of an architecture that grows "out of the ground into the light"[6] and arises "from within out"—an architecture that "continuously begins at the beginning," that "fearlessly accepts the laws of change inherent in all nature"—an architecture that, according to these principles, will conceive every building problem as a new one, as an individual case to be dealt with according to its own laws, the laws of its individual existence.

This concept of organic architecture is a dynamic one, in contrast to the academic concept that is based on the static laws of geometry imposed upon the structure. It is life and not a preconceived scheme or dogma that is on the basis of this concept. The house, instead of being composed of a series of rooms conceived as boxes arranged on a system of coordinate axes, was now defined as life-space, as interior space separated from outer space by enclosing and protecting walls and roofs. Within this interior space the rooms are to be so arranged as to lay out the pattern of domestic life, to order and control the movements, the comings and goings of those who live in it. If the house is conceived as an organism, the rooms are to be interpreted as its organs. Their individual form and their interrelationship are determined by the function they have to fulfill for the whole. Superseding Sullivan's famous formula, Wright states that "form and function are one"[7] which, according to his interpretation, means that the purpose and pattern of the building are one. And as the rooms inside are organized into an organic whole, so the inside is related to the outside. Inside and outside are "of each other."

In discussing the new concept of organic architecture, I have closely followed Wright's own terms. To understand what they mean and to realize the fundamental change of structure brought about under the impact of this new concept, one must, however, study the plans and buildings themselves. In all his plans the chimney and its fireplaces are made the center of the house around which the rooms are grouped. In the larger houses there is often more than one such center. But always the rooms stretch out from this center toward the garden, opening themselves to the light and the view on all sides. With the interior space showing only minor or subordinate subdivisions, the rooms, interspersed with low galleries or short passages as connecting links, flow into each other, penetrating each other and interlacing with indissoluble cohesion. And their uninterrupted flow does not stop at the enclosing walls, but continues over terraces, loggias, and balconies into the outer space of the surrounding landscape.

As the rooms are no longer conceived as boxes in an organic architecture, their enclosing walls change into light screens, and the windows, formerly holes punched in the walls, appear within these screens as large transparent areas frequently extending around the corners of the building.

The idea of organic structure implies a new attitude toward the material, too. It means that material is to be used according to its organic nature: brick as brick, or wood to look like wood, showing its finished surface or the ornamental effect of its natural grain instead of being covered with a coat of paint. Or when natural stone is used, it means following the pattern of the strata and the natural ledges, with the edges left natural, in order to utilize not only the physical but also the physiognomical properties of the material.

However, one has not done full justice to this new concept if one interprets it only as an architectural theory. It is much more. Wright's theory of architecture is an integral part of Wright's philosophy of life. This philosophy is based on moral and intellectual concepts which center around the fundamental conditions of life, of man and nature. And the same concept which he follows in his plans and structures, the concept of organic order, he also visualizes as the basis of our social structure. Architecture, he once stated, is a true expression of the life of the human and social world. And so is organic architecture integral to a life lived as organic.

Wright's philosophy and architectural theory are no less admirable as the extraordinary achievement of a profound thinker than his creation of an organic architecture is as the work of a great artist. With his ideas demonstrated in practical examples he gave the modern movement a new impetus, particularly in Europe. Guided by the principle of organic structure and inspired by his practical examples, it soon gained so much momentum that it totally changed the appearance of contemporary architecture.

IV.

With his architectural theory clearly defined, Wright, devotedly and conscientiously, put himself under the severe discipline of his ideal. The theory, of course, grew and developed on the practical problems which came to the workshop. And the work of his lifetime, from his earliest building, the unprecedented windmill tower Romeo and Juliet (1896), on the hill of his family's farm in Wisconsin, now the famous landmark of Taliesin, is one continuous adventure in experiment.

Set at the task of making architecture a genuine expression of the machine age, he readily accepts modern building techniques and materials and explores their constructive possibilities. He experiments with glass, steel, and concrete. In designing his first public building, Unity

Temple (Oak Park, 1905[–1908]), he was faced with the narrow budget of a small community. He experimented with concrete as building material and cast it in wooden molds, the cheapest of its many techniques. Until that time concrete had been used only in utilitarian engineering structures. As a church scheme the building is just as unique in its plan (with two-leveled aisles and cloister corridor) as it is in its construction. Cast concrete was used for the walls, reinforced concrete slabs for the roof. By developing skillful devices for surface treatment, enlivening the large unbroken areas of the walls through the coarse texture of gravel, the architect succeeded in ennobling the profane nature of the commonplace material. And by adapting scale and proportion to the inherent character of the material, he imbued the whole structure, though rather modest in its physical dimensions, with a quality appropriate to its noble purpose, monumental both in mass and in detail. The experiment proved to be a thorough success: there is hardly another contemporary church building which in its structure is expressive of its modern building technique, in its form one with its function, and in both its interior and exterior full of emotional appeal.

He experimented with construction. In designing the Imperial Hotel in Tokio, his ambition was to develop an earthquake-proof structure, flexible enough to resist the most formidable enemy that threatens building in that country. By an ingenious device the building was set on a shockproof foundation, with its outer walls separated from the floors by the use of the cantilever. Although at first no native contractor was to be found to take the risk of this experiment, the building finally was erected according to Wright's plan, and the architect found himself most splendidly rewarded for having insisted upon his courageous experiment when, two years later, the Imperial Hotel proved to be one of the few buildings in Tokio that survived the notorious catastrophe of 1924.[8]

Another experiment, never attempted before, was made in one of Wright's most recent buildings: the administration building of the Johnson Wax Company in Racine, Wisconsin. Glass tubing is used all over the building for lighting. Two continuous bands of horizontal glass tubing encircle the building, one at eye level, the other at the junction of the walls and the roof. Set in two layers, they serve as the sources of natural light as well as artificial, eliminating all other fixtures and affording a pleasantly diffused light. Since the glass tubing is not designed to open like regular windows, the building is air-conditioned and equipped with two circular shafts, reaching from the roof to the basement, which, like nostrils, function as breathing organs for the building. For the same building Wright used a new kind of construction unit, a mushroom-shaped hollow concrete column, forming post and ceiling together. In the main office room several hundred desks are arranged between the slender shafts of these columns. The large concrete circles at the top are tangent to each other, and through glass tubing set between the circles a gentle light floods down from the ceiling: a light and elegant construction, appropriate for the purpose, making the room spacious and easy to oversee.

And so it goes all through the long list of Wright's works: fascinated by the possibilities offered by modern technique, curious to explore the properties of new building materials, anxious to take advantage of modern building construction and to interpret its character in an expressive form, Wright goes from experiment to experiment. He, the individualist par excellence, does not hesitate to utilize modern industrialized methods: he accepts standardization and prefabrication without depriving his buildings in the least of their individuality. For him, every new problem is another opportunity for experiment. And it is characteristic of his conception that he always approaches his problem by intuition, starting from the particular nature of the problem, and not vice versa, that is, making the problem subject to a preestablished theory taken at face value.

For the client it is no easy task to work with an architect who is such a passionate experimenter. On his part, too, it needs a lot of patience, confidence, and a good deal of personal interest in the problem. He has to be willing to put up with disappointment, inefficacy, wearisome detours, perhaps even failure. However, experiments are needed if we desire to progress, and no progress can be obtained without taking a risk. A leaking roof matters little when a new building material is tried out for the first time. The way to experience is through initial mistakes. In the development of Gothic construction the occasional collapse of vaults of daring new construction was, as an experience, an important stimulant to further exploration.

All through his life, Wright has been fortunate in finding congenial clients who, captivated by his genius, faithfully supported his experiments and helped him through. In this regard, such names as Darwin D. Martin, the vice-president of the Larkin factory; Baron Okura, the main figure in the exciting story of the Tokio Hotel; the most extraordinary Miss [Aline] Barnsdall, patroness of the Hollyhock House in Hollywood; Paul Mueller, the inventive contractor; Edgar Kaufmann, Herbert Johnson, and many others, are closely connected with Wright's achievements. It is to their undying credit that they gave their mental and material assistance in full faith to a genius who is permanently and passionately experimenting toward a new organic architecture.

V.

Always searching for other opportunities to test his inventive power on new problems hitherto unsolved, Wright began, in recent years, to interest himself in the problems of the small house, the house of moderate cost, which he declares is America's most pressing contemporary building problem. "As for me, I would rather solve this with satisfaction to myself and Usonia than build anything I can think of at the moment except the modern theater now needed by the legitimate drama."[ii]

The first result of his studies and experiments in this field was a small house in Madison, Wisconsin, designed for Mr. Herbert Jacobs, a journalist, and his small family, a house built on contract for $5,500, and a surprise for all those who had previously seen this architect associated with the most affluent customers. With this house he created a new type, demonstrating that, besides satisfying all vital necessities and requirements for comfort, he could offer a more livable house than anything that is on the market at this price. Of course, "more livable"[9] it will appear only to those who are willing to accept "a pattern for more simple

ii. ["Frank Lloyd Wright,"] *Architectural Forum*, January 1938 [p. 78. The quote is cut off; it ends, "unless 'the stage' is to be done to death by 'the movies.'"]

and more gracious living." More livable it will be for those who prefer to have their house built at one level, with greater spaciousness because no space is wasted for stairs to climb up to the bedrooms. More livable it will be for those who are satisfied with one large living room, well lighted and opened out fully to the garden on its south side, with a section set apart for dining and a kitchen large enough to prepare a good meal.

In short, to be ready to accept that new type of house means to be mentally prepared for a new form of society. Here it becomes manifest that the concept of an organic architecture involves the concept of a new society, a society also based on organic order. To use Wright's own phrase: "Architecture which is a genuine interpretation of the present is a prophecy of social structure yet to come." In fact, many of Wright's projects, audacious creations, demonstrating a form fit for and expressive of a new mode of life, are anticipating, within society as it is, the ideal of a new society to come.

Most illuminating in this regard are Wright's prospective studies and tentative projects in the field of city planning: projects which, upon their realization, make obligatory an antecedent change of some at least of our most important social institutions. It is but logical that Wright, devoted to a concept of organic planning, condemns the big city as a form of settlement characteristic of an "inorganic society." The big city he considers as an obsolete institution, "a temporal hangover from the infancy of the race, when the herd instinct triumphed over humanity."[10] In our time, however, the big city, in his opinion, is no more a necessity since a decentralized form of settlement has become possible with the advances of technology. Our machines will furnish the greatest service they can do to man if we will use them to carry through decentralization at a large scale. In his project for Broadacre City he has indicated what a community planned for the decentralized life of an organic society would look like. Instead of being crowded with structures tipped up edgewise and piled to the sky, it will be built up with houses spreading horizontally, naturally developed on the ground, surrounded by large gardens and open areas, offering to the inhabitants the most natural way of living in closest contact with the nourishing soil and organic nature. "Ruralism," he once stated, "as distinguished from 'Urbanism' for future machine-age development, is the business of the modern architect."[11] And this new ruralism finally will provide a social condition enabling the architect "to build into his structures the good life as a new kind of beauty."

In fact, if we were to indicate the specific character of Wright's art, we would call it rural. Based on a principle of organic order, it evidently loses its finest values when it is diverted to projects of typical city building. It is most characteristic that Wright, when faced with the problem of designing a tall apartment house, logically reverted to the most rigid geometrical form, the rectangular box: incidentally this is the most perfect form in regard to function, when the packing problem is to be solved—that problem which is at the basis of all present city building.

VI.

It is the study of nature on which Wright's art is founded, and it is the principle of organic growth as manifest in nature from which this art takes its structural as well as its aesthetic concept. Logically from his creative observation of nature, Wright arrives at the conclusion that "every true aesthetic is an implication of nature."

On another occasion–in my book *Modern Building*,[12] where I have set forth at length the nature and essence of Frank Lloyd Wright's work–I have pointed out that in describing his architectural creations one is, again and again, urged to a comparison with the world of plants. Wright himself once suggested THE TREE as an image and ideal for "American" building. In this image the rooms in his houses are arranged around the nucleus of the chimney part, like the leaves of a plant around the stem. Treelike, indeed, are his buildings, firmly rooted in their ground. Treelike, they grow up from the earth to the light, adapting themselves to their environment, following the natural conditions of the site, so that at the end they become an integral part of the scene in which they are set. And again, as the tree is not just an example of a species but also an individual growth, so each house of Frank Lloyd Wright is an individual organism. In such a sense, Taliesin, for instance, the architect's own house, is not just a house on the hill, but it really is The House of The Hill.

The comparison, which links the artistic vision to the world of natural growth, holds true for the detail of the architectural form. As the bulky stem of a tree ramifies into the light boughs that form its crown, so the bulk of Wright's buildings, as they rise higher from the ground, becomes lighter and lighter, while the detail becomes more elaborate and tenuous. Compare the change in the design of the windows from the lower to the upper floor, with their treelike arrangement–in the [Avery] Coonley House [Riverside, Illinois, 1906–8], for instance, and in many other examples: a device which, besides its practical purpose, has the aesthetic function of loosening the building bulk into greater lightness. Over the bulk of the building the roofs spread with their widely overhanging projections like lofty treetops. As they appear, in their multiform arrangement, in which the void plays just as important a part aesthetically as the mass, these roofs seem to be of Japanese ancestry: in fact, Wright's country houses often recall the Japanese house, another highly developed example of organic structure.

With a florid and exuberant imagination, which is the strongest among his manifold talents, Wright created a new architectural form expressive of the organic, a form of fresh beauty enchanting with its sensual and emotional effect. So strong and forceful is this imagination that, in humoring his great artistic talent, Wright easily opens himself to a betrayal of his own theory. Although he seems to believe, concluding from his own statement, that "any style is offensive now," as an artist he is apparently so much of an individualist as not to see that, when forcing his personal style upon his clients, he is acting against his belief. In Wright's houses, as a matter of fact, the interior is not fully neutralized into life space, but still used by the architect as a vehicle for personal expression. As long as in a Frank Lloyd Wright room no other furniture is permissible but that of Frank Lloyd Wright's design, the interior space is still subject to the idea of style, be it only that of a personal style. And for us, today, and particularly in architecture, as correctly stated by Wright himself, any style has become offensive, and most of all the personal one.

This does not diminish the value of his artistic achievement. On the contrary, it clearly brings out the remarkable fact that the form in which Wright for the first time expressed the idea of an organic architecture is a thoroughly personal creation, a creation of his own, and as such deserving our fullest admiration and gratefulness as it opened to us a fresh source of that fine delight that goes with the enjoyment of beauty.

Frank Lloyd Wright is one of the most imposing figures from the past period of individualism who has lived on into our time, a personality of such overwhelming greatness as we will not see soon again. As an artist he is an emotionalist. It is for that reason that the younger generation is inclined to distrust him. In their judgment he passes as a romantic: which only means that the world today has begun to lose the sense for that kind of romantic beauty he has to offer as the most precious gift of his extraordinary talent. But even if the form in which he presented his ideas should prove to be evanescent, the principle on which his work is founded will continue to be upheld in all future efforts directed toward making architecture again a living art.

1. In 1910, Ernst Wasmuth, of Berlin, published the monograph *Ausgeführte Bauten und Entwürfe von Frank Lloyd Wright*, a two-volume book often called the Wasmuth Portfolio. In 1911 Wasmuth published a second edition of the book that in addition to being reduced to one volume was smaller in dimension, and since Behrendt refers here to a "small monograph" he may be thinking of this version. Behrendt's original text indicates that he intended a footnote here but he had not yet supplied one.

2. McKim, Mead & White, *A Monograph of the Work of McKim, Mead & White* (New York: Architectural Book Publishing Co., 1915).

3. During his lifetime Wright gave 1869 as his year of birth, but he was actually born in 1867, making him twenty-six when he finished the William H. Winslow House, in 1893.

4. "The United States were being swept into one grand rubbish heap of the styles." Wright, *An Autobiography* (New York: Longmans, Green and Company, 1932), p. 151.

5. Wright's nickname for Louis Sullivan, his "beloved master."

6. Wright, *Modern Architecture: Being the Kahn Lectures for 1930* (Princeton: at the University Press, 1931), n.p. (frontispiece). Also in Wright, *An Organic Architecture: The Architecture of Democracy* (London: Lund, Humphries and Co., 1939), p. 6.

7. "Frank Lloyd Wright," *The Architectural Forum* 68, no. 1 (January 1938): 100. Also in Wright, *An Organic Architecture*, p. 4.

8. The earthquake in fact took place on September 1, 1923.

9. Wright, *Modern Architecture*, p. 72.

10. Wright wrote in the Kahn Lectures, "Is the city a natural triumph of the herd instinct over humanity, and therefore a temporal necessity as a hangover from the infancy of the race, to be outgrown as humanity grows?" Ibid., p. 101.

11. Wright, *An Autobiography*, p. 321.

12. Behrendt, *Modern Building: Its Nature, Problems and Forms* (New York: Harcourt, Brace and Company, 1937).

I.

That Frank Lloyd Wright's architectural work was an individual achievement of national importance that soon would prove to be of international influence, was recognized and announced earlier abroad than in his native country. When, in the early years of this century, his name was known in America to only a few people who found themselves deeply impressed by the bold novelty of his work, his fame had already spread over Europe. Particularly in those countries where the spirit of modern building had already gained a strong foothold he was readily accepted as a leading avant-guardist, and his work was eagerly discussed among the progressive groups as a challenging example to be studied and followed.

Though on the Continent his work and message was received as a revelation, in this country his contemporaries, almost up to the present day, took him for a venturous eccentric who was making a point in being different. Though the Japanese government appointed him as architect for the Imperial Hotel in Tokio, he has never been asked by his own government to design one of the public buildings in the capital. To the man who is reputed and celebrated abroad as the creator of a new architecture, no invitation was extended in his own country to participate in one of those recent fairs which pretended to demonstrate the Century of Progress or the World of Tomorrow. Though documents of his work, drawings, plans, and selected photos had been shown in numerous exhibitions all over Europe, he had to reach the biblical age before he was given in this country the opportunity of a one-man show displaying to the public the results of a lifetime's work, a work overwhelming by its sheer size and its far-reaching scope.

It is about time for the Americans to realize that amidst them there is living a great genius, one of the greatest architects of all history.

II.

The scanty public appreciation, amounting to almost complete neglect, that was given to Wright's work, at least until recent years, throws an illuminating light on the development of architecture in this country.

In their slavish dependence on the standards of taste set by the old countries, standards which were incontestably accepted, American architects as well as art critics were completely unaware of the fresh sprout that was growing in virgin soil of their own country. America was proud of the high level of taste reached in its public buildings. These were designed by the Ecole des Beaux-Arts architects who, imitating in their designs the Classic and Renaissance pattern, accomplished little more than a pretentious monumentality. These academic standards of taste were already strongly questioned and partly undermined in Europe when, in 1910, the early work of Frank Lloyd Wright was first shown in a small monograph published in Berlin. In 1915, however, a publishing house in New York still found enough subscribers for a monumental publication of the complete works of McKim, Mead and White, edited in three large-sized volumes.

This American brand of Beaux-Arts architecture, it must be admitted, was perfect in design and faultless in detail, but how fake in its vaunting idealism, how meaningless as an interpretation of actual life, let alone modern American life. While the conspicuous creations of this academic architecture were widely celebrated, the early beginnings of realistic and indigenous building in this country were hardly noticed.

Frank Lloyd Wright, when he started, had Sullivan's shoulders to stand on; and Sullivan, for his part, was in many ways indebted to John Edelman and also somewhat to H. H. Richardson, who had been the first in this country to restore straightforwardness to architecture. (?) Richardson and Sullivan both attended the Ecole des Beaux-Arts, and all through their life remained under the influence of this great academic tradition of Europe. (Sullivan openly condemned it.) ~~Certain European influences can be traced in Wright's work too: those of Art Nouveau, for instance, and of the English Arts and Crafts movement. But this applies mainly to some details of interior decoration, and the~~ The fact remains that, right from the beginning, the houses designed by Frank Lloyd Wright showed a specific character which, unmistakably and irrefutably, marks them as products of the American soil.

Here was the first indication of a new architecture definitely distinguished from any European style,: a genuine expression of American spirit. How was it possible to overlook these striking characteristics in Wright's first houses built around Chicago, in Oak Park and Riverside? How was it possible to miss their novel features? Little critical discernment was needed to perceive the sense of their momentous message. Here was a new type of domestic architecture, and a vernacular one at that. With their low building masses stretching out over the ground and with their far-projecting eaves guarding them from an abundant sun, these houses, in an intimate union with soil and landscape, strike a new regional note belonging to the prairie lands of the Middle West.

Incidentally, some interesting discoveries were to be made in studying the structure of these houses. Unusual, too, were their aesthetic qualities: there was a stunning variety of form, indicating the abundant imagination of the designer; there was the superior manner in which the scale was handled. Compared with their neighbors, haughty imitators of the Georgian or Colonial manner, prettified by a finical detail, Wright's houses look like giants among dwarfs.

The first test Wright gave of his extraordinary talent revealed him as a great architect. His promising debut, however, was not accompanied by the cheering approval of his confrères, nor was it followed by the encouraging appreciation of art critics. In splendid isolation he started his career, pushed on only by his ~~stolid self-assurance.~~ *stolid self-assurance.* (?)

III.

When Wright, at the age of twenty-three, had just finished the Winslow house in Oak Park, he was offered the opportunity to go to Paris for several years to attend the Ecole des Beaux-Arts on some sort of private fellowship, sponsored by "Uncle Dan" (Daniel H. Burnham). He refused on the ground that Sullivan had spoiled him for that fountainhead of architectural doctrine. His refusal proves that he was already sure of himself, that he saw his way clear ahead and that nothing could distract him any more from the great aim he had set himself–not even such a splendid and big-hearted offer as would have tempted any other young man.

He was right: the teaching of Louis Sullivan had turned his mind in a direction incompatible with academic doctrine. Wright had no use for academic architecture and its modern species of eclecticism. For him it was a meaningless elaboration, nothing but "a rubbish heap of styles." Conscious of his own creative power, he was out to "formulate, not to reformulate."

The idea of architecture, born dormant within him and awakened by his "lieber Meister," had already germinated and taken shape so that he was now able to define it. His was a concept of organic architecture–of an architecture that grows "out of the ground into the light" and arises "from within outward"–an architecture that "continuously begins at the beginning," that "fearlessly accepts the laws of change inherent in all nature"–an architecture that, according to these principles, will conceive every building problem as a new one, as an individual case to be dealt with according to its own laws, the laws of its individual existence.

This concept of organic architecture is a dynamic one, in contrast to the academic concept that is based on the static laws of geometry imposed upon the structure. It is life and not a preconceived scheme or dogma that is on the basis of this concept. The house, instead of being composed of a series of rooms conceived as boxes arranged on a system of coordinate axes, was now defined as life-space, as interior space separated from outer space by enclosing and protecting walls and roofs. Within this interior space the rooms are to be so arranged as to lay out the pattern of domestic life, to order and control the movements, the comings and goings of those who live in it. If the house is conceived as an organism, the rooms are to be interpreted as its organs. Their individual form and their interrelationship are determined by the function they have to fulfill for the whole. Superseding Sullivan's famous formula, Wright states that "form and function are one" which, according to his interpretation, means that the purpose and pattern of the building are one. And as the rooms inside are organized into an organic whole, so the inside is related to the outside. Inside and outside are "of each other."

In discussing the new concept of organic architecture, I have closely followed Wright's own terms. To understand what they mean and to realize the fundamental change of structure brought about under the impact of this new concept, one must, however, study the plans and buildings themselves. In all his plans the chimney and its fireplaces are made the center of the house around which the rooms are grouped. In the larger houses there is often more than one such center. But always the rooms stretch out from this center toward the garden, opening themselves to the light and the view on all sides. With the interior space showing only minor or subordinate subdivisions, the rooms, interspersed with low galleries or short passages as connecting links, flow into each other, penetrating each other and interlacing with indissoluble cohesion. And their uninterrupted flow does not stop at the enclosing walls, but continues over terraces, loggias and balconies into the outer space of the surrounding landscape.

As the rooms are no longer conceived as boxes in an organic architecture, their enclosing walls often change into light screens, and the windows, formerly holes punched in the walls, appear within these screens as large transparent areas frequently extending around the corners of the building.

The idea of organic structure not only demands a new integrity of purpose but implies a new attitude toward the use of material, too. It means that material is to be used according to its organic nature: brick as brick, or wood to look like wood, showing its finished surface or the ornamental effect of its natural grain instead of being covered with a coat of paint. Or when natural stone is used, it means following the pattern of the strata and laid on its natural bed as in the natural ledges, with the edges left natural, in order to utilize not only the physical but also the physiognomical properties of the material.

However, one has not done full justice to this new concept if one interprets it only as an architectural theory. It is much more. Wright's theory of architecture is an integral part of Wright's philosophy of life. This philosophy is based on moral and intellectual concepts which center around the fundamental conditions of life, of man and nature as one. And the same concept which he follows in his plans and structures, the concept of organic order, he also visualizes as the essential basis of our social structure. Architecture, he once stated, is a true expression of the life of the human and social world. The center line of any true culture. And so is organic architecture is integral to a life lived as organic.

Wright's philosophy and architectural theory are no less admirable as the extraordinary achievement of a profound thinker than his creation of an organic architecture is as the work of a great artist. With his ideas demonstrated in practical examples he gave the modern movement a new impetus, particularly in Europe. Guided by the principle of organic structure and inspired by his practical examples, it soon gained so much momentum that it totally changed the appearance of contemporary architecture.

IV.

With his architectural theory clearly defined, Wright, devotedly and conscientiously, put himself under the severe discipline of his ideal. The theory, of course, grew and developed on the practical problems which came to the workshop. And the work of his lifetime, from his earliest building, the unprecedented windmill tower Romeo and Juliet (1896), on the hill of his family's farm in Wisconsin, now the famous landmark of Taliesin, is one continuous adventure in experiment in search of more simple methods of construction and greater integrity of form.

Set at Setting himself the task of making architecture a genuine expression of the machine age, he readily accepts modern building techniques and materials and explores their constructive possibilities to simplify and improve them. He experiments with glass, steel, and concrete in reasonable ways often objectionable to building codes. In designing his first public building, Unity Temple (Oak Park, 1905), he was faced with the narrow budget of a small community. He experimented with concrete as building material : he used concrete, a new building material then, and cast it in wooden molds, the cheapest of its ~~many~~ old techniques. Until that time concrete had been used only in utilitarian engineering structures. Unity Temple was the first concrete structure to come finished and complete out of its forms. As a church scheme the building is just as unique in its plan (with two-leveled aisles and cloister corridor) as it is in its construction. Cast concrete was used for the walls, reinforced concrete slabs for the roof. By developing skillful devices for surface treatment, enlivening the large unbroken areas of the walls through the coarse texture of gravel, the architect succeeded in ennobling the profane nature of the commonplace material. And by adapting scale and proportion to the inherent character of the material, he imbued the whole structure, though rather modest in its physical dimensions, with a quality appropriate to its noble purpose, monumental both in mass and in detail. The experiment proved to be a thorough success: there is hardly another contemporary church building which in its structure is expressive of its modern building technique, in its form one with its function, and in both its interior and exterior ~~full of emotional appeal.~~ an expression of the concept that "the reality of a building does not consist in walls and roof but in the space within to be lived in."

He has always judiciously and carefully experimented with construction. In designing the Imperial Hotel in Tokio, his ambition was to develop an earthquakeproof structure, flexible enough to resist the most formidable enemy that threatens building in that country. By an ingenious device the building was set on a shockproof foundation, with its ~~outer walls separated from the floors~~ floors extending through the outer walls by the use of the cantilever and supported from within on posts much as a waiter poises his tray on his upraised fingers. Although at first ~~no native contractor was to be found~~ the Tokio building department would not allow him to take the risk of this experiment, officials finally relented and the building ~~finally~~ was erected according to Wright's plan ~~and the~~ . The architect and his clients found ~~himself~~ themselves most splendidly rewarded for having insisted upon his courageous experiment when, two years later, contrary to dire prophecies from engineering experts the Imperial Hotel proved to be the only one of the few buildings in Tokio that survived the notorious catastrophe of 1924 totally unharmed.

Another experiment, never attempted before, was made in one of Wright's most recent buildings: the administration building of the Johnson Wax Company in Racine, Wisconsin. Glass tubing is used all over the building for lighting. Two continuous bands of horizontal glass tubing encircle the building, one at eye level, the other at the junction of the walls and the roof. Set in two layers, they serve as the sources of natural light as well as artificial, eliminating all other fixtures and affording a pleasantly diffused light. Since the glass tubing is not designed to open like regular windows, the building is air-conditioned and equipped with two circular shafts, reaching from the roof to the basement, which, like nostrils, function as breathing organs for the building. For the same building Wright used a new kind of construction unit, a ~~mushroom shaped~~ dendriform hollow concrete column, forming post and ceiling together. In the main office room several hundred desks are arranged between the extraordinarily slender shafts of these columns, which are ten times the height allowed by the building code for their diameter. The large concrete circles at the top are tangent to each other, and through glass tubing set between the circles a gentle light floods down from the ceiling: a light and elegant construction, appropriate for the purpose, making the room spacious and easy to oversee.

And so ~~it goes all~~ the search goes on through the long list of Wright's works: fascinated by the possibilities offered by modern technique, ~~curious~~ gaining experience to safely explore the properties of new building materials, anxious to take advantage of the economies of modern building construction and to interpret its character in an truly expressive forms, Wright goes from ~~experiment to experiment~~ building to building. He, the individualist par excellence, does not hesitate to utilize modern industrialized methods: he accepts standardization and prefabrication now able to use both without depriving his buildings in the least of ~~their~~ individuality. For him, every new problem is another opportunity for ~~experiment~~ a better way of building. And it is a characteristic of his conception that out of the vast resources of his experience he ~~always~~ approaches his problem by intuition, starting from the particular nature of the problem, and not vice versa, that is, making the problem subject to ~~a~~ some preestablished theory taken at face value.

For the client, then, it is ~~no easy task~~ not always easy to work with an architect who is ~~such a passionate experimenter~~ so devoted to the nature and possibilities of his building problem. On his part, too, it needs a lot of patience, confidence in his architect's experience, and a good deal of personal interest in the problem besides. He has to be willing to put ~~up with disappointment, inefficacy,~~ faith in his architect, wearisome detours and delays, perhaps. ~~even failure. However,~~ But though failure is yet to be recorded it is only fair to say, experiments such as Wright makes are needed if we desire to progress, and no progress can be obtained without taking ~~a~~ some risk. A leaking roof matters little when a new building material is tried out for the first time. ~~The way to experience is through initial mistakes. In the development of Gothic construction the occasional collapse of vaults of daring new construction was, as an experience, an important stimulant to further exploration.~~ It can be fixed.

All through his life, Wright has been fortunate in his building experience in finding congenial clients who, captivated by his genius and believing implicitly in him, faithfully supported his ~~experiments~~ efforts in their behalf and generously helped him through. In this regard, such names as Francis W. Little; Darwin D. Martin, the vice-president of the Larkin factory; Aisaku Aayashi and Baron Okura, the main figures in the exciting story of the Tokio Hotel; the most extraordinary Miss Barnsdall, patroness of the Hollyhock House in Hollywood; Paul Mueller, the inventive contractor; Edgar Kaufmann, Herbert Johnson, and ~~many~~ hundreds of others, are closely connected with Wright's achievements in the field of architecture. It is to their undying credit that they gave their mental and material assistance in full faith to a genius who is ~~permanently~~ wisely and passionately ~~experimenting~~ growing toward ~~a~~ the new organic architecture of his dreams.

V.

Always searching for other opportunities ~~to test his~~ where inventive power ~~on~~ is needed most and where new problems are hitherto unsolved, Wright began, ~~in recent years~~ some twenty years ago to interest himself in the problems of the small house, the house of moderate cost, which he declares is America's most pressing contemporary building problem. "As for me, I would rather solve this with satisfaction to myself and Usonia than build anything I can think of at the moment except the modern theater now needed by the legitimate drama."

The first result of his studies and experiments in this field was a small house in Madison, Wisconsin, designed for Mr. Herbert Jacobs, a journalist, and his small family, a house built on contract for $5,500, and a surprise for all those who had previously seen this architect associated with the most affluent customers. With this house he created a new type, demonstrating that, besides satisfying all vital necessities and requirements for comfort, he could offer a more livable house (and more of it) than anything that is on the market at this price. Of course, "more livable" it will appear only to those who are willing to accept "a pattern for more simple and more gracious living." More livable it will be for those who prefer to have their house built at one level, with greater spaciousness because no space is wasted for stairs to climb up to the bedrooms. More livable it will be for those who are satisfied with one large living room, well lighted and opened out fully to the garden on its south side, with a section set apart for dining and ~~a~~ the kitchen a ventilating shaft for the house; large enough to prepare a good meal.

In short, to be ready to accept ~~that~~ his new type of house means to be mentally ~~prepared~~ preparing for a new form of American society. Here it becomes manifest that the concept of an organic architecture involves the concept of ~~a new society~~, a society also based ~~on~~ upon some comprehension of an organic order. To use Wright's own phrase: "Architecture which is a genuine interpretation of the present is a prophecy of social structure yet to come." In fact, many of Wright's projects, audacious yet reasonable creations, demonstrating a form fit for and expressive of a new mode of life, are anticipating, within themselves and society as it is, the ideal of a new society to come.

Most illuminating in this regard are Wright's prospective studies and tentative projects in the field of city planning: projects which, upon their realization, make ~~obligatory~~ feasible an antecedent change of some at least of our most important social institutions. It is but logical that Wright, devoted to a concept of organic planning, condemns the big city as a dated form of settlement characteristic of an "inorganic society." The big city he considers as an obsolete institution, "a temporal hangover from the infancy of the race, when the herd instinct triumphed over humanity." In our time, however, the big city, in his opinion, is no more a necessity since a decentralized form of settlement has become possible with the advances of technology. Our machines will furnish the greatest service they can do to man if we will use them to carry through decentralization at a large scale. In his project for Broadacre City he has indicated what a community planned for the decentralized life of an organic society would look like. Instead of being crowded with structures tipped up edgewise and piled to the sky, it will be built up with houses spreading horizontally, naturally developed on the ground, surrounded by large gardens, little farms, and open areas, associating with pleasant factories, clinics, markets, etc., offering to the inhabitants the most natural way of living in closest contact with the nourishing soil and organic nature. "Ruralism," he once stated, "as distinguished from 'Urbanism' for future machine-age development, is the business of the modern architect." And this ~~new~~ forward-looking ruralism finally will provide a social condition enabling the architect "to build into his structures the good life as a new kind of beauty.": a highly developed landscape on the terms of human occupation and cultivation.

In fact, if we were to indicate the specific character of Wright's art, we ~~would~~ might call it rural in the sense that he himself uses the word. Based on ~~a~~ principles of natural organic order, it evidently loses its finest values when it is congested or diverted to projects of typical city building. It is most characteristic that Wright, when faced with the problem of designing a tall apartment house, logically reverted to the most rigid geometrical form, ~~the rectangular box~~: incidentally, ~~this is~~ the most perfect form in regard to function, when the parking problem is to be solved–that problem which is at the basis of all present city building.

VI.

It is the study of nature on which Wright's art is securely founded, and it is the working principle of ~~organic~~ growth as manifest in nature from which ~~this~~ art takes much of its structural as well as its aesthetic concept. Logically from his creative observation of nature, Wright arrives at the conclusion that "every true aesthetic is an implication of nature." The building itself must be supremely natural.

On another occasion–in my book *Modern Building*, where I have set forth at length the nature and essence of Frank Lloyd Wright's work–I have pointed out that in describing his architectural creations one is, again and again, urged to a comparison with the world of plants. Wright himself once suggested THE TREE AS an image and ideal for "American" ~~building~~ culture. Figuratively we might say that ~~In~~ in this image the rooms in his houses are arranged around the nucleus of the ~~chimney part,~~ living space like the leaves of a plant around the stem. Treelike, indeed, are his buildings, firmly rooted in their ground. Treelike, they grow up from the earth to the light, adapting themselves to their environment, following the natural conditions of the site, so that at the end they become an integral part of the scene in which they are set to serve the life to be lived in them, which has given them the pattern they have. And again, as the tree is not just an example of a species but also an individual growth, so each house of Frank Lloyd Wright is an individual organism, true to its function and making. In such a sense, Taliesin, for instance, the architect's own house, is not just a house on the hill, but it really is The House of The Hill.

The comparison, which links the artistic vision to the principles underlying the world of natural growth, holds true for the details of the various architectural forms. As the bulky stem of a tree ramifies into the light boughs that form its crown, so the bulk of Wright's buildings, as they rise higher from the ground, becomes lighter and lighter, while the detail becomes more ~~elaborate~~ delicate and tenuous. Compare the change in the design of the windows from the lower to the upper floor, with their screenlike arrangement–in the Coonley House, for instance, and in many other examples: a device which, besides its practical purpose, has the aesthetic function of loosening the building bulk into greater lightness and breadth of repose. Over the bulk of the building the roofs spread with their widely overhanging projections like lofty treetops. As they appear, in their multiform arrangement, in which the void plays ~~just as~~ far more important a part aesthetically ~~as~~ than the mass, these roofs seem to be of Japanese ancestry: in fact, Wright's country houses often recall the Japanese house, ~~another~~ perhaps because it is another highly developed example of organic structure. His buildings knew nothing of them when originally conceived.

With a ~~florid~~ fertile and exuberant imagination, which is ~~the~~ strongest among his manifold talents, Wright created a new architectural form expressive of the organic, a form of fresh beauty enchanting with its sensual and emotional effect at the same time as its definite appeal to reason. So strong and forceful is ~~this~~ imagination that, in humoring his great artistic talent, Wright easily opens himself to the accusation of a betrayal of his own theory. (?) Although he seems to believe, concluding from his own statement, that "~~any~~ a style is offensive now," because we want style all the while, a style is the death of Style"—as an artist he is apparently so much of an individualist as not to see that, when forcing ~~his personal~~ organic style upon his clients, he ~~is~~ seems to be acting against his belief, though in reality this is again natural and inevitable. In Wright's houses, as a matter of fact, the interior is ~~not~~ fully neutralized into life space ~~but~~ while still used by the architect as a vehicle for ~~personal~~ individual experience and its expression. As long as in a Frank Lloyd Wright room no other furniture is permissible but that of Frank Lloyd Wright's design, the interior space is ~~still~~ simply subject to the ~~idea of style, be it only that of a personal~~ same conditions as give its enclosure always individual style. And for us, today, and particularly in architecture, as correctly stated by Wright himself, ~~any~~ a style has become offensive, ~~and most of all the personal one.~~ although style itself has not, and is more than ever the need. Most of all, style is needed as the most precious of democratic privileges extended to the individual.

So ~~This~~ this does not diminish the value of his artistic achievement. On the contrary, it clearly brings out the remarkable fact that the form in which Wright for the first time expressed the idea of an organic architecture, is a thoroughly ~~personal~~ individual creation, ~~a~~ his buildings being creations of his own, and as such ~~deserving~~ inspiring our fullest admiration and gratefulness as ~~it~~ they opened to us a fresh source of that fine delight that goes with the practice of principle and the enjoyment of beauty.

Frank Lloyd Wright is one of the most imposing figures ~~from~~ in the ~~past~~ period of individualism we call democratic who has lived on into our time, ~~a personality~~ an individual of such overwhelming greatness as we will not see soon again. As an artist-architect he is an emotionalist and a romantic individual guided by principles that are not personal but primal. It is for that reason that the younger generation is inclined to ~~distrust~~ idolize him. ~~In their judgment he passes as a romantic: which only means that~~ Over 400 young aspirants have applied for admission to his Fellowship at Taliesin, where only a few could be taken.[1] Youth crowds the rare occasions upon which he speaks although the world today ~~has~~ seems to have begun to lose the sense for that kind of romantic beauty as an expression of principle which he has to offer as the most precious gift of his extraordinary talent. But even if the form in which he presented his ideas should prove to be evanescent, and the quality of individuality be replaced by the totalitarian or communistic or socialistic ideal of architecture, the principle on which his work is founded will continue to be upheld in all future efforts where they are sincerely directed toward making architecture again a ~~living~~ *living* art.

1. Here Wright added in pencil in the margin, "For your information, in case you might not know—F.LL.W."

TO MY CRITICS

Frank Lloyd Wright

September 14, 1940

Reading many criticisms of my work now standing among you, I realize I should talk to you myself.

Appreciation from you is not lacking, nor generosity . . . I am not ungrateful.

But a mystery is still made of what is extremely simple and natural, if difficult. I should explain that I have let my work go into exhibition here and now because I felt the force of my example either confused or no longer clearly felt. And because I have noticed of late years concentration upon appearances that do not grow outward into manifold richness of expression but that tend to concrete on the barren bands and box-outlines of a calculated style. Another academic for schools, administrated by professors.

Any tyro may emulate any calculated superficial style. While much talk of principle goes with such calculated effort it is definitely a rationalizing after the fact because principles, if involved in this effort at *a* style, do not fructify creation.

What has happened?

The usual abuse: the straight line and the flat plane—necessary basis of forms for our machine age, capitalized as something by, for, and in themselves.

The T-square, triangle, and the flat of the paper had been "stylized" and there the matter stays—a negation. Sterile!

Negation is good sometimes, for a time.

But affirmation of more than mere negation is needed, in Usonia[1] at least, if human life is going beyond its own machinery. So this friendly warning and brotherly protest against the kind of protestant who continues to protest the human riches involved in genuine creative endeavor, and implies that certain impersonal universalities, which they understand, can take its place in our brave new world.

Do not imagine, my critics, that mathematics is music, although music is sublimated mathematics.

No more is the geometry of the straight line and flat plane applied to the bare facts of the machine age in itself architecture, however academic you make it.

Once the now easy rejection of former insignificance, waste, and lying by way of functionless ornament is effected, there the matter seems to rest with you. You get no further on. You seem content with that, especially you of the Old Europe.

And some of you seem to imagine that by renouncing such individualities as you possess (I think you confuse personality with individuality) you may *calculate* a style for our Usonian future. Nothing could be more absurd.

While the machine is become the tool of the age a new ideal has grown up beside it out of the grass roots of the new ground. We call that ideal Freedom! The word most often going with it is Democracy: an interior evolution of the individuality commanding the personality. That evolution was ever the human core of such limited cultures as the ages have developed.

Are we now reaching a point where man, to be free, must triumph over you and your new aesthetic abstractions as well as those naturally made by the machine? Or is man to triumph over all machinery and give human significance to all abstraction over your decent but dead bodies?

■ ■ ■ ■

I say, *a* style is no longer necessary because it cannot be individual and therefore cannot be free. Why let Style die that way again as it has died so many deaths heretofore?

The thought of an "international style"[2] is a horrible nightmare; again the sensibilities and potencies of vibrant human life imprisoned by the narrow vision and impotence of small men.

Life cannot be straightened out and tipped edgewise to be surveyed in the vertical flat for longer than a brief period while novelty is a satisfaction. Better turn the flat plane parallel with the Earth.

I believe that notwithstanding educators and educated, the wellsprings of human activity lie as deep and are more thirst-quenching than ever before, when found.

But that thirst for more life is at once intensified and now denied by the engine we live by, the machine.

I am sure it is our office as creative artists to overcome the machine by intelligent use of that engine and, by means of it, using it as a new tool, gratify the natural longing of the human soul for beauty: yes, for sentient, living beauty, to live in, to live by, and to live for. Compositions, gestured simplicities, affectations, negations, and lies, however pretentious of universal common sense they may be, cheat this finer sense of the man himself. So the thought at the center of the buildings and these plans and models you may see in this exhibition is wasted on you if you gauge their worth by the negation you mistake for affirmation, "universalities" you have mistaken for the individual creative impulse that alone can give them validity or human desirability.

I have seen and used the straight line and flat plane only as humble enough new means to a greater end. But that end is not an international style nor *a* style at all. All that I have done is aimed at greater individuality by way of greater imagination because of greater resources and the demands of the deepening sense of life that freedom, when it is realized, must bring with style all the while.

So in any new freedom for life, abstractions, especially those now academic, are to be regarded with doubt and suspicion, held well under or again they become prison-houses for the mind. Not by way of any momentary thrill of discovery are they to be made into *a* style.

So, instead of trying to put the world into new prisons for greater academic convenience, why not liberate the world by way of greater imaginative vision—new and better technique, mastering new and greater resources in order to make no more prison-houses with professors for wardens.

Such liberation means no emulation of emulation by emulation, such as men used to call and professors continue to call a style.

No, my critics, the matter is already more truly simple and therefore infinitely more difficult.

Liberation means the free exercise of whatever resources of imagination happen to be your individual gift, disciplined by your new tool, the machine, but never mastered by it. Such wealth of significant form as the world never saw before will in those circumstances belong to our coming of age.

■ ■ ■ ■

Do not take from one another more than common knowledge.

Do not take from any source more than inspiration.

Do not try to take from life more than you can put into it because the natural thief is always severely punished by Nature herself.

I say this to you out of an intensely joyous—if turbulent—personal experience.

Great appreciation I have given to life and have received from it. Life is no niggard except to the niggardly. The more one gives to life in free spirit, the more he will receive from life. Strength increases by way of exercise of strength, never by way of keeping an eye on the other fellow, to do as well or better than he.

In the arts of life, emulation is cowardice. To be a coward is to die continually and never be quite dead because one never was quite alive.

If my buildings and these plans and models have any significance to you—my appreciation of life is that general significance. But there is much in them all to help the young man to form a technique, because he may see, here, form taking shape out of the nature and character of materials and material conditions as naturally as a flower takes shape from the principle committed to its seed. But where a man builds with organic character there will be style—all the while and by way of technique—every builder his own.

My critical contemporaries: criticize me as I am. Do not criticize me as you would have me. Because I would not be as you would have me. Unless you change we could not help each other. It does not thrill or even please me to see myself referred to as one of the greatest architects on earth or in heaven or in hell. Because no architect such as I must be has ever been. To be an architect heretofore has been relatively simple. All were in command of an established craftsmanship pursuing a preferred style established by the order of the times. I have had to cut my way through degenerate confusion and enmity to prophesy order anew and conceive new form according to a complete change of ways and means in this world and try to live by it. That means a new architecture for a new life. So no bouquets if you please. You have none in your baskets at all becoming. I am not sure that any that could be forthcoming at this time would be becoming to me. Occasionally a remark is dropped which finds a mark though seldom as intended.

Criticism, after all, like Autobiography, is best read between the lines and when it is so read it reveals not the criticized but the critic.

And why not realize that I am still at work with greater appreciation of life than ever?

What you have seen from my hand is yet unfinished.

1. Wright's term for the United States of America, borrowed from Samuel Butler and developed in the 1920s. See Wright, *An Autobiography* (New York: Longmans, Green and Company, 1932), p. 22.

2. The Museum of Modern Art organized its famous "International Style" exhibition, actually titled *Modern Architecture, International Exhibition*, in 1932. The exhibition was accompanied by a publication, *Modern Architects* (New York: The Museum of Modern Art, 1932), and by an independently published book, *The International Style: Architecture since 1922* (New York: W. W. Norton, 1932). Hitchcock coorganized the exhibition, with Johnson, and was a coauthor of both books.

FRANK LLOYD WRIGHT: HIS INFLUENCE IN AMERICA

Talbot Hamlin

In one sense, the influence of Frank Lloyd Wright pervades the whole of American architecture today. It is seldom we find one man who during his own lifetime sees his name become a byword, almost, as the architect *par excellence*. Even those who are hostile to his ideas do him the credit of a violence in controversy which reveals their sense of his power. Yet, in another sense, the relationship of the Wright influence to actual work constructed today is more difficult to trace. For forty years his views and his achievements have been almost constantly before the architects of the United States. The peculiar individuality and extraordinary capacity for growth which have always characterized Wright make imitations of his work almost impossible and, when attempted, seldom successful. What one has, as the enduring body of his influence, is something much deeper than mere imitations of plan types or details; it is a whole philosophy of building, a general theory of the oneness of structure, use, and effect, which Wright himself calls "organic architecture."[1] This ideal has come to be accepted among large numbers of American architects, almost as a matter of course; and, in its many ramifications in ways of using materials as well as in ways of putting spaces together in a building, it is visible in the work of many architects who themselves would perhaps even warmly deny that Wright had anything to do with the way they design.

And the influence itself has suffered many vagaries. Wright came into the practice of architecture at almost the perfect time and in almost the perfect place. The early [18]90s in America were years of high artistic adventure. The Richardsonian movement had brought, in architecture, a new feeling for materials. Louis Sullivan was creating extraordinarily successful new formulae for business buildings, and decorating them with a vivid originality that was widely welcomed. Louis Tiffany, in industrial art, was producing silverware, lamps, and glass which sought, all of it, to be practical and beautiful in a new way; the windows which he made, often for his own pleasure, out of pebbles and natural translucent stones, were immensely significant of a widespread search in America for new expressions of materials to serve a new kind of life. Publishers like Stone and Kimball, of Chicago, were attempting to make the book a work of art. These were the years, too, of extensive enthusiasm for Japanese prints and Japanese decorative ideas, popularized in all sorts of misunderstood and sometimes caricatured ways. And it was a time when, in the mountains and along the New England shores, summer cottages of wide, many-windowed rooms, with spreading roofs, covered with silver-gray weathered shingles, were rising–not all beautiful, but all frank attempts to create a new kind of building rooted in use and materials.

Chicago, in those years, as for another decade or two, was of all the cities in America, the one in which this new spirit, this frank search for a new and American artistic expression, was most brilliantly aflame. From the memoirs of Edgar Lee Masters, from Harriet Monroe's biography of her brother-in-law John Root, from many other sources one may gain a picture of this strange inchoate city, half mad with moneymaking and half drunk with new visions of political advance or artistic creation. This was the city and this the atmosphere into which Wright came to offer his services; and it is little wonder that his gifts were welcomed and that the list of the work which he did between 1893 and 1915 is so long.

Nor is it strange, given this accomplishment, given these houses which rose in so many Chicago suburbs and sometimes far afield as well, with their exquisite proportions, their lovely long lines, their merging and marrying of landscape and garden and building, their wide-open, inviting interiors and their strong and simple furniture, that their beauty and their perfect fittingness should have been almost at once recognized as expressive of a new vision, a new creative genius. The *Architectural Review* of Boston, in May, 1900, published an enthusiastic monograph on Wright's work, written by Robert C. Spencer, Jr.[2] It is interesting to note how in this article so many of the essential qualities of Wright's genius were already set forth. Five years later the *Architectural Record* of New York has an article entitled "The Work of Frank Lloyd Wright, Its Influence,"[3] in which the superficial copying of Wright details is deplored, but the essential soundness of Wright's own creation is recognized and applauded. And from then on until the coming of the World War the articles and illustrations of Wright's work become more and more common and more and more adulatory in nearly all of the American architectural publications.

One can divide a man's influence in art into two different classes: first, the influence exerted by his basic thinking–the real expression and reworking of his ideals in accordance with each individual's own personality–and, second, the actual copying of his mannerisms or his details. It is the bane of much art criticism that it concentrates too definitely on the latter, because it is easier to trace and to illustrate. In the case of the work of Wright, the problem is especially difficult, since Wright was not an isolated artist. Working for years in Sullivan's office, he himself fell deeply under the sway of his "*lieber Meister*"; and early followers of Wright often imitated the more Sullivanesque mannerisms, so that it is difficult to discriminate between the direct and the indirect Sullivan influence and the direct Wright influence. So with the work of [William Gray] Purcell and [George Grant] Elmslie. Elmslie had been a coworker with Wright in the Sullivan office and an intimate friend, and like Wright was deeply under the Sullivan influence; yet in the domestic work of the firm the forms used are frequently so similar to those which appeared in the Wright houses that one is tempted to think the influence at work rather that of his friend and contemporary rather than that of his earlier employer, Sullivan. So the Decker House at Lake Minnetonka or the beautiful Community House at Eau Claire, Wisconsin, might be thought of either as developments of Sullivan training by a contemporary of Wright's with much the same artistic aim, or else as more direct results of the inspiration received from the earlier houses of his friend, Wright. Certainly here the influence is from the general philosophy, and the work is no slavish copy of Wright details. In such a design as that for the Riverside Country Club the ideal of organic architecture, which is Wright's, received one of its most charming early expressions and would be "modern" even today.

The touches of "Japanese" forms or atmosphere, which one comes upon in the interiors of that time again and again, may be either results of the direct influence of Wright's own "Japanese" effects or, on the other hand, merely, like his other expressions of a widely held impulse. Moreover, Wright's interiors and furniture, like those of Charles Rennie Mackintosh in Scotland a little later, seem to have flowed from some feeling about craftsmanship, which has definite relationships to the whole English Arts and Crafts movement initiated by William Morris. This same movement, itself, had other American expressions forty years ago. The *Craftsman* magazine of Gustav Stickley, for instance, sought for open interiors and simple rectangular furniture, not without resemblances, at least in general idea, to the work of Wright; and the *Craftsman* influence was extremely broad. "Mission furniture" at its best was founded on the same principle of simplicity of line and construction which is evident in the Wright furniture, and over and over again in looking at photographs of interiors of the early 1900s one is hard put to it to discriminate between the influence of the one and the influence of the other. Yet the *Craftsman* magazine turned definitely away from America toward England, and later toward the Art Nouveau of the Continent, for its essential inspiration, whereas Wright's work seems always to have remained free from sentimentalities of the English movement and the incoherencies of the Art Nouveau. It is possible, of course, that Stickley fell, himself, under the influence of Wright's early interiors and in the sane simplicity of his best work was paying his own tribute to Wright's originality.

In the sense of close emulation if not imitation, Wright's power was strongest during the period between 1905 and 1914. It was definitely regional in character. All through the Middle West one finds evidences of it in the work of architects like Purcell, Feick, and Elmslie (afterwards Purcell & Elmslie), Dwight Perkins, or in the work of Robert C. Spencer, Jr. (author of the 1900 monograph), all of them striving for the accented horizontal, the broad eaves, the low hipped roofs, the strong masonry lower portions contrasted with lighter walls above, the large low chimneys, which characterized the Wright houses of that time. Many go much further in imitation, attempting the quick nervous ornament with its simple geometry and sharp staccato accents which Wright developed to such a high degree in grille work or glass leading. And the Bunte Brothers Candy Factory in Chicago, by Schmidt, Garden & Martin, one of the earlier attempts to make factories works of architecture as well as of engineering, bears definite evidence of a study of Wright's Larkin Soap Company administration building in Buffalo and acts as a connecting link between Wright's original revolutionary work of 1903 and the whole movement toward making industrial buildings decent and beautiful, which is a growing trend today.

Nor is this early influence limited to the work of known architects; it permeated much of the speculative building of the region as well, and it is here that the sometimes disastrous results of unintelligent emulation or imitation can best be seen. Wright had designed a number of group housing developments, prophetically independent in plan and unusually simple and straightforward in detail. Many speculative builders in Middle Western cities hastened to follow the example he had set. Wright had sought for buildings relatively low, and covered them with low-pitched hipped roofs and wide eaves. The broad, square windows, the wide surfaces of gray or yellow brick, the flat bands and surface ornament which Wright used in this work can be found again and again in the strangest guise in speculative building of the early twentieth century in that section of the country. Almost everywhere speculative builders, seizing upon details of the Wright work and wedding it to the planless and awkward bungalows that were increasingly the fashion, produced a type the endless proliferation of which covers untold square miles of the Plains cities. Thus, Wright suffered the fate of all great men in having his ideas caricatured and prostituted. In the second article of his series "In the Cause of Architecture," which appeared in May, 1914, in the *Architectural Record*,[4] Wright himself complains bitterly of unthinking imitations of his mannerisms. A new style, he claims, can only flow from new conceptions organically expressed; a mere imitation of forms is never enough. "As for the vital principle of the work," he says, "–the quality of an organic architecture–that has been lost to sight even by pupils . . . In any case, judging from what is exploited as such, most of what is beginning to be called the 'New School of the Middle West' is not only far from the ideal of an organic architecture, but getting farther away from it every day."[5]

This first wave of influence, this first grasping for Wright's details and ideas, died out little by little from 1914 on, as more and more the new fashions of eclecticism swept over the thoughtless and drowned out the earlier ardent Americanism of the Middle Western taste. In the sense of actual constructed buildings, the Wright influence lay perhaps at its lowest ebb during the decade following 1916. Yet this was precisely the period when the other and more important side of Wright's effect–the growing appreciation of his basic philosophy–was becoming increasingly important and exerting among the young men and the architectural students a growing power. Despite the apparent complete triumph of superficial eclecticism in the schools, there was hardly one in which there were not young men who were more and more restless under the imposed discipline, more and more questioning its aims and its methods, and more and more conscious of the continuing creative work which came from the Wright studio. The exciting quality of the Midway Gardens in Chicago, its vivid and human gaiety, its disciplined exuberance, fired the imaginations of thousands, architect and layman alike; and it was perhaps only the accident that Wright was absent in Tokyo working on the Imperial Hotel for a long period from around 1916 which prevented this growing interest, this increasing admiration, from coming into flower earlier than it did.

Another source of direct Wright influence was developing–that of his own "graduates" and, later, of his own sons John and Lloyd. Thus, the work of Guenzel & Drummond shows unmistakable evidence of [William] Drummond's seven years with Wright, as in the Brookfield Kindergarten or River Forest Woman's Club; and the work of Walter Burley Griffin (later the architect of Canberra, the Australian capital) indicates similarly his training under Wright. Further west, Francis Byrne, who had been with Wright five years, and Andrew Willatzen, who had three years in the Wright office, formed a partnership in Seattle which built many houses that carried the Wright message to the Pacific Coast. In the 1920s, [Albert Chase] McArthur used modifications of the textured concrete block in the romantic layout for the Arizona Biltmore Hotel [in Phoenix]. Similarly, in more recent years, Alden Dow, under the direct influence of Wright, his former master, has been producing in Midland, Michigan, a series of brilliant and imaginative, if somewhat fantastic, houses which serve to show the almost unlimited possibilities in American house design.

Another line of influence flows directly from the concrete block houses which Wright designed in Los Angeles and its vicinity in 1920–25. These brought the brilliance of Wright's organic integration, of structure and design, graphically before the architects and the prospective clients of a region particularly ready for it–the Pacific Coast. Architectural work on the Pacific Coast had partly escaped the complete domination of eclectic ideals: [Bernard] Maybeck in San Francisco, and Elmer Grey, Irving Gill, and others in the Los Angeles neighborhood, had still been trying to preserve in much of their domestic work something of the true feeling for materials and their use that is such an important part of good architecture; [Bertram Grosvenor] Goodhue had persuaded Los Angeles to give up the eclectic Spanish design he had made for the public library and substitute another founded on the natural forms of concrete construction. These new Wright houses, these splendid new examples of what exquisiteness could flow from a new structural method and from the brilliance of the open plan conception which characterized them, had an almost immediate effect.

R. M. Schindler, who had worked with Wright, went on to produce house after house in California, none imitating or closely resembling the Wright work, but all seriously attempting to work with something of the same freedom, the same organic quality. Neutra also had worked with Wright and perhaps from him gained that interest in construction methods and the frank use of new materials which has controlled his work. He has used different materials from those Wright loves, to be sure; and, differing in personality, has sought for different aesthetic expressions. Yet the influence is there, nevertheless. Harwell Hamilton Harris was turned from sculpture to architecture by his enthusiastic admiration of Wright's Barnsdall House [in Los Angeles], and the Wright lessons of honest use of materials, imaginatively and creatively handled, have been a controlling element in his work. In a larger sense, and perhaps almost unconsciously, the same influences have formed and vitalized nearly all the free contemporary house design which is the glory of the San Francisco region; and one can say that without a doubt these lovely and open houses, so beautifully amalgamated with their gardens and their sites, so simply built of pleasant materials frankly expressed, so freely and openly planned, so attractively roofed (like the work of William Wurster, Michael Goodman, Hervey Clarke, John Funk, John Ekin Dinwiddie, or John Yeon of Portland) would never have achieved their present form or their present excellence without the inspiration which the Wright work furnished.

With recent years, as the true ideals of contemporary architecture are more and more widely accepted by the most creative architects, the Wright influence in this broader sense becomes more and more triumphant. For the ideas of contemporary architecture owe much of their basic validity to the original fertilization of European experiments by the strong, new personality from across the sea, and in Germany and Holland alike the Wright influence played an important part in forming the whole body of international modern architecture. Thus when American architects, especially of the East, themselves fall under the influence of the International Style, they are, at least in some measure, however unwittingly, falling under the influence of their compatriot, Frank Lloyd Wright. Wherever architects strive to build with true organic vision; wherever they attack a problem of building design, not as a style matter, not to produce modernism or eclecticism, but to produce integrated and beautiful buildings; wherever they delight in the qualities of materials and base their design on them both structurally and aesthetically–there the spirit of Wright is at work.

1. Frank Lloyd Wright, "In the Cause of Architecture, Second Paper," *The Architectural Record* 35, no. 5 (May 1914): 406.

2. Robert C. Spencer, Jr., "The Work of Frank Lloyd Wright," *The Architectural Review* 7, no. 5 (May 1900): 61–72.

3. "The Work of Frank Lloyd Wright: Its Influence," *The Architectural Record* 18, no. 1 (July 1905): 60–66.

4. Wright, "In the Cause of Architecture, Second Paper," *The Architectural Record* 35, no. 5 (May 1914): 405–13. The earlier essay in the series had appeared in 1908: Wright, "In the Cause of Architecture," *The Architectural Record* 23, no. 3 (March 1908): 155–220.

5. Ibid., p. 408.

WRIGHT'S INFLUENCE ABROAD

Henry-Russell Hitchcock, Jr.

Although we are far from appreciating yet the true significance of many American developments in structure or of the particular ways in which American buildings of the seventeenth, eighteenth, and nineteenth centuries differ from their foreign prototypes, it is evident that the United States was, before the twentieth century, a debtor nation in architecture.

Skyscraper construction, invented in the [18]80s in Chicago, paralleled but hardly affected the feats of metal construction in later-nineteenth-century Europe. It was not until about a generation ago that American leadership in engineering was generally recognized and influential abroad. Moreover, it was hardly until after the last war that the more subtle appreciation of American engineering achievements, the superb but unintentional beauty of grain elevators and factories, the vital possibilities beneath the derivative surfaces of skyscrapers, became an active force in the development of modern architecture in Europe. Such influence was in any case almost extra-architectural, effectively anonymous in its sources, generic rather than specific, and accepted with Le Corbusier's proviso: "N.B. Let us listen to the counsels of American engineers. But let us beware of American architects."[i] Sullivan's work, although often more intelligently admired abroad than at home, was never adequately published in Europe, and had little or no real influence apart from the general technical influence of skyscraper construction.

If America in the twentieth century is no longer architecturally in debt to Europe, the credit is predominantly due to one man and to one man alone, Frank Lloyd Wright. It is characteristic and proper that our debt should have been paid by a man who in his own formation owes little or nothing to Europe, beyond his debt to a few great writers and musicians. Though Wright's architecture includes no European elements, Wright was not and is not completely typical of America as Americans in all parts of the country know it. The very strength of his regionalism and his individualism have made him seem an exotic to some of his compatriots. Because of the intensity of his genius and the fact that its pattern conformed more closely to what Europeans hoped of America than to the expectations of many Americans of his own generation, his achievement, like that of [Walt] Whitman and of F. W. Taylor, could perhaps be more justly evaluated in Europe than at home. This was particularly true in the years 1910 to 1925 when his influence on Europe was strongest.

The Publication of Wright's Work Abroad and Its Importance

The most important channel by which knowledge of Wright and his work was brought to Europe was the great German monograph *Ausgeführte Bauten und Entwürfe*, published by Wasmuth in

i. Le Corbusier, *Towards a New Architecture*, [trans. Frederick Etchells] (New York: Payson & Clarke, Ltd., n.d. [1927]), p. 42.

1910.[1] All who have used this book have cursed its confused organization and pretentious format as well as its inaccurate or nonexistent dates, but its completeness is remarkable. The many important projects which are included in it were studied abroad as avidly as the plates of executed work, though many critics since have forgotten the testimony those unexecuted projects gave of Wright's broader sociological interests in a period when his actual production was chiefly of middle class suburban houses. Such a tribute to a foreign architect of forty must be unique. It was apparently Kuno Francke who suggested the publication of Wright's work to the younger Wasmuth. In any case Wasmuth invited Wright to prepare such a volume in 1909, and Wright went to Europe in 1910 to bring it to completion. Wright's introductory text was written, of all places, in Florence. And this introductory text was very important, for the younger European architects were soon to distinguish between the ideas of Wright, as set down here and in the *Architectural Record* articles of 1908 and 1914,[2] and the realization of those ideas in his own work.[ii]

The next year, 1911, Wasmuth brought out a small and less expensive book, rather confusingly entitled *Frank Lloyd Wright Ausgeführte Bauten* (the 1910 portfolio was called *Ausgeführte Bauten und Entwürfe*). This was illustrated with photographs and had a considerable text by the English architect and critic C. R. Ashbee.

In the same year [Hendrik Petrus] Berlage, the greatest Dutch architect of the period, visited America and on his return to Europe spread the gospel of Wright by lectures and by three articles in the *Schweizerische Bauzeitung* in 1912.[iii] The next year in his book on America he referred to Wright as "a master without an equal in Europe."[3]

Wright's great foreign prophet in the '20s was the Dutch architect H. Th. Wijdeveld, who claimed to have seen the light of Wright's genius when he was only fifteen (presumably in the Boston *Architectural Review* article of 1900).[4] He published important Wright material in the magazine *Wendingen*, of which he was editor, in 1921 and 1925 and in the latter year brought out a large book on *The Life Work of the American Architect Frank Lloyd Wright*, in which several of Wright's own early articles were republished as well as tributes by the editor, by Berlage, by Lewis Mumford, by [Robert] Mallet-Stevens, by [Erich] Mendelsohn, and by [J. J. P.] Oud.[iv]

Thus, the executed buildings and projects of Wright's first great period of maturity, as well as many of his preparatory steps of the [18]90s, were made available in Europe at a time when a general stirring in architecture made their appreciation and understanding both possible and profitable. These publications were little known in America, for the fatal fire at Taliesin (whose concomitants had so much to do with Wright's social isolation in the Middle West where he had been hitherto chiefly employed) destroyed most of the copies of the foreign publication which had been reserved for American distribution.

In 1927, when the *Cahiers d'Art* in Paris brought out a book on Wright, an American[v] was asked to provide the introductory text; the illustrations were brought together by André Lurçat.[5] Like the Morancé volume three years later,[6] this already treated Wright (more than a little prematurely, as his work of the late '30s has shown) as an "old master."

ii. Younger European architects later made the same distinction when reading Le Corbusier's equally influential books.

iii. H. P. Berlage, "Neuere amerikanische Architektur," *Schweizerische Bauzeitung* 50, nos. 14, 21, 28 (September 1912): 148–50, 165–70, 178, also issued together as an offprint.

iv. Le Corbusier when invited to write a tribute disclaimed all knowledge of Wright.

It was also essentially as an "old master" (with more chronological justification, but without a full comprehension of the extraordinarily renewed vitality of his current production) that Wright was received two years ago into Honorary Fellowship by the Royal Institute of British Architects in London.[7] This academic honor, like those he had received earlier in Japan and from several European academies, is hardly an important element in his foreign influence. It merely records a recognition of prominence.

The Japanese monographs, which had no effect outside that country,[8] and the Berlin book of 1926, edited by H. de Fries,[9] may also be largely ignored. Both were less significant than the reprint of the 1910 monograph, which Wasmuth brought out in 1924 as an indication of the con-tinuous interest in Wright's work abroad. The text of these two volumes has little of the profound revelation of what Wright's influence in Europe had really been in the fifteen years between 1910 and 1925 which marks what Berlage and Oud wrote for Wijdeveld's *Wendingen* volume.

In Germany, Holland, France, and Japan, new publications as well as magazine articles continued to be devoted to his ideas and to his work both new and old. Nor has this foreign interest ceased in the last decade (when finally in America books by Wright began to be pub-lished during the early years of the Depression).[10] Only a year ago there appeared in England the lecture he delivered in London in the spring of 1939,[11] thus rounding out the important pub-lications which have been devoted to him since 1910 in the chief countries of Europe. It has been in England that his influence has been least traceable, although curiously enough it was the Englishman C. R. Ashbee who, having met Wright in Chicago in 1900, became perhaps the first foreigner to appreciate his significance. Nikolaus Pevsner, in "Frank Lloyd Wright's Peaceful Penetration of Europe" published in the London *Architects' Journal* for May 4, 1939,[12] the best summary of Wright's influence abroad, tells of Ashbee's relations with Wright, contin-ued by correspondence through the years.

Early Influence on European Architects 1910–1925: Imitation vs. Understanding

The stage had been set in 1910 and 1911 for the study of Wright's work by German and Dutch architects, as well as by many in Switzerland and other German-speaking countries to whom the first books and articles were available. The effect of this study was very soon apparent in Holland and Germany, and as these countries were then much more active than any others in architecture, this positive influence was more significant than the lack of Wrightian influence in England or France.

The overt copying of Wright's mannerisms which soon appeared in some European buildings is not perhaps intrinsically significant, but it proves the strong impression the study of his work was making. It also offered to Europeans at second hand some sense of what Wright's architecture could offer.

Berlage's own style was already too mature to be much modified and the slightly Wrightian character of the house he built in the Prinse-Vinkenpark in The Hague in 1913 is of less interest than the increased sense of structural articulation and regularity of rhythm in his masterpieces of these years, the W. H. Müller offices of 1914 in Bury Street, London. Even here the influence is apparently as much from Sullivan as from Wright.

v. The writer of this article. –Ed.

Another important building of 1914, Gropius's Deutz Motor Pavilion at the Werkbund exposition in Cologne, shows more obviously Wrightian elements. But just in so far as it does so, it represents a recession from the extreme point of his advance toward a rational industrial architecture marked by his Faguswerk building at Alfeld of 1911. The real influence of Wright upon Gropius was of a more subtle and less definable nature than the horizontal eaves and the clustered windows flanking the portal of the Pavilion.

The outright imitations of Wright by [Robert] Van't Hoff in 1915, the projects by Oud in 1919, the work of [J. B.] van Loghem, [Jan] Wils, [Willem Marinus] Dudok, and many others in Holland in the early '20s firmly reject the wild romanticism of the more native Fantastic School of [P. L.] Kramer and [Michel] de Klerk.

In Germany it was above all Mendelsohn and Mies van der Rohe, as they moved away from the extremes of postwar Expressionism, who owed the most to Wright. These were Wright's own years of romantic exuberance; but his influence abroad, deriving from his early work and his writings, was all in the direction of simplicity and clarity. Yet in some sense these imitations of Wright's mannerisms are but the outward sign and the aftermath of the more serious digestion of his ideas and of the essentials of his architectural methods which went on in men's minds during the last war and which by the early '20s was all but complete.

Thus when further foreign books devoted to Wright's work appeared in the mid-'20s, the heyday of his influence was already past, although a considerable group of Dutch architects remained for many years markedly Wrightian in the derivative sense.

Wright and the "International Style"

The years 1910–1925 were the crucial ones in the development of modern architecture. In 1910 there were no flourishing national schools of modern architecture, except perhaps in Holland and Austria. Art Nouveau and Jugendstil were somewhat in retreat. There were, however, several important foci of architectural innovation: [Charles Rennie] Mackintosh in Scotland, [Charles F. A.] Voysey in England, [Auguste] Perret and [Charles] Garnier in France, [Henry] van de Velde and [Peter] Behrens in Germany, [Josef] Hoffman and [Adolf] Loos in Austria, Berlage in Holland, not to speak of the Scandinavians. Each had his own markedly personal style and his own groups of disciples. But despite mutual respect there was little as yet to bring the independent lines of development together, so different were the backgrounds, so superficially opposed were the theories, upon which these men worked. By 1925, on the other hand, all relevant lines of development had come together into that synthesis which was to be known as the "International Style"[13] (Gropius's book entitled *Internationale Architektur* appeared in 1925).[14] In Holland, in France, and in Germany a new architecture was by then manifestly in existence and already rapidly succeeding the various nationalistic movements of the previous decade. Moreover, it was already spreading beyond the countries in which it originated over all of Western Europe, and was destined to spread through the world until political reaction began to circumscribe it.

In the formation of this new architecture four new elements, over and above the valuable elements in the existing confusion of individual innovation, were important between 1910 and 1925: (1) a more intensely sociological approach; (2) an aesthetic as well as instrumental respect for the possibilities of engineering; (3) the influence of Cubism and derived forms of abstract art; (4) and finally the influence of the American, Wright. By 1925 the integrating force of these new elements had clearly done its work. A positive and universal theory of modern architecture existed, so rigid in its doctrine that much of the most characteristic work of Wright, as well as of the great Europeans of his generation to whom almost as much was owed, could be and was most ungenerously read out of the canon.

If, as we must believe, the work of Wright is again at the forefront of the world's architectural achievement, there may well be a new wave of influence from that vital source still to come, a wave whose strength and virtue must be adjudged in later years. But the first great international force of Wright's influence spent itself and was absorbed into the main current of modern architecture in Europe in the years between 1910 and 1925.

Character of Wright's
Influence as Seen by Berlage and Oud

How Wright's influence was received can be no better summarized than by a few direct quotations and paraphrases from the articles of Berlage and Oud in the *Wendingen* monograph of 1925, with interpolated comments.[15]

Berlage wrote (in English): " . . . A strong personality obtains not only superficial followers–the admirers of the exterior revelation only" (i.e. the greater part of the Dutchmen and Germans who were Wrightians in the early '20s) "–but also they who in virtue of their talent, probe to the essence of the new form from the very start" (i.e. Oud, Gropius, probably Mies, possibly even Le Corbusier, despite his denials). "It is the fascination of the new gift which attracts, which, with one stroke stimulates change and propagates itself with inconceivable rapidity."[vi] (That is why it is so hard to define precisely an influence such as Wright's, which was as much that of a catalytic agent as of a positively borrowed element).

"For, although Wright has certainly created a center of art of the first importance for his country, yet the character of his art cannot be considered typically American. In that case its character would bear a more mechanical stamp; . . . In any case I find it difficult to see Wright otherwise than as a romanticist and to see him as his very antipode, that is, as an industrial architect, as many like to see him–as he likes to see himself."[vii] (Wright's work does not answer the mechanical ideal set by himself in 1908 as the inevitable product of the machine.[16] Indeed, in the '20s, he consistently decried the work of such Europeans as took, in part from his own writings, the mechanical ideal as their own).

In appreciation of Wright's early work Berlage justly pointed out that, like the work of the men of his generation in Europe, Wright's art was personal and not universal. The chief formal and easily imitable elements in Wright's personal style were the dominant horizontalism,

vi. *Wendingen*, p. 79. [Republished as Berlage, "Frank Lloyd Wright," in Hendrikus Theodorus Wijdeveld, ed., *Frank Lloyd Wright: The Life Work of the American Architect Frank Lloyd Wright* (Santpoort: C. A. Mees, 1925), p. 79.]

vii. *Wendingen*, p. 80, ff. [ibid., pp. 80–81].

the consistent grouping of small windows in rows, the low-pitched roofs and immensely projecting eaves, with their special tridimensional effect.

But Berlage saw that the relation of rooms was of the essence of Wright's contribution, the low areas opening into one another through doorless apertures to form a "poem of space."[18] Although never previously given such positive aesthetic form, this interconnection of rooms was, as Berlage knew, an American tradition. Almost equally significant were the exterior terraces with their flower bowls and flower boxes, extending the composition out into surrounding nature and bringing the elements of nature into the realm of architecture.

It is characteristic of Berlage's generation, as opposed to the younger men such as Oud, that Berlage found the Tokio Hotel the apotheosis of Wright.

Oud's article in the *Wendingen* volume, "The Influence of Frank Lloyd Wright on the Architecture of Europe" expresses clearly the point of view of the men of the new generation who had just crystallized their ideals of modern architecture in books and in actual building. Although Oud felt that Wright towered as one of the very greatest architects of the time, although he praised the remarkable unity that pervades all Wright's building down to the last details, and stressed the straight line his development had followed, he could already state that Wright's influence on Europe had been far from happy in some respects. Just because of Wright's vigorous and consistent individualism, which seemed a complete revelation after the preceding European eclecticism, just because his work and his ideas convinced at once, there was the danger, particularly well illustrated in Holland, of the development of a Wrightian rather than of a universal modern architecture.

Also significant are the qualities of Wright's work which Oud chose to emphasize: the "cinematic" interlacing of planes;[18] the contemporaneity of his ideals of convenience and comfort. The shifting of planes, the projecting eaves, the masses interrupted and continued again in predominantly horizontal compositions—all were to Oud of essential importance to the new architecture; but in the particular form they took in Wright's work they were not, as too many had assumed, the only possible realization of Wright's own ideals and intentions.

It was admiration for Wright, even direct emulation of his methods, that had broken the ground for what seemed to Oud the broader and sounder influence of Cubism, or more accurately of the various more advanced types of abstract painting which had grown out of Cubism. Wright's lyric charm had opened to Oud and to many others a new road. But once on that road they found themselves more inspired by Wright's writing than by the forms of his work, particularly those exuberant and exotic forms he was developing during the very years when these progressive young architects were most intensely the disciples of his ideas. The situation is not an infrequent one in modern architecture, and Wright is not the only twentieth-century architect who has been accused of unfaithfulness to his own ideals as expressed in written prophecies or programs.

"That which Wright desires, viz. an architecture based on the needs and possibilities of our own time, satisfying its requirements of general economic feasibility, universal social attainableness, in general of social-aesthetic necessity, and resulting in compactness, austerity and exactness of form, in simplicity and regularity; that which he desired, but from which he continually escapes on the wings of his great visionary faculty, was tried in more actual consistency in Cubism."[viii] Thus ran Oud's critique.

An architecture of right angles, clearly three-dimensional, its forms produced by breaking up bodies and recombining their parts, synthesis following upon analysis, but without dissolving entirely the constituent elements, could perhaps have been derived either from Wright alone or from an intelligent application of Cubism. But in historic fact it was developed chiefly by those who found in Wright a stimulus wholly architectural and not decorative and in Cubism a strand of puritanic asceticism which immunized them against the plastic exuberance and sensuous abundance of much of Wright's work. To this aspect of Wright's work the nationalistic and romantic architects of the early '20s–those architects to whom Oud and his associates were opposed–were only too sympathetic. In retrospect, however, we may find significance in Oud's admission that with Wright romantic exuberance grew out of fullness of life, while the "mental abstinence" of the more advanced young Europeans such as he, the "humble level" on which they saw the new architecture growing, were in part a reaction against the postwar hysteria of Dutch Fantasy and German Expressionism.[19]

In Oud's estimation the fact that by 1925 Wright's influence had already played its role in the formation of the new architecture in Europe did not justify the fashionable condemnation of Wright's own continuing work. With him, he wrote, "Life escapes from the dogma of theory."[ix] But what was important in 1925 was to carry further the good work in Europe and for that Wright's aid was no longer necessary; rather a danger lay in the continued temptation to imitate him: "More harmful, indeed, than the impediments which an academic architecture puts in the way of a rising functional art of building are the works of those who imitate modern masters."[x]

Wright, the International Style, and Architecture Today

After fifteen years the architecture which was new in 1925 has suffered two opposed and equally dangerous attacks. On the one hand it has been proscribed in large areas of the world for ideological reasons and on the other it has tended to freeze into a sort of academicism based too largely upon imitation of the modern masters of fifteen years ago.

In concluding this discussion of the foreign influence of Wright, it may be well to state that the renewed admiration for Wright's work now so widespread, if coupled with such a reasoned and critical appreciation as that of Oud fifteen years ago, might again help to lift modern architecture (if anything outside of the economic or ideological realm can now be effective) over the impasse of dogmatic rejection and dogmatic conformity which faces the young architects of the world today.

viii. *Wendingen*, p. 88 [Oud, "The Influence of Frank Lloyd Wright on the Architecture of Europe," p. 88].

ix. Ibid., p. 89. [Oud writes, ". . . because of the beautiful result, because the basic idea of his work is a reasonable one, not confused by aesthetic premises, because, lastly, life, which has not become rigid and fixed, continually escapes the dogma of theory."]

x. Ibid.

1. Frank Lloyd Wright, *Ausgeführte Bauten und Entwürfe von Frank Lloyd Wright* (Berlin: Ernst Wasmuth, 1910).

2. Wright, "In the Cause of Architecture," *Architectural Record* 23, no. 3 (March 1908): 155–220, and "In the Cause of Architecture, Second Paper," *Architectural Record* 35, no. 5 (May 1914): 405–13.

3. H. P. Berlage, *Amerikaansche Reisherinneringen* (Rotterdam: W. L. & J. Brusse, 1913).

4. Robert C. Spencer, Jr., "The Work of Frank Lloyd Wright," *Architectural Review* 7, no. 5 (May 1900): 61–72.

5. *Frank Lloyd Wright* (Paris: Editions Cahiers d'art, 1928). The book was published in 1928; possibly Henry-Russell Hitchcock was approached to write for it in 1927, and was relying on his memory in dating the book to that year.

6. *Frank Lloyd Wright: Architect américain* (Paris: Editions Albert Morancé, 1932).

7. Wright received this honor in 1939.

8. Wright's bibliography in the catalogue for the Museum's *Modern Architecture* exhibition, organized by Hitchcock and Philip Johnson in 1932, lists the following: "(Monograph in Japanese on the Imperial Hotel.) Tokyo, n.d."; "(Another Japanese monograph similar to the German one of 1910.)" *Modern Architects* (New York: The Museum of Modern Art, 1932), p. 39. Robert L. Sweeney, in Sweeney, *Frank Lloyd Wright: An Annotated Bibliography* (Los Angeles: Hennessey & Ingalls, Inc., 1978), p. 29, gives the date of the first as 1923.

9. H. de Fries, ed., *Frank Lloyd Wright: Aus dem Lebenswerke eines Architekten* (Berlin: E. Pollak, 1926).

10. Hitchcock is presumably referring to Wright's books *Two Lectures on Architecture* (Chicago: The Art Institute of Chicago, 1931), *Modern Architecture: Being the Kahn Lectures for 1930* (Princeton: at the University Press, 1931), *The Disappearing City* (New York: William Farquar Payson, 1932), *An Autobiography* (New York: Longmans, Green and Co., 1932), and, with Baker Brownell, *Architecture and Modern Life* (New York: Harper and Brothers, 1938).

11. Wright, *An Organic Architecture: The Architecture of Democracy* (London: Lund, Humphries and Co., 1939).

12. Nikolaus Pevsner, "Frank Lloyd Wright's Peaceful Penetration of Europe," *Architects' Journal* 89 (May 4, 1939): 731–34.

13. The Museum of Modern Art organized its famous "International Style" exhibition, actually titled *Modern Architecture, International Exhibition*, in 1932. The exhibition was accompanied by a publication, *Modern Architects* (New York: The Museum of Modern Art, 1932), and by an independently published book, *The International Style: Architecture since 1922* (New York: W. W. Norton, 1932). Hitchcock coorganized the exhibition, with Johnson, and was a coauthor of both books.

14. Walter Gropius, *Internationale Architektur* (Munich: Albert Langen Verlag, 1925).

15. These articles were originally published as seven special issues of *Wendingen* dedicated to Wright. They were subsequently bound together into a single volume: Hendrikus Theodorus Wijdeveld, ed., *Frank Lloyd Wright: The Life-Work of the American Architect Frank Lloyd Wright* (Santpoort: C. A. Mees, 1925).] Berlage's essay, "Frank Lloyd Wright," appears on pp. 79–85 of that volume; J. J. P. Oud's, "The Influence of Frank Lloyd Wright on the Architecture of Europe," on pp. 85–89.

16. In Wright, "In the Cause of Architecture."

17. Berlage writes, "And while looking, admiration increases for the poet of this poem of space." "Frank Lloyd Wright," p. 83.

18. Oud writes, "So natural was the interlacing of the elements shifting as on a cinematographic screen, so reasonable was the arrangement of the spaces, that nobody doubted the inevitable necessity of this form-language for ourselves too." "The Influence of Frank Lloyd Wright on the Architecture of Europe," p. 86.

19. Oud writes, "What was with Wright, however, plastic exuberance, sensuous abundance, was in the case of cubism—it could not for the present be otherwise—puritanic asceticism, mental abstinence. What was with Wright out of the very fullness of life developed into a luxurious growth which could only suit American 'high-life,' compelled itself in Europe to the humble level of an abstraction which had its origin in other wants and embraced all: men and things." Ibid., p. 88.

BUILDER AND POET—
FRANK LLOYD WRIGHT

Fiske Kimball

To understand Frank Lloyd Wright, whose own effort at self-understanding we have in his autobiography, we must turn to the writers of another period of storm and stress—the great German thinkers of the eighteenth century who divined the nature of poetic or artistic creation, and who so deeply influenced Wright and, before him, Louis Sullivan.

It was in the later eighteenth century that reaction against an exclusive worship of reason led [Friedrich Gottlieb] Klopstock to realize that "true poetry must spring from the deeply agitated heart, in order to stir the hearts of men." Thus arose with [Johann Gottfried] Herder the conception of the genius, who by the totality of his faculties, by his senses, his feelings, imagination, and reason, could draw upon the primal sources of nature and humanity to bring forth creative works of deep originality, akin to those of nature herself. "The poetic genius," wrote Goethe, "became fully aware of himself and, conscious of his dignity, would create the conditions of his existence independently and thus found a new epoch of intellectual life."

"To create the conditions of his existence independently": that indeed has been the striving of Frank Lloyd Wright, giving unity to his work, to his life. Personality is one; the work and life cannot be separated. "To create the conditions of his existence independently": that makes us understand the building, at twenty-one, of Wright's own first house at Oak Park; the genesis of Taliesin, at once home and workshop; its tenacious rebuilding after tragedy and calamity; the creation of the Tokio studio, of the desert camp Ocatilla. More deeply, it makes us understand the loyalties underlying the struggle for freedom in life by "this unconventional believer in the Good, the True, the Beautiful, as work and life and love."

One condition of his existence, indeed, he could not control or escape: the heritage of pioneer independence, the heredity of the protestant, the rebel, and the preacher. But it led him to rebel against that very heritage itself in its sterner Mosaic aspects, to demand that beauty should be admitted as well as truth. Society too has been loath to permit him independent control of the conditions of personal existence, and has imposed its penalty, not only on him, but on itself by the loss of many a work.

"To arrest and typify in materials the harmonious and interblended rhythms of nature and humanity": that is how Sullivan, Wright's "beloved Master," expressed the task of architecture—architecture which Wright himself once called "the Idea of the thing—made to sing to heaven." With what freshness of intuition Wright seized on the idea or essence of the thing in each work he attacked, his book, like his work, bears ample witness. The early houses, in their articulated union of the elements of use, in their harmonious outgrowth of the site, in their multiplied planes, their energized gathering of pier and opening–the Larkin [Company Administration] Building [Buffalo, 1902–6], in its humanization of mechanized business, its richly plastic embodiment–the Unity Temple [(Oak Park, Illinois, 1905–8], with use and form so genially fused–the joyous exuberant phantasy of abstract geometric elements in the Midway Gardens [Chicago, 1913–14, demolished 1929]–the elemental clarity and simplicity of the National Life Insurance [Company] Building [project, Chicago, 1924–25]–the infinite significant variety of so many other buildings–all these leave us astounded at the imaginative penetration of practical and ideal requirements, flowering in organic form.

"To typify *in materials*," Sullivan had said–but here it was Wright who was to practice what Sullivan had preached. "As to relying on them for beauties of their own," says Wright, "he had no need, no patience. All materials were stuff to bear the stamp of his imagination and bear it they did–cast iron, wrought iron, marble, plaster, concrete, wood pretty much alike . . . his sensuous ornament . . . his own . . . so lovely a smile evoked by love of Beauty."[1] To Wright the thought of materials is primary and instinctive–the design takes form only in an appropriate material, which itself suggests both structure and pattern. And what a fertility of suggestion and invention!–monolithic, form-cast concrete; concrete precast in permanent forms; reinforced cantilevered slab-roofs; poised cantilevered floors with wall-curtains of glass, copper, and insulation; woven block-construction. No limited canon; "Stick. Stone. Steel. Pottery. Concrete. Glass. Yes pulp, too, as well as pigment."[2] "Inventing new construction to make itself beautiful as architecture." We cannot, to be sure, agree with Wright in believing that "there never was, there is no architecture otherwise"–in rejecting the great plastic or even sculptural works of certain past epochs which have no constructive basis. But we have the work of Wright and of the Gothic architects to prove that construction itself can be made to sing.

First, perhaps anywhere in the world, to welcome "The Art and Craft of the Machine"[3] as the tool of a craftsmanship not confined to "handicraft," Wright does not allow the machine age to demand the rejection of all but machine products: "the ideal does *not* require that buildings must be of steel, concrete, or glass. . . . Nor does it even imply that mass is no longer a beautiful attribute of masonry materials genuinely used. We are entitled to vast variety in our buildings in our complex age."[4] Sullivan, confusing art with science, sought "the rule so broad as to admit no exceptions"; his reasonings tended to confine his imagination, wrongly, within "Types" he himself had first created as individual institutions. Wright says, "For the life of me I could not help, then or now, being interested in the exception as proving any rule both useful and useless." "Consistency? It is seldom the word for the imaginative mind in action." Thus he rejects every demand for a new "style" or "unity of style" to be held in common by the architects of our day and conceived as to be valid also for the future: " . . . the sentimentality that tries to hold life by 'institution' and establishment–are they not all punishment for violation of the first simple law of Freedom: the law of organic change?"[5]

One may object that all this is merely the view of a period–a bygone period–of romanticism, individualism. Alas for such an objection: if we know anything of philosophy it is that individualism is rooted in the very nature of art itself. What is deeply true of art is that individual creation is of its essence. What distinguishes it from science, which seeks universal laws and universal forms, is that art seeks individual forms, each differing in synthesis from every other, each henceforth endowed with its own organic life and participating, with nature itself, in the miracle of creation.

No preoccupation with practical problems alone, no merely mechanical expression of function, will produce this work of art. It only can be when the practical elements have been fused in the soul of the artist that the work of art–essentially, vitally new–can appear. We speak of the influence of economic and material forces as if merely to incorporate them were the province of art. So long as the new works remain merely a product of law, of mechanism, of economics, they will never constitute a new art.

The problem of artistic merit is independent of "styles." We know that it rests on the personal force and fire of the individual artist, which can transmute and rekindle old elements, just as it can with new elements create something new under the sun. We may agree, for convenience, to distinguish "types" and "styles"–we recognize, for example, obvious instances in archaic Greek and Gothic art–but we know that, in art, the superior merit of any given work lies not in its exemplification of such a "type" or such a "style." Its merit lies just in its differences from any prevailing formula, differences which give it a unique character and make it a creative expression. Indeed the philosopher [Benedetto] Croce has, in our day, insisted with striking emphasis on excluding from the realm of art any work in which generic formulae have not crystallized in individual entity. "In the end, of course," we must agree with Goethe, "it is only through the spirit that technique becomes alive."

It is an artist of such creative spirit that America has in Frank Lloyd Wright. From the depths of bitter personal experience Sullivan wrote: "To the master mind . . . imbued with the elemental significance of nature's moods, humbled before the future and the past, art and its outworkings are largely tragic." In Wright too we have a master who has not escaped inherent tragedy, but has enriched us with the only gifts which art can bring, the individual creations of the inspired artist.

1. Wright, "Louis Henry Sullivan: His Work," *The Architectural Record* 56 (July 1924): 29–30.

2. Wright, *An Autobiography* (New York: Longmans, Green and Company, 1932), p. 357.

3. Kimball is referring to Wright's essay "The Art and Craft of the Machine," *Catalogue of the Fourteenth Annual Exhibition* (Chicago: Chicago Architectural Club, 1901), pp. 8–20.

4. Wright, *An Autobiography*, p. 357.

5. Ibid., p. 363.

THE EARLY IMPRESS OF JAPAN
ON WRIGHT'S ART

Grant Manson

Although the architecture which Frank Lloyd Wright evolved in his maturity is so personal and so radical that it defies any attempt to explain it as a synthesis of influences, to infer that nothing extraneous helped him to give expression to what he had, by nature, to say, is a form of idolatry which Wright himself does not admire. The more acute is a man's perception, the more significant his gifts, the better he will know how to evaluate and to adapt the best that he sees in his lifetime; part of the purpose of this work is to explore the experiences which Wright underwent prior to 1910 and to suggest the ways in which they could have added to the development of his style. Of these experiences, Wright's engrossing interest in the art of Japan is fraught with possibilities–it is, at the same time, one of the most provocative and controversial elements in his artistic personality. It was at the World's Fair of 1893 that his Japanophilia received its first real stimulus.[1]

A good way of recapturing the spirit of the Fair is to look through any of the illustrated guide-books which were taken home by visitors to lay upon the parlor table. Expunging such symbols of another age as the costumes and the arc-lights and the divertissements of the Midway, it appears, like all great fairs, to have been a stupendous and overwhelming collection of things, a sort of cosmic magpie's nest of the good, bad, and indifferent. There is something in such an agglomeration to appeal to every taste. Wright, dismayed as he was by the trumpery classicism of the buildings, must nevertheless have entered the gates many times to be instructed and entertained. One remarkable exhibit was that which was sponsored by the Japanese Imperial Government. It was housed in a structure called the "Ho-o-den,"[i] which was a half-scale replica of its namesake in Japan, a wooden temple compound of the Fujiwara Period (c. 1000 A.D.). The Ho-o-den itself, together with the objects which it contained, was the first wholesale introduction of Japanese art to the Middle West. For Wright, what he saw there was an enlightenment and a confirmation of a dawning enthusiasm; he had already acquired a taste for Japanese things by general reading and by contact with some people of advanced tastes like his early employer, Joseph Silsbee, whose house in Edgewater was crammed with Japanese objects by the end of the eighties.

i. Okakura Kukudzo, "The Ho-o-den" (An illustrated description of the buildings erected by the Japanese Government at the World's Columbian Exposition, Jackson Park, Chicago), Tokyo, 1893 [Okakura Kakuzo, The Ho-o-den (Phoenix Hall): An Illustrated Description of the Buildings Erected by the Japanese Government at the World's Columbian Exposition, Jackson Park, Chicago (Chicago: W. B. Conkey Co., 1893)]. P. B. Wight: "Japanese Architecture at Chicago," Inland Architect and News Record, vol. 20, Dec. 1892, pp. 49-50, and Jan. 1893, p. 61.

There is an affinity between Wright's conception of a house and the domestic architecture of pre-Perry centuries in Japan.[2] Whether this amounts to an actual indebtedness is a very moot question, and one which Wright has always hotly debated. "No, my dear Mrs. Gablemore, Mrs. Plasterbilt, and especially, now, Miss Flattop, nothing from 'Japan' had helped at all, except the marvel of Japanese color-prints."[ii] Nevertheless, [H. P.] Berlage, [Henry-Russell] Hitchcock, [Thomas] Tallmadge, [Walter Curt] Behrendt, [P. Morton] Shand, and other critics of Wright's architecture have all touched upon the matter to some extent, as if impelled to do so by the evidence of their eyes; and the consensus of their opinions is that a debt does exist. Tallmadge finds Japanese influence in the "intimate liaison between art and nature"[3]; Behrendt says, "The domestic buildings of Wright are like Japanese houses . . . Wright's art is, in fact, similar to the Japanese"[4]; Shand says that "it must not be forgotten that the dominant influence on Wright (as on [Charles Rennie] Mackintosh) was Japanese."[5]

Thus, it is impossible to dismiss the question of Japanism as cavalierly as Wright would like to have us do. He himself makes no mystery of his pronounced Japanophilia, referring to it frequently in his writings; but he keeps it on a nonpractical basis. He relates, in *An Autobiography*: "During the years at the Oak Park workshop, Japanese prints intrigued me and taught me much. The elimination of the insignificant, a process of simplification in art in which I was engaged, beginning with my twenty-third year, found collateral evidence in the print. Ever since I discovered the print, Japan has appealed to me as the most romantic, artistic country on earth. Japanese art, I found, really did have organic character, was nearer to the earth and a more indigenous product of native conditions of life and work, therefore more nearly modern as I saw it, than any European civilization alive or dead."[6] Upon arriving in Japan for the first time in 1905, he exclaims, "It all looks just like the prints! [. . .] The quiet but gay life of the ancient modern capital is aware of Toyonobu, Harunobu, Shunso, and Shigemasa."[7] He analyzes the style of Japanese architecture as a natural function of its adaptation to the national religion of cleanliness: "Here you have a kind of spiritual ideal of natural and hence organic simplicity. . . . The plan of any Japanese dwelling was an effective study in sublimated mathematics."[8]

The Ho-o-den at the World's Fair was a source of fascination for all the progressive young members of the "Chicago School" of architects.[9] They remarked upon its strange construction. Beneath its ample roof, which served no purpose but to shelter, and above the platform on which the temple stood, was the area where people moved about and lived—an open and ephemeral region of sliding screens which could change its appearance according to the activity of the hour, and which, in occidental terms, was not architecture at all. In this region between roof and platform, solid walls were practically nonexistent. The plan of the Ho-o-den opened outward toward innumerable rows of sliding paper windows and away from its base-screen which formed an impasse to the prevailing wind; the main room and the flanking tea-rooms were in no sense boxes, but they were, instead, devices for living in comfort and intimacy with the out-of-doors. The only part of the interior which was not subject to change

ii. Wright, "Recollections–United States, 1893–1920," *Architects' Journal* (London) 84 (July [16,] 1936): 76–78 [quote on p. 78].

was the *tokonoma*, or shrine, which was the focus of group-life within the temple. Light did not enter these rooms in isolated spots, but continuously, throughout most of their perimeters. Illumination was a pliant band of daylight wrapped around the building and freed from glare by the overhanging eaves, which were like awnings. Because there were no solid corners, there were no dark pockets. The consequent lack of wall-space was no objection to the Japanese, who regarded their furniture, like other household objects, as things to be used when needed and then stored away. The simplicity of these airy rooms was reiterated in the materials of which they were constructed: plain paper and unpainted wood. To inspect the Ho-o-den was a happy confirmation of what certain young architects of Chicago had dimly envisioned through the medium of Japanese architectural prints of the eighteenth century. There was a large collection of contemporary and antique prints on display from time to time in the Ho-o-den with which to make comparison between the imaginary and the actual of Japanese architecture.

What lesson, then, could the progressive "Chicago School" deduce from the resources of the Japanese Exhibit of 1893? Nothing less than the essential formula for a new Western architecture in the sympathetic affinity of the Japanese house with immense quantities of light and air.[iii] To symbolize this affinity, Japanese fenestration is liberated from the rest of the building by means of strip-windows, in what was, to them, an unprecedented way. The sills of these strip-windows are suppressed to become only a part of the base of the building; the eaves of the building are restored to their function as awnings for the house, rather than, as in European precedent, as mere boundary lines for abstract areas of the design.

Four years prior to the time that the attention of a small vanguard of Chicago's architects was focused upon Japanese architecture by the Ho-o-den, Wright had built his Oak Park house [the Frank Lloyd Wright House, Oak Park, Illinois, 1889–90]; two years before, he had designed the Charnley house.[10] In both of these buildings he had stated his belief in a new openness of plan and a new functional simplicity. All the germs but one of his coming Prairie House were contained in them. What Wright had arrived at spontaneously was a bold and vigorous expression based upon his confessed tendency to turn all that he touched into his beloved geometric forms. The result stopped just short of perfection because it was too self-contained. The ideal house, he knew, must surrender more to the earth beneath it and the atmosphere around it—in brief, it must be more pliant. Japan had as an age-old heritage a form of fenestration which had plasticity, which could be bent around corners, which opened the house to the outdoors anywhere and everywhere, and which contributed by its horizontality to that level domestic line which Wright felt was essential to a good house. Japanese architecture must have been as sympathetic to Wright's ideas as air is to the wing of a bird, and it had the one definite gift of plastic fenestration to offer him.

Whether the gift was welcome, or whether it had already been anticipated, is the question. At any rate, early in the '90s Wright began to discard the guillotine window in favor of the casement to prepare his art for the change from fenestration by spots to fenestration in strips.

iii. Jean Badovici ("Frank Lloyd Wright," Morancé, Paris, 1932) says that Wright, in his plans, loses something of the quality of intimacy "que nous (i.e. Europeans) aimons trouver dans nos demeures," because he sees the house as an indivisible part of its natural setting, to which it must be opened up. [See Badovici, *Frank Lloyd Wright: Architect américain* (Paris: Editions Albert Morancé, 1932), p. 50.]

This change, once accomplished, automatically erased the severity and resistance of sheer wall, fostered the free, plastic handling of sills and bases, and lent itself readily to the triumphant establishment of the horizontal as the dominant line of a style. Henceforth, Wright's architecture was to be a perfect fusion of crisp planes and plasticity. The Winslow house of 1894 [the William H. Winslow House, River Forest, Illinois, 1893–94] is an interesting example of this transformation at its halfway point: the second-story wall is conceived as a setting for continuous fenestration, and the first-story wall as its sill–but the tradition of isolated guillotine windows, which are used instead, is yet too strong to be rejected. The beauty of the Winslow house is, therefore, the less-than-perfect beauty of any great art just at the moment of its transition.

Because he was endowed by nature and by childhood training with a deep understanding of all these new forms, it is perfectly possible that he might have arrived at them had there never been any Japanese art to be seen in America; but assuming that Japanese art *was* the final hint that was required to give to his architecture its lifelong direction, many steps in its evolution become easier to understand. For example: the translation of the *tokonoma* into its Western equivalent, the fireplace; the final frank revelation of the brickwork of the fireplace as the only permanent substance in an interior of increasing fluidity; the opening out of the interior away from the fireplace toward shifting areas of glass at its outer limit; the division of a given room into living and dining spaces by means of low screen-walls rather than partitions; the change from varnished trim to natural, unpainted wood–all these could have been suggested by the Ho-o-den as salutary modifications in Wright's art. If so, the credit goes to Wright alone among all the other members of the young "Chicago School" who observed the lesson of the Ho-o-den for carrying Japanese inspiration to its ultimate good in the evolution of an American architecture.

In the field of publication, the early lead of the brothers de Goncourt in disseminating Japanese concepts had been followed up by men of a more practical bent who had gone to spend some years in Japan for the purpose of direct research into Japanese art, architecture, and *moeurs*. In England, the artist Mortimer Menpes was such a connoisseur; his London house, designed by [Arthur Heygate] Mackmurdo, contained interiors carried out quite faithfully in the Japanese manner, although somewhat too crowded with objects in the inevitable exuberance of the '90s. Menpes's house, and the illustrated chronicle of his travels in Japan, appeared often in print; they were featured in the early editions of *The International Studio*, beginning in 1897,[11] and were thus made available for study in the United States. But, many years previous to this, America had actually seen the publication of a careful, objective text on Japanese domestic architecture: this was Edward Morse's *Japanese Homes and Their Surroundings*, which appeared in 1885.[iv] The fact that this book ran into at least two editions postulates that it enjoyed a considerable circulation; it must have come to the attention of architects like Silsbee and Wright, who were alert to the possibilities of the Japanese touch in home decoration. Morse's attitude toward his research was that of the practical architect, and his book is distinguished by its consideration of the minutiae of construction and furnishing, and by its copious illustrations. It

iv. Edward S. Morse, *Japanese Homes and Their Surroundings* (Boston: Ticknor & Co., 1885).

could well have served as a manual for constructing facsimiles of Japanese dwellings of all sorts, from the palace of a *daimio* to a peasant's hut. A few illustrations from Morse's book are here reproduced to suggest the possibility of their application to a new form of American domestic architecture.[12] What was said concerning the lesson of the Ho-o-den is equally valid in the case of the precedent of Japanese dwellings such as those reproduced in Morse's book, since the basic principles are the same as those involved in temple construction; in fact, the transfer of ideas is easier and less devious.

By these various methods, the seeds of a noticeable Japanism in Wright's style could well have been sown. In the beginning, he invigorated his architecture by the basic principles of Japanese buildings, which he immediately grasped; it was later, after his first sojourn in Japan in 1905, during which he "went native" with a tremendous delight and absorbed all he could of the Japanese way of life, that a certain specific use of Japanese motifs began to appear in his designs.

Wright's connoisseurship of Japanese art became well recognized, both here and in Japan. Starting with the prints which he purchased at the Fair of 1893, Wright made a famous collection of Japanese masters for himself, and he has supervised many of the great collections in the country. In 1912 he established his name as a writer on Japanese prints by publishing a slim volume of criticism and appreciation.[13] His astuteness as a collector is seen in the fact that he was able to realize large sums of money on his prints whenever he was in need of cash or pressed by debts. The catalogue of the last and largest of these sales, in 1927, for which Wright wrote the description and foreword, makes interesting reading for anyone who is curious to know which of the famous Japanese printmakers Wright studied and admired; in that year, more than twenty-five masters were represented in the collection.[14] The effect of these prints upon Wright's drawings and perspectives is striking. At times he borrowed foliage and flowers from a print to decorate a drawing; he became fascinated by casual, off-center arrangements and occasionally it interested him to cast the whole drawing into a Japanese composition. The perspective of the Hardy house [the Thomas P. Hardy House, Racine, Wisconsin, 1905], which is the complete antithesis of the usual architectural "rendering," is disposed picturesquely like a panel of a Japanese screen.

Next to the materialization of his architecture, Wright's second concern has continuously been his unbounded love of Japanese things. No one can enter "the House" at Taliesin without realizing at once that he is in the sanctum of a great Japanophile; that this interest is closely bound up with the evolution of Wright's professional character is certainly indicated but the reality and extent of the influence is something at which a critic can only guess. The true answer is known to Wright alone.

1. The World's Columbian Exposition, Chicago, May 1–October 31, 1893.

2. Manson is referring to the American Commodore Matthew Perry, whose landing in Japan in 1854 opened the country, previously closed off from contact with the West, to diplomatic connections and trade.

3. Thomas E. Tallmadge, *The Story of Architecture in America* (New York: W. W. Norton and Company, 1936), p. 229.

4. Walter Curt Behrendt, *Modern Building: Its Nature, Problems and Forms* (New York: Harcourt, Brace and Company, 1937), pp. 134–35.

5. P. Morton Shand, "Scenario for a Human Drama," *Architectural Review* 77 (February 1935): 64.

6. Frank Lloyd Wright, *An Autobiography* (New York: Longmans, Green and Company, 1932), p. 194.

7. Ibid., p. 206.

8. Wright, *Modern Architecture: Being the Kahn Lectures for 1930* (Princeton: at the University Press, 1931), p. 34.

9. A term coined by Tallmadge to refer to Chicago-area architects from the generation after Louis Sullivan and Burnham and Root—architects such as Wright, George R. Dean, Hugh M. G. Garden, Myron Hunt, George W. Maher, George C. Nimmons, Dwight H. Perkins, Richard E. Schmidt, and Robert C. Spencer. See Tallmadge, "The Chicago School," *The Architectural Review* XV (1908): 69–74.

10. Wright designed the James Charnley House, Chicago (1891–92), while he was working for Adler and Sullivan.

11. Work by Mortimer Menpes in *The International Studio* included a series of illustrated letters, partly made in Japan, partly made later but based on his visit there. See Menpes, "A Letter from Japan," *The*

International Studio 1 (1897): 32–36, and "A Letter from Japan," *The International Studio 3* (1898): 21–26. The journal also published an illustrated article on his Japanese works: "Mortimer Menpes' Japanese Drawings," *The International Studio 1* (1897): 165–77.

12. What images Manson planned to reproduce is not recorded.

13. Wright, *The Japanese Print: An Interpretation* (Chicago: Ralph Fletcher Seymour, Co., 1912).

14. See *The Frank Lloyd Wright Collection of Japanese Antique Prints* (New York: Anderson Galleries, 1927).

EXCERPT FROM MUSEUM PRESS RELEASE
"Museum of Modern Art Opens Large Exhibition of the Work of Frank Lloyd Wright"
John McAndrew

Wright created a new kind of open plan for the house. Instead of being measured out into many boxlike rooms, the living space flowed freely from hall to living room to dining room, reaching out for abundant light and air whereever needed. Continuous long bands of windows brought indoors and outdoors intimately together. . . . This open plan gave spaciousness to many new small houses, and grandeur to large ones. His easy but disciplined compositions, with their long low sweeping eave-lines, have become part of our modern American idiom. His sympathetic use of wood, stone and brick, traditional materials avoided by the stricter functionalists, has been a refreshing example to many younger men. Opposed to the International Style is his warm, humanitarian approach to architecture, his insistence on providing not only for the physical needs of a family but also for the more subjective comforts—softer light, surfaces pleasant to touch, intimacy with nature, and even release from the very Machine Age the functionalists were domesticating. . . .

If one were to make a small crystal model of the air in the main spaces of one of his early Prairie Houses, one would see a carefully composed piece of abstract sculpture, with long rectangular prisms harmoniously united, side by side or interpenetrating. The main forms would be bold and clear, yet indissolubly welded to one another. Episodes of smaller angular shapes might enliven or emphasize the whole.

The space-conception created by Wright in 1904 was destined be the most characteristic one of modern architecture, above all, of the modern house.

In its great beauty and in its originality, this idea is one of the great creations of recent architecture, and one of the most fruitful.

Though made up of straight-edged and angular parts, these compositions of Wright's appear to have grown more than to have been built from carefully ruled blueprints. He thinks of their creation as a sort of natural process: "Conceive now that an entire building might grow up out of conditions as a plant grows up out of soil, as free to live its own life according to Nature as is the tree."[1] A house and a plant "both unfold similarly from within."

The whole form, seeming so closely related to natural forms, is never an imitation of them; its organic arrangement *rivals* rather than imitates the organic arrangements of nature.

Perhaps this is why the houses of Wright more than those of any other architect unite with their natural surroundings in serene and effortless harmony. The pantheism of their author is poetically expressed in their oneness with nature. He has reestablished the ancient lost collaboration between the builder of a structure and the character of a site, and has served in an ancient office, as interpreter between nature and man, translating the spirit of places into shapes that are habitable.

1. Wright, *An Autobiography* (New York: Longmans, Green and Co., 1932), p. 146.

STRUCTURE AND DESIGN IN THE WORK OF FRANK LLOYD WRIGHT

Richard Neutra

The intimate relation of architectural design and expression to problems of construction and production has been of central interest both to Mr. Wright and to those who honor his leadership and contributions.

Frank Lloyd Wright's speeches and conversation, even before 1900, his grand summary of principles in 1908,[i] so magnificent in its gripping sincerity, and the forceful reiteration of principles in his later writings–these might well have discouraged other less experienced minds from further defending a position already so effectively fortified by himself, or to assail it again with criticism of small details.

As a prophetic *formulator of basic principles*, he interpreted for the designer many potentialities of industry which had been only very superficially noticed by professionals of the country. As an *architect*, he had to educate laboriously crews of assistants in his office–general and subcontractors, foremen, workmen, bankers, building department officials and last but not least, consumers, or clients. This second and main function of his architecture called for endless economic sacrifices on his part; for constant winning over of many different individuals; for

i. Frank Lloyd Wright, "In the Cause of Architecture," *The Architectural Record* [23, no. 3] (March 1908), [pp. 155–220].

fighting off frontal and whispering attacks; for never-ending patience in the face of stupid inertia and in the face of a building routine which was, and still is, far below the possible technological level of the age.

"So," wrote Mr. Wright thirty-two years ago, "in addition to the special preparation in any case necessary for every little matter of construction and finishing, special detail drawings were necessary merely to show the things to be left off or not done—and not only studied designs for every part had to be made, but quantity surveys and schedules of millwork furnished the contractors besides. This, in a year or two, brought the architect face to face with the fact that the fee for his service 'established' by the American Institute of Architects was intended for something stock and shop, for it would not even pay for the bare drawings necessary for conscientious work.

"It is perhaps significant that in the beginning it was very difficult to secure a building loan on any terms upon one of these houses, now" (in 1908!) "it is easy to secure a better loan than ordinary."[ii] (This last half-sentence seems in 1940 a historical "stranger than fiction!")

During the period of this perpetual struggle the means, tools, and materials on which Mr. Wright desired to base a program for contemporary structure were not a simple given quantity. Far from it!

New methods of statical computations for continuous skeletons, for thin-shell domes and vaults in reinforced concrete; the transition in steel construction from screwing and riveting to welding; light-gauge structural sections of less corrosive, exposable metal; prefabricated steel truss joists and vibrated concrete joists; air-compressed cement and a host of other significant innovations—all these were either unheard of in 1908, or were rarities like residential metal windows. It is for example difficult to appreciate fully today Mr. Wright's early struggle against the old double-hung sash of Oak Park:

" . . . The poetry-crushing characteristics of the guillotine window, which was then firmly rooted, became apparent, and single-handed I waged a determined battle for casements swinging out, although it was necessary to have special hardware made for them, as there was none to be had this side of England."[1] "Steel sash came within reach for the first time" in Fallingwater (Bear Run) [the Edgar J. Kaufmann House, Mill Run, Pennsylvania, 1934–37], in 1937.[iii]

The ever-swelling volumes of the yearly building catalogues like Sweet's have been indicators of the increase and diversification in the American manufacture of novel building materials and equipment. An integrated architectural design in proper adjustment to technological advance, and creatively inspired by it, remains a burning problem, and solutions are speedily threatened by—may we call it: *obsolescence praecox*.

Naturally it is easy to know things better a few years later, and to excel in criticism *post festum*. To dwell on the fact that [Eugène Emmanuel] Viollet-le-Duc or Gottfried Semper did not reach in actual practice the mark which they had set in theoretical formulation is beside the point and unjust. Even if Frank Lloyd Wright—all difficulties considered—was born into a time more mature, more receptive to the realization of a design philosophy recognizing Technique, Material, and Function, he could not possibly accomplish single-handed that full

ii. Ibid. [p. 159].

iii. ["Frank Lloyd Wright,"] *Architectural Forum* [68, no. 1] (January 1938), [p. 36].

adjustment to industrial production which he himself had set before the eyes of a young generation. It is truly an immense task beyond the capacity of any single individual or even any one generation. To have visualized a new spirit, and to have stated so early some of its fundamentals, motives, and consequences, is indeed a high accomplishment of the first order.

To single out and merely report some of Mr. Wright's structural proposals and systems as I have done in earlier publications[iv] is therefore arbitrarily limiting his accomplishment and distorting it by such limitation. Of primary significance remains his *structural design attitude*, which derives creative inspiration from the organic nature of true integration.

As Lewis Mumford stated fifteen years ago, Frank Lloyd Wright is not a "mechanist."[v] His faith and approach are rather of a biological character not only in intimately and superbly relating architectural space to nature, landscape vegetation, air, light; he conceives a structural scheme and its execution as an extension of natural phenomena instead of seeing it in stark contrast and opposition to them.

A parallel taken from another field perhaps will indicate well this direction in architectural evolution, with–to quote Mumford again–"science and poetry" converging into "synthesis."[2]

Wright and "Naturalism"

More than two generations ago a school of "naturalism" appeared in literature simultaneously with the *plein air* revolution of the French Impressionists. Emile Zola in one person was the founder of the first and the violent, vociferous defender of the second. He pronounced in manifestoes his opposition to the history-flavored romanticism of Victor Hugo's era, his antagonism to the historical and eclectic in pictures and novels. He claimed that the contemporary constellation of "this day" and "the nearby" was entitled to creative loyalty–was in fact full of vital inspiration. There was the "natural environment" around the artist which would mold his mind and his work, just as the then fashionable Darwinian research claimed for any and all organic growth and evolution. It was again a return to nature. But not by means of a sentimental speculation in the vein of Jean Jacques [Rousseau] a century earlier.

It was a return to nature by proud scientific systems in the light of contemporary life; by–so to speak–taking a railway train into the country; by looking through a microscope; by compiling exact statistics on heredity! To write a cycle of novels on the "Rougon-Macquart," the fate of a spreading French family tree, Zola would study biology, [the early psychologist Wilhelm] Wundt, [the criminologist Cesare] Lombroso, experimental psychology, genetics, and even agricultural and industrial economics. To explain the *plein air* painting of Monet, the pointillism of Seurat, scientific color optics and spectroscopic findings would be cited.

Alas, the naturalistic attitude of those days did not yet extend to architecture! Emile Zola actually died of suffocation in a late Victorian bedroom, with narrow windows tightly

iv. From "Lifework of an Architect" [*Frank Lloyd Wright: Aus dem Lebenswerke eines Architekten*], ed. H. de Fries (Berlin: Ernst Pollak, 1926), and [Neutra], "American New Building in the World" [*Amerika, die Stilbildung des neuen Bauens in den Vereinigten Staaten*] (Vienna: Anton Schroll Co., 1930).

v. *Wendingen*, 1925. ["Unlike the mere mechanists, he recognizes the value of living processes." Lewis Mumford, "The Social Background of Frank Lloyd Wright," *Frank Lloyd Wright: The Life-Work of the American Architect Frank Lloyd*

Wright, ed. H. Th. Wijdeveld (Santpoort, the Netherlands: C. A. Mees, 1925), p. 75. This book collects seven special issues of the magazine *Wendingen* on Wright.]

shut behind heavy velour draperies, and on his writing desk–where he wrote his daily 2,500 revolutionary words on behalf of scientific naturalism–was accumulated the dusty eclectic, historical bric-a-brac and the dry Makart bouquets of the '80s.[3] The human mind after all has a compartmental constitution and it is probably a biological rule that man can emancipate himself in some, but not in all compartments at the same time.

"Naturalism," the return to nature with scientific enthusiasm, has meanwhile reached architecture, and Frank Lloyd Wright represents far more than Zola.

It is not mechanism. Artistic creativeness and the urge toward scientific precision, from which technological procedure derives, are merely two emanations from the same organically evolved human brain; when biologically understood, they are not of two different worlds, not really hostile to each other. Rather they are twins, exfoliating from the very same physiological roots.

"Primarily," Wright said in 1908,[vi] "NATURE furnished the materials out of which the architectural forms we know today have been developed,[4] and, although for centuries our practice has been to turn from her . . . adhering slavishly to dead formulae, her wealth of suggestion is inexhaustible.

"There is no source so fertile so suggestive to the architect as comprehension of natural forms. . . .[5] A sense of the organic in nature is indispensable to an architect. . . . Where can he find the pertinent object lessons nature so readily furnishes? . . . Bring out the nature of materials, always let their nature intimately into your scheme.[6] . . . Reveal the nature of wood, plaster, brick, or stone in your designs; they are all by nature friendly and beautiful. No treatment can be a matter of fine art, when these natural characteristics are, or their nature is, outraged or neglected."[7]

And half a dozen lines later: "Above all integrity. The machine is the normal tool of our civilization, give it work that it can do well–nothing is of greater importance. To do this will be to formulate new industrial ideals, sadly needed.

"The aim is that the designs shall make the best of the technical contrivances that produce them. . . .[8] The machine is here to stay. It is the forerunner of the real economic democracy that is our dearest hope. There is no more important work before the architect than to use this normal (natural) tool of civilization to the best advantage.[9]

"Certain facilities, too, of the machine, which it would be interesting to enlarge upon, are taken advantage of and the nature of the materials is usually revealed in the process. . . .[10]

"I have observed that nature usually perfects her forms. . . . She rarely says a thing and tries to take it back at the same time."[11] (Such as classic supports reduced to a decorative order of pilasters.)

Whenever Wright speaks of technology, industry, structure, he uses words borrowed from the organic world, thinks in naturalistic terms: "The old structural forms which up to the present time have spelled 'architecture' are *decayed. Their life went from them* long ago and new conditions industrially, steel and concrete, and terra-cotta in particular, are prophesying a more plastic era wherein as the flesh is to our bones, so will the covering be to the structure."

vi. Wright, "In the Cause of Architecture," [p. 155].

"Beautifully expressive" but no mechanistic exhibitionism or baring of structural or other utilities as a purpose in itself![12] That outside "covering" is conceived rather as an epidermis nurtured from the inner essentials below than as an application from without.

It is characteristic to call the columns of the new Johnson Administration Building [the S. C. Johnson & Son, Inc., Administration Building, Racine, Wisconsin, 1936–39] tree-shaped, "dendriform." And Mr. Wright's early interest in cantilever systems from the [Avery] Coonley Playhouse [Riverside, Illinois, 1912] to the Edgar Kaufmann House on Bear Run reaches perhaps its fullest expression in the St. Mark's apartment skyscraper (1924?) [St. Mark's-in-the-Bouwerie Towers project, New York, 1927–31] with eighteen reinforced-concrete floor slabs projected from an internal structural trunk, following the freely balanced and continuous statics of organic plant structure, where bilateral supports are unknown!

Prefabrication

But Wright recognized also the precedent of physiological *growth on the spot.* Our production methods with most preparation far from the premises called for some effective restudy; machines, "the normal tools of our civilization," operated more frequently in factories than on the building site, but the creative mind could jump the distance and, shuttling between the two poles, still weave an organic fabric. Prefabrication, in the sense of shop-fabrication for consistent integration on the actual job, has occupied Wright's mind again and again. Of course plumbing fixtures, doors, windows, and hardware might be standardized, but also structural framing and wall materials, from Wright's "Ready-Cut" dwelling designs a quarter century ago [the American System-Built Houses for the Richards Company, 1915–17] to the reinforced concrete-block system of the California houses and the plywood wall-sections of his $5,000 [Herbert] Jacobs House [Madison] ([1936–] 1937) and recent "Usonian" houses. Even *floors* and *roofs* could be similarly conceived, although they offer perhaps a more difficult problem.

Roof Design

Abandoning the simple boxlike type of house as found on the Continent and in New England, and adopting the articulated plan and plan outline, Mr. Wright has experimented with roof formations more inventively and imaginatively than any other architect. From the steeply pitched roofs like that of the [Chauncey I.] Williams House in River Forest [Illinois] (1895) he proceeded to the ever flatter, many-gabled solutions of the [B. Harley] Bradley or Warren [Hickox] houses in Kankakee [Illinois] (1900), and the still flatter hip-roofs of the magnificent Prairie style, which to his grief was speedily vulgarized by superficial imitators.

Finally the roof surface disappeared from sight, and despite his ingenious ability in the handling of pitched roofs, the accomplished master recognized the simple, *logical relation of the flat roof to the articulate floor plan of his own creation.* Most roofing materials of the past had required steep pitch and logically produced prominent roof areas. The asphalt and other ply-composition materials of minimum joining removed that cumbersome restriction, against which classic architecture had aspired in vain for lack of the now common "normal tool."

From early building in Glencoe [Illinois], from Unity Church [Unity Temple, Oak Park,

Illinois, 1905–8] to the House on the Mesa of Broadacre City[13] or to the houses in Los Angeles–where the flat roof was instinctively felt by Mr. Wright as indigenous (and indeed once had been used as exclusively as in Mexico City), the decision went to the structural simplicity and consequent economy of level cover. He had expressed himself against "tortured abortions of residential skylines" already in 1908.[14]

Thirty years later, luxurious Fallingwater or the simple Jacobs House were level-topped without losing charm: "There should be no complicated roofs. Every time a hip or valley . . . is allowed to ruffle a roof, the life of the building is threatened."[vii]

The flat roof, target of stern attack by busy European dictators in their off-hours, appalling to artistic FHA [Federal Housing Administration] appraisers and some local housing authorities, has become a tragicomic issue: amusingly incongruous to the fundamental problems on hand–and less amusing in view of the misguided industrial inventiveness that is geared to roofing a third of a nation with composition shingles, pink, green, and blue.

Considering by contrast Wright's *truly unique mastery of pitched-roof design*, his self-chosen abstinence from it after having achieved brilliant formal solutions shows the rare intrinsic sincerity of his genius; he recognized the threat of structural complications of an obsolete order. In the long run he could refrain from concessions even to his own splendid skill! In an accomplished manner he tries diverse solutions before his decision: "Visible roofs are expensive and unnecessary."[15]

His expression for the level domestic roof is a symbolic example. It bears testimony to Wright's profoundly sacrificing, incorruptible search, to his affirming faith: ARCHITECTURAL AMBITION WELDED TO PRODUCTIONAL LOGIC OF THE AGE.

vii. ["Frank Lloyd Wright"], *Architectural Forum*, January 1938 [p. 79].

1. In his footnote to this quotation Neutra gives its source as Wright's book *An Autobiography*. In fact, although that book includes a similar sentence (*An Autobiography* [New York: Longmans, Green, 1932], p. 141), the version quoted comes from Wright's "In the Cause of Architecture," *The Architectural Record* 23, no. 3 (March 1908): 159.

2. "Science and poetry, knowledge and the humane arts are divided in our own time as they were perhaps never divided before. . . . The task of the original artist today, and in essence it is the same in literature, in philosophy and in architecture, is to bring 'science' and 'poetry' together again. . . . Mr. Wright's buildings, it seems to me, are essays towards this synthesis." Mumford, "The Social Background of Frank Lloyd Wright," pp. 78–79.

3. Makart bouquets were bunches of dried flowers, grasses, reeds, palm fronds, and so on, bound together with wire. They were named after the Austrian artist Hans Makart because of his many representations of bouquets of flowers.

4. Neutra has omitted a phrase: the quotation should read, "NATURE furnished the materials for architectural motifs out of which the architectural forms we know today have been developed. . . . "

5. Wright actually wrote, " . . . comprehension of natural law."

6. Wright actually wrote, "Bring out the nature of the materials, let their nature intimately into your scheme."

7. Wright, "In the Cause of Architecture," p. 157.

8. Ibid., p. 161.

9. Ibid., p. 163. The word "natural" in parentheses is added by Neutra.

10. Ibid., p. 162.

11. Ibid., p. 160.

12. Ibid., p. 163. The italics are added by Neutra.

13. The House on the Mesa project (1931) was originally designed for a site in Denver and was later incorporated into the Broadacre City project (1934–35).

14. Ibid., p. 157. Wright wrote, "The skylines of our domestic architecture were fantastic abortions, tortured by features that disrupted the distorted roof surfaces."

15. "Frank Lloyd Wright," *Architectural Forum* 68, no. 1 (January 1938): 79.

MY FRANK LLOYD WRIGHT

Alvar Aalto

One would naturally have to be a scientist to analyze the works of Frank Lloyd Wright. But I would not wish to be this scientist even if I possessed that gift of limitation which every scientist requires—even the science of Architecture. However, I would suggest that some gifted person do an analysis of F.L.W. Certainly I wish someone would do this because to my surprise I have not found a complete analysis of this kind in America. I would probably not read his book, but there is one thing in this connection which I would like to do. I would like to have lunch with Wright and his dissector shortly after the first copy of the book reached Taliesin. I doubt whether Wright would read the book either, but he would instinctively know enough about the product to make the luncheon the most interesting I have ever attended.

There would naturally be beautiful flowers on the table, and glasses, and silver, and everything else. But I would probably start with rye whiskey and have my army pistol with me, for you never know what might happen.

This is the country of Mark Twain. . . .

There is a nice museum at Harvard full of flowers, but all the flowers are made of glass.[1] They are mostly enlargements of microscopic elements, like the findings of a surgeon's knife. They are beautiful and mysterious. They show the rationalism of nature as well as its prolific waste and chaos. It is dramatic; it appeals to both my mental and emotional being. Still, I like the living flowers more.

To try to analyze the elements of Wright's architecture would be like dissecting the flowers. I like flowers too much to dissect them.

I like Wright's houses as I like the flowers. Cutting them apart would not improve them for me.

There is a great deal in the new architecture which reminds me of the flowers in glass. Every element is visible, every corner's function and construction can be explained. But there still remains something artificial—like flowers of glass.

There are elements visible in Wright's architecture. You can explain some of the functions, but never all. His elements form a totality more like the assembling in Nature. There are rational things, but there is chaos also.

There are many tendencies in the new architecture toward a more complete and clear mechanism than the human being itself. Never so with Frank Lloyd Wright. His works have always, without a single exception, the limitations of the human being. They are our friends, on an equal standing. There is always something which reminds us of the unknown depths of our own being.

1. Aalto must be referring to the Ware Collection of Glass Models of Plants at the Harvard Museum of Natural History. Made outside Dresden, Germany, by Leopold Blaschka and his son, Rudolph, between 1887 and 1936, these life-sized, highly accurate models of hundreds of different plants and flowers include anatomical sections and enlarged flower parts.

UNTITLED

Harwell Hamilton Harris

A youth trudged slowly up a winding road. The road encircled a low hill. The hilltop was covered with groves of tall pines and eucalyptus, the slopes with gray green olives. Below the hill, on three sides, were busy thoroughfares and beyond these stretched the city; the hill with its groves rose like an island out of the flat gridiron of sun-baked streets.

The youth paused often and looked above him. He had been told that hidden among the trees on the top of the hill was a building that would interest him as a sculptor. He doubted it. What had he ever found to interest him in a building? Is architecture an art? It possesses the same elements of three-dimensional form as sculpture—theoretically the same means of abstract statement. Why then are there no examples of architecture as art? Architecture, he decided, is for practical purposes too impure to be an art. Arguing to himself, he reached the top of the hill.

Through a screen of tall trees he glimpsed fragments of a low building with sharp outlines. He forgot his argument and hurried along the road, pausing every few steps to peer. He came at last to a break in the planting and stepped through.[1]

Within an open grassy space, strongly silhouetted against the circle of dark trees, lay a long low building, its creamy walls golden in the afternoon sunlight. Its low wings were extended and paralleled by high garden walls. In the foreground was a pool as sharply rectilinear as the building; joining the building to the pool was a large plantbox. Building, pool, and plantbox were one material. Above the plantbox was a broad opening; within the opening was a pair of square vertical mullions covered with intricate square ornament in low relief. Above the line of the opening the walls broke back, and on the ledge thus created the square sharp ornament appeared again, this time in bigger scale and in high relief. Like a wreath, the ornament moved lightly across the broad brow of the building, continuing in quiet, unbroken rhythm from one wall to the next and from one wing to the next. The ornament which he had followed through its developments in relief now burst into full round—not singly, but in pairs—high up in the interior of the building. No sooner had he discerned it once than he discovered it again—always in pairs, always silhouetted against a background of trees or of sky. Stunned, he watched climax follow climax.

He was alone with his discovery, striding in rhythm to inaudible music. Forms gathering in procession and pouring themselves out in melody; climax following climax. No halt, no uncertainty, no fumbling, no struggle, only melody, pouring itself out endlessly. With racing pulse he saw life as form, union, plan; and architecture as a kind of crystallized play, regulating life as though it were music.

Gradually he returned to earth. Recumbent upon her green carpet and screened by trees from the gaze of all others, the Sleeping Beauty smiled on her youthful discoverer. And so

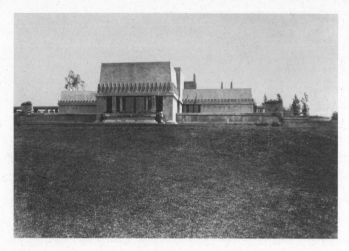

Frank Lloyd Wright. Aline Barnsdall House (Hollyhock House),
Los Angeles. c. 1916–1921

began the metamorphosis of a youthful sculptor into a still
more youthful architect.

As in the life of the youthful sculptor, so in the
lives of countless others, the work of Frank Lloyd Wright
has been the revelation of architecture as art. Not the art of
books or of classrooms, but the art that proceeds from the
very fiber of things. An art from within. Filling the imagination with a swirling stream of living images. Arousing an
intense desire to body them forth in living buildings.
Energizing their possessor with a feeling of the reality of the
self. Making him a part of the living stream. Sensitive to the
aliveness of all things. Projecting himself unconsciously into
all things. Feeling the oneness and continuity of all things. Delighting in the rediscovery of his
own self in these expressions. Delighting in the richness and multiplicity of being of which he
finds himself capable.

In Wright, the architect becomes the free spirit, the creator, the uniter of living impuls-
es, evoking a new sense of mystery from the familiar–his buildings, like all living things, born
rather than contrived. To the young man in architecture he is the yea-sayer, giving affirmation to
the expansive yearnings of the spirit; his work a presence, not confined to any time or place, but,
like a current, sweeping into a single expressive gesture the real of the past and the present.

Stretched at their ease upon the ground, seemingly absorbing energy from the contact
of their broad surfaces with the earth and the air, these buildings express in their naturalness,
casualness, amplitude and democratic acceptance of sun, wind, rain, vegetation, a quality singu-
larly American. There is in them a [Walt] Whitman's "contempt for statutes and ceremonies," a
"beauty of independence, departure, actions that rely on themselves."[2] They are laws unto
themselves and depend on themselves. There is in them an instinct for order and also an
instinct for freedom. In a world absorbed with devices, these buildings exhibit a singular clarity
regarding fundamentals. Their pattern is the pattern of a free man, striding abroad in the open.
Their spread is the spread of creation. All else is impudence.

To the youth in architecture these buildings are evidence of the existence of the art of
architecture and of the nature of creation. As personal responses to a primordial impulse they
will fasten upon him for a time their idiosyncrasies. Painful as this must be to Wright, it seems
to be temporarily inevitable.

1. A handwritten note in the original manuscript indicates an illustration here.
Presumably this would have been a photograph of "Hollyhock House"—the Aline
Barnsdall House, Los Angeles (c. 1916–21).

2. Harris is quoting Walt Whitman's poem
"Song of the Broad-Axe," in *Leaves of Grass*,
1855 (reprint ed. Philadelphia: Rees Welsh &
Co, 1882), p. 149.

1940: FRANK LLOYD WRIGHT

Ludwig Mies van der Rohe

About the beginning of this century, the great European revival of architecture instigated by William Morris grew overrefined and began gradually to lose its force. Distinct signs of exhaustion became manifest. The attempt to revive architecture from the standpoint of form was apparently doomed. Even the greatest efforts of artists could not overcome the patent lack of any usable convention. Then, however, these efforts were limited to the subjective. But the authentic approach to architecture must always be the objective. Accordingly, the only valid solutions at that time were in cases such as industrial building, where objective limitations made subjective license impossible. Peter Behrens's significant creations for the electrical industry are a vivid illustration. But in all other problems of architectural creation, the architect ventured into the dangerous realm of the historical; to some architects the revival of classic forms seemed reasonable, and, in the field of monumental architecture, even imperative.

Of course this was not true of all early-twentieth-century architects. [Henry] Van de Velde and [H. P.] Berlage especially remained steadfastly loyal to their own ideals. Once a way of thinking had been accepted as essential, Van de Velde's intellectual integrity and Berlage's sincerity and almost religious faith in his ideal allowed no compromise. For these reasons the former won our highest respect and admiration, the latter our special veneration and love.

Nevertheless, we young architects found ourselves in painful inner discord. We were ready to pledge ourselves to an idea, but our enthusiastic hearts demanded an unqualified ideal. And the potential vitality of Van de Velde's and Berlage's ideals had by that time been lost.

This, then, was the situation in 1910.

At this moment, so critical for us, there came to Berlin the exhibition of the work of Frank Lloyd Wright. This comprehensive display and the extensive publication of his works enabled us really to become acquainted with the achievement of this architect.[1] The encounter was destined to prove of great significance to the development of architecture in Europe.

The work of this great master revealed an architectural world of unexpected force and clarity of language, and also a disconcerting richness of form. Here finally was a master-builder drawing upon the veritable fountainhead of architecture, who with true originality lifted his architectural creations into the light. Here again, at last, genuine organic architecture flowered.

The more deeply we studied Wright's creations, the greater became our admiration for his incomparable talent, for the boldness of his conceptions, and for his independence in thought and action. The dynamic impulse emanating from his work invigorated a whole generation. His influence was strongly felt even when it was not actually visible.

After this first encounter, we followed the development of this rare man with eager hearts. We watched with astonishment the exuberant unfolding of the gifts of one who had been endowed by nature with the most splendid talents. In his undiminishing power he resembles a giant tree in a wide landscape, which, year after year, ever attains a more noble crown.

1. Research by Anthony Alofsin indicates that there was no formal exhibition of Wright's work in Berlin until 1931. On February 16, 1910, the architect Bruno

Möhring lectured on Wright's work and showed a selection of his drawings. It is possible that this is what Mies is referring to here. See Anthony Alofsin, *Frank Lloyd Wright: The Lost Years, 1910–1922. A Study of*

Influence (Chicago: at the University Press, 1993), p. 34. The publication referred to is *Ausgeführte Bauten und Entwürfe von Frank Lloyd Wright* (Berlin: E. Wasmuth, 1910).

TO MEET–TO KNOW–TO BATTLE–
TO LOVE–FRANK LLOYD WRIGHT

Edgar J. Kaufmann, Sr.

1934

In the fall of 1934 Mrs. Kaufmann and I traveled to Taliesin to visit our son, who was there as a member of the Taliesin Fellowship. We were met by the charming and beautiful Mrs. Wright, her daughters, Iovanna and Svetlana, and the police dog.

During the afternoon we became gradually acquainted with some of the fellows, and had a visit with the Master and his family before an informal dinner with him and the children. I remember distinctly the homemade wine. Mr. and Mrs. [George S.] Parker (of the pens)[1] joined the weekend.

After dinner, conversation in small groups. Then sudden silence. Music. Edgar Tafel, one of the fellows, playing Bach–then Beethoven. Silence again. A semicircle was formed and the Master spoke.

He discussed with the fellows the reconditioning and the rehabilitation of the model of Broadacre City [project, 1934–35]. The Master called upon Mr. Parker. The fellows listened attentively. I realized I was in for something. What should I say? The Master gave the cue and I expressed my interest in the rehabilitation of the Broadacre model. I wanted to know more about it, and the fellows promised to show me the model and explain it the following day. It was whispered that money was needed. I listened but was not particularly interested.

The fellows retired. The house was quiet. Around a smoldering fire, one of the many delightful ones in the house of Taliesin, sat the Master, Mr. Parker, and myself. The conversation was general. Finally the Master challenged me–"What are your interests besides selling rags?" At that particular time, I told him, I was deeply interested in the Allegheny County Authority, which had come into existence partly through my efforts and which was contemplating building a number of bridges and a viaduct around the riverfronts of Pittsburgh's Golden Triangle; I had been negotiating for a planetarium in Pittsburgh. Furthermore, I hoped to find a scheme to recondition my own office. The one I was using I had lived with for ten years. And, not least, we had been dreaming of a lodge to take care of the family all year round near the waterfalls at Bear Run. Bear Run is a stream about five miles long, gathering water from innumerable mountain springs and finally emptying into the Youghigheny River. The Master was interested. He wanted to talk more about it the next day.

Sunday morning, immediately after breakfast, cars and trucks were loaded with lunch baskets and equipment for a morning in the Wisconsin woods. It was a beautiful day, with clear-cut skylines and big trees. Extreme informality prevailed. On the way one gets better acquainted with the fellows and the Master. Then a hurried trip back to Taliesin for Sunday afternoon moving pictures. Visitors from everywhere. Finally a late inspection and explanation of the Broadacre model. It intrigued me and I committed myself to help to rehabilitate it. In the morning the Master promised to send it to Pittsburgh for exhibition to the citizens of the Tri-State area.

After dinner and more music from records and from Edgar Tafel, we had to depart. A promise was exacted that I should visit the workshop at Chandler, Arizona, during the coming winter, where the Broadacre model was to be worked on. In return a promise from the Master to come to Pittsburgh within the next fortnight to meet the Allegheny County Authority Commission. There might be hope of making some arrangement for him to become consulting engineer and architect. The two-day meeting in December 1934 ended without success. They simply did not understand.

The Master looked at my office and made suggestions for a new one. I did not understand but he promised to put it on paper. We discussed a planetarium and he made rough sketches. But we left that for the moment because we were hurrying to Bear Run to look over the possible site of the lodge, later to be known as Fallingwater.

The sun was shining when we started, unusual for Pittsburgh in December. We traveled through Clairton Valley along the Monongahela River admiring the powerful steelworks along its banks. A slight rain began to fall. On to Connellsville, where it turned into a light snow. Up over Chestnut Ridge—still snowing—then down toward Bear Run. Light rain with a magnificent rainbow which crossed the mountains and dipped into both valleys greeted us as we arrived. The Master in a comfortable seat had been relaxing. With the rainbow he became alive. Turning to me he said, "Surely something will come out of this journey; after all the elements through which we have traveled, the end is crowned with a rainbow."

We tramped around the terrain of the waterfalls. The Master was amazed at the beauty and the forceful contours. His first idea was a house suspended by cables from cliff to cliff, facing the falls. I stood amazed. We talked and disagreed. It ended by my promising to send a topographical map which was to include everything 100 feet above and 200 feet below the falls, showing every tree more than 2" in diameter, and every stone and boulder permitted, by the ages, to rear its head above the ground.

1935

In February we spent two weeks in Arizona, eighteen hours a day with the Master and the fellows. It was the busiest workshop I have ever lived with. Planning, thinking, discussing–Broadacre City was gradually being rehabilitated with fury. Larger models explaining certain features were being constructed. It was a fascinating fortnight.

Further discussions of the office, the planetarium, and the Allegheny County Authority projects. The Master asked how we wanted to live in our Bear Run house. I explained we had been living in a 40 x 40' Aladdin House[2] with screened sleeping porches on three sides. On the fourth side had been constructed a living room 40 x 60', with solid logs for three feet, and above that removable windows. A little pool, fed by mountain spring water, ten steps away from my bed. We had been living and sleeping practically in the open, bathing in cold water before breakfast, all day, and after dinner. Simplified housekeeping, a minimum of servants and house cares.

We discussed material. There was plenty of native stone handy to the site; plenty of river sand within less than half a mile; plenty of white and black oak, poplar and fir, and a saw mill within ⅛ of a mile. I asked what he had in mind. Where would the house be placed? What would it look like? The Master was silent. How many rooms do you want? We need a utility room, a kitchen, a living room large enough for eating, living, and music, a double guestroom and bath, a double master's bedroom and bath, a single master's dressing room and bath for overflow guests, a single bedroom and bath for Junior. I stressed our habit of living outdoors, behind screens, or behind glass. We had learned to allow the outside to come in. More discussion. What would it look like? Where would we place it? Again the Master was silent. Wait until the contour plan comes.

On March 9 the topographical survey was sent to Mr. Wright. During April the fellows were working on the project.

On April 27 a letter arrived: "We are ready to go to work on the waterfall cottage at Bear Run and the planetarium. Also we are like the little Mississippi River steamboat Lincoln told about–every time she blew her whistle she had to heave to at the bank for steam. We blew our whistle so long and loud on Broadacre that we have nothing left." Fifteen hundred dollars needed, forty oriental prints as security–the loan to be paid off in eighteen months, the prints to be returned. Instead, I sent the $1,500.00 as an advance on the house.

May: Broadacre completed. Caravan from Arizona to New York.

June 15: Broadacre came to Pittsburgh for a two-week exhibit. Howling success. Miners, mill workers, white-collar workers deeply interested; few architects during the first week; few of the upper crust. Second week–more architects, plenty of upper crust. Exhibit closed in a blaze of glory.

September 15: Floor plans and colored elevation of Fallingwater arrived. The next few nights were sleepless. Finally I began to understand the plan partially. The Master's conception–the colored elevations fascinated me. At least I thought I understood.

On September 16 I could not work. I thought of nothing but the house.

September 21: The Master arrived. Went over the plan thoroughly. Allowed me to drink in his conception and the meaning. My first lesson in organic architecture. It was plain I did not understand—it required the Master to open my eyes.

He also discussed his idea of an all-wood office. Again I did not understand at all. He talked about a plywood mural at one end. I was more confused than ever. My mind was on Fallingwater. The office had to be pushed aside.[i]

The following Sunday a new vision of the house grew upon me and I stood on the rocks with Junior and Mrs. Kaufmann—we read the plan and discussed it.

The Master came to Pittsburgh to speak at the Hungry Club in October; he demanded the destruction of all Pittsburgh and its rebuilding. He caused consternation to the reading public of the evening and morning papers and provoked many editorial comments pro and anti.

In December we decided to quarry stone during the winter for a possible beginning of Fallingwater the following spring. The walls to be minimum 18" thick; stones to be the run of the quarry. Those split thinner than 4" to be kept aside as paving stones throughout the house and terraces.

1936

Late February finally a letter from Chandler with a package, "We have sent you in this morning's mail two complete sets of blueprints of Fallingwater. Three copies of specifications."

In May the quarrying had been completed. A sample wall had been constructed at the quarry.

The Master arrived on his way to Philadelphia to inspect the sample wall for an hour. Not satisfied, he made corrections. "I don't have much confidence in any of the usual estimates you can get on this work. We will have to plan some way of taking it up more directly with some interested competent builder who is small enough to stay on the job and experienced enough to know what to do and how to do it with our help." I query, "Where do you find such?" The Master answers, "I had one but he is too old. He has built many of my buildings. We will have to find a new one."

This was very discouraging because I realized that the proper man was needed to interpret, and to understand how to build according to the Master's interpretation.

The latter part of April we turned over plans and specifications to our estimating, purchasing, and building department. They, in turn, wrote a four-page letter to the Master asking for further explanation. The Master returned the original letter to me with priceless marginal notes.

Early in May a letter came from Taliesin:

i. It was built in 1936? [Kaufmann may have inserted the question mark here because the construction of his office was long drawn out: originally planned for 1935, it didn't begin until early 1937 and wasn't finished until the end of that year. See Christopher Wilk, *Frank Lloyd Wright: The Kaufmann Office* (London: The Victoria and Albert Museum, 1993).]

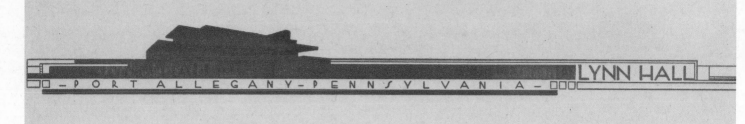

Lynn Hall letterhead, designed by Walter J. Hall

You seem to forget all I said about building an extraordinary house in extraordinary circumstances. Having been through it scores of times I know what we are up against and decline to start it unless I can see our way. The same to you.

Now suppose I were a sculptor and you would say "Carve me an extraordinary statue." I would accept. Then you hand me a pantograph and say—"Use this. I have found the use of the pantograph a good way to carve statues. It saves time and money." Then I would say—"But in this case it will waste time and money and ruin the statue." You would come back with "But when I have statues made I have the pantograph used."

Well E. J., you would have the sculptor where you have me now with your Thumm.3 I can't build this extraordinary house with a Thumm. Read the enclosed correspondence and note the pantograph punctilio for only one thing. There is no sense whatever of the things he should know after studying the plans.

Now a pickaxe is more suited to my style of labor than a pantograph. But, for a fact, I can't use either.

Your Thumm won't do. I must have my own fingers. . . .

This ought to clear up point one and get me a modest builder with brains—not too anxious to show off—willing to learn new ways of doing old things: able but wise to the fact that his previous experience might fool him in this case. . . .

Finally first check sent on account for bridge detail and specifications. Taliesin wires two days later—"Check has been mislaid, please send duplicate."

May 15: Ten strikes. The Master writes that his son from California had been motoring through Pennsylvania near Port Allegany, McKean County, when he stopped his car abruptly because he recognized the earmarks of the Master's design on what was called a Tea House and Filling Station. He inquired of the two maiden ladies who built the building. It had been a local contractor by the name of Walter J. Hall & Son.4 The son immediately wired the Master, "Here is a possible builder for the Kaufmann project." The Master corresponded with Hall and Hall said he was interested.

On May 27 I telephoned Hall asking him to come to Pittsburgh and he was most eager to build a building designed by Frank Lloyd Wright.

I tried to get him to give us a bid at once. By June 13 his estimates were received. In the meantime I looked up his references and personal credit rating. He had always been known as an efficient carpenter and builder, and had done some contracting on his own account, but during the last eight years had little to do. His reputation was good; he was well liked by the workmen.

I communicated with the Master. He was happy with the results. This was exactly the kind of man he wanted. Mr. Hall became superintendent in charge of construction.

He accepted and by July 13 he started work and the building was begun. He organized local farmers and their boys to do the carpentry, smithing, masonry, and concrete work. (Plumbing, electrical work, and heating were of course installed by trained workmen.)

There was some question about the safety of the site for the type of building the Master submitted, so I commissioned an engineer's report. It arrived on July 18 and did not recommend the site for an important structure, for the rate of recession of the falls, although slow, could not be predicted with any degree of safety. There was evidence of minor spalling off of the rock at the face of the falls and a possibility of further disturbance of the rock strata if channels were cut in the surface to provide necessary keyways for the foundation walls.

> The question of utilizing the boulder as a base for the fireplace is perhaps a detail, but we do not consider the boulder suitable for incorporation into the foundation of the building.
>
> Of course there is a possibility, or even a probability, that future deterioration of the rock ledge will not be sufficient to endanger the foundations; but in our opinion there could be no feeling of complete safety and consequently we recommend that the proposed site be not used for any important structure.

I was in a quandary. I did not communicate with the Master. I figured periodic inspections could be made regarding recession and if any alarming condition did arise it could be caught and rectified. I knew it was difficult to say just what nature might do, but in most cases there was always evidence showing before any real danger. No record as to when the minor spallings referred to by the engineer had occurred—but they were due to frost action in the upper stratifications as verified by the profile of the falls. The engineer misinterpreted Wright's plan, for it had not been intended to use keyways in the foundation work. Moreover, I was not prepared to sacrifice using the boulder for the fireplace under any circumstances.

We did not stop work. We filed the engineer's report.

On July 27, Bob Mosher, one of the fellows at Taliesin, arrived to interpret the plans and assist Mr. Hall. From now on the work became exciting. I spent most of my days helping in the interpretation of the plans and in the construction.

On August 2, the steel diagrams arrived. They were sent out for estimates.

Steel engineers questioned the specifications of reinforcing as well as the general steel-and-concrete construction. Hall, Mosher, and myself got into a huddle one afternoon and decided to proceed with the Master's specifications. To cap the climax the engineers who had condemned the site appeared, were surprised that we had started work, and began to tell their story to Hall and Mosher.

Word reached Taliesin. Out of the blue on Sunday morning came the following telegram to Mosher: "The battle of Bear Run is on. Drop work and come back immediately. We are through until Kaufmann and I arrive at some basis of mutual respect. You are needed here.

Do not delay one hour and bring in all the plans you can get. . . . Frank Lloyd Wright."

We were crestfallen. The day became bluer. We suggested that Bob telephone. The result—another telegram: "You are at least able to get off job as expected. Neither explanation nor argument should be necessary. Affairs there are more serious than you comprehend. If you are unable or unwilling to carry out my instructions your connection with me ends. I am not coming to Pittsburgh. Frank Lloyd Wright."

More sleepless nights.

August 27: The following letter from Taliesin:

If you are paying to have the concrete engineering done there, there is no use whatever in our doing it here. I am willing you should take it over but I am not willing to be insulted.

So we will send no more steel diagrams. I am unaccustomed to such treatment where I have built buildings before and do not intend to put up with it now so I am calling Bob back until we can work out something or nothing. . . .

August 28: How should I answer? I did the best I could:

If you have been paid to do the concrete engineering up there, there is no use whatever of our doing it down here. I am not willing to take it over as you suggest nor am I willing to be insulted.

So if you will not send any more steel diagrams, what shall I do? I am unaccustomed to such treatment where I have been building before and I do not intend to put up with it now so I am calling you to come down here, which I hoped you could have done during the past few weeks, to inspect the work under Mr. Hall's direction who is an unknown foreman to you, instead of allowing the entire responsibility of his craftsmanship to rest upon us here. So if you will come here perhaps we can work out something or nothing. . . .

P.S. Now don't you think that we should stop writing letters and that you owe it to the situation to come to Pittsburgh and clear it up by getting the facts? Certainly there are reasons which must have prompted you to write as you have.

I am sorry that you are calling Bob back. He seems entirely wrapped up in his work and in its progress but this is beyond my control and you must use your own judgment. . . .

August 29: Bob, finally, with the help of the family, packed his two shirts, his one pair of work pants, two sweaters—we could not find his socks and his work shoes—and reluctantly put on his first Pittsburgh outfit for traveling back home. We all stood at the gate and waved him goodbye. It was not an easy moment. . . .

August 31: Another letter from Taliesin only partly quoted:

Apologies are nothing to a man like yourself. But explanation seems to be in order. The atmosphere should be cleared. Lightning and inevitable thunder may help to clear it. Anyhow that's what it is as I see the way it is. The thing hurts me in this instance I assure you. I am sure it hurts you.

Meantime your letter shows me that I do owe it to you and to myself to get on that job. I'll come soon. Sincerely, Frank Lloyd Wright.

The armistice is on. The Master leaves for Pittsburgh in early September. The parties to the armistice: Mr. Wright; Edgar Tafel, a fellow of Taliesin; Mr. Hall; and myself. It is not held in a railroad coach but under a majestic oak tree. The conditions are discussed and agreed to. Mr. Hall remains superintendent, Edgar Tafel is to take Bob Mosher's place on the first of October. Mr. Hall is to be sent to Taliesin in the early winter to absorb the spirit in which the drawings are turned out. I agreed not to inject myself or any of my "yes" men, as the Master called them, except through Edgar Tafel.

Much progress was made during Edgar's direction. Unfortunately he was called back to Taliesin November 20. The Master was confined with a slight cold. In December word reached us that he was bedridden with pneumonia.

In a letter of November 2, the Master wrote:

I think you fail to realize how well off you have been in the execution of this building so far. Hall is rough but pretty good and all the mistakes made including the crooked bridge rails don't add up to enough to form a fair basis for complaint.

Perhaps you don't quite realize the nature of what is being done for you and still imagine it could have been done without error or waste by way of the present system. No more possible than for Franklin D. Roosevelt to give us a better government by way of "politics." Hall is doing remarkably well with awkward material.

During the last week of Edgar's stay checks in the concrete work appeared on the terrace of the master bedroom. Edgar was concerned.

Before leaving we discussed with Edgar an arrangement to have engineers make computations of the structure every three months to see what was happening. In spite of the Master's illness the following telegram December 29:

KINDLY REFRAIN ALL INTERFERENCE WITH ME IN MY WORK AT THIS TIME. SEND ME WHAT I ASK FOR. HAVE NO RESPONSIBLE·REPRESENTATIVE. IN THESE CIRCUMSTANCES EASY TO SPOIL THE ENTIRE WORK BY LACK OF CONFIDENCE IN MY ABILITY TO HANDLE MY OWN WORK. KINDLY STAND BY. CUT AND SEND ME THE CONCRETE SAMPLES AS DIRECTED. they will not harm the structure. I WILL PAY FOR THEM IF IN THE OUTCOME IT SEEMS NECESSARY. I WANT AN UNCRACKED STRUCTURE. KNOW HOW TO GET IT. INTEND TO HAVE IT. READ MY LETTER MAILED YESTERDAY. IN CIRCUMSTANCES LIKE THESE THERE IS ONLY ONE DOCTOR. BE THANKFUL YOU DIDN'T LOSE HIM. NOW BE GOOD ENOUGH TO REALIZE THE TRUTH OF WHAT I SAY.

1937

The engineers, late in December 1936, made complete investigation of the engineering features of Fallingwater, together with several loading tests of the structure itself. They made similar computations again on January 6, 1937, January 13, and May 21. Deflections at various points of the building showed only from 3/16" to 3/4" maximum. The report: "The structure does not have a satisfactory factor of safety, or what might be termed reserve strength."[ii]

On January 2, we sent samples of concrete to the Master, as he asked. He had them analyzed and they proved satisfactory.

The house was completed during the spring of 1937.

That summer Mr. and Mrs. Wright were invited to Russia for an International Conference of Architects.

On September 7, we had been wiring back and forth because the Master had not been to see the completed work.

On December 19 he finally came and spent the day inspecting and re-arranging many things. Nevertheless it was a day of rejoicing for both of us.

We discussed the extension. The Master surveyed the hillside on which it was to be built. He gave me a sketchy outline of what was in his mind.

1938

The winter closed us in at Bear Run. Hall was living like a squirrel in his little house on the terrace.[5]

February 22: from Taliesin-in-the-Desert, Scottsdale, Arizona, comes the following letter: "When do you want to build extension? We will try to have the plans then."

Letter relayed to Sun Valley, Idaho, where I was trying to learn to ski. I answered the Master, "Intend to build at once."

April 26: Letter from Taliesin, Wisconsin: "Plans are in work."

May 25: Plans arrived with elevations. I wrote the Master that we were very enthusiastic about them but we find the addition too large.

On July 27 the Master came. We discussed revision of the guest wing, servants' quarters, and garage.

On August 20 a letter reading "All going well. Revision to guesthouse complete."

1939

On January 6, I informed the Master that Mr. Hall had agreed to start to build the guest wing, servant's quarters, and garage at once. This was the beginning of our second building operation. I spent most of January and the first two weeks in February on the site. I had been having trouble with my back, probably from falling off horses during the past thirty years, aggravated by having fallen not less than thirty times a day learning to ski.

ii. July 5, 1938, the same engineers took level readings and found them the same as a year before. They also inspected the building thoroughly for cracks and any other signs of distress, and, as far as they could see, the structure was in remarkably good condition. A further reading of May 21, 1940, quoting the engineer's report: "The results of these levels indicate that the structure has suffered a further settlement of 1/4". We further investigated the structure for cracks and other signs of distress, but, as far as we could determine, it is in very good condition."

The scene changes in March, to a hospital in New York. I am to undergo an operation—the first in my life. The Master has been called to England for a series of lectures—sailing April 25. Mrs. Kaufmann and the nurses say that coming out of the anesthesia that very morning, I shouted, "Send for Frank Lloyd Wright—send for Frank Lloyd Wright—there is something structurally wrong with me." That evening, when Mrs. Kaufmann bade Mr. and Mrs. Wright goodbye, she mentioned it to them.

From the R.M.S. *Queen Mary* I received the following letter, dated April 25, 1939:

I meant to get around to see you in New York before embarking on this errand to England but, as usual, got late and had to run.

I was shocked to hear of so serious an operation but glad to know that you had it over with and now heading in for an end to physical torture. You must have suffered! The house addition was going swell when I saw it. Stonework beautiful. Hall doing as well as could be, etc., etc.

Junior is running things all right.

Mrs. Kaufmann told me your remark when coming out from under ether—so apparently I have made a deep impression. Anyhow here's to you man. I hope this finds you cheerful and coming along to everybody's satisfaction—yours most of all. I expect great things of you—and Pittsburgh—I'll not forget the hand you gave me in my work and besides I like you a lot. To you, Liliane, and Junior, faithfully, Frank Lloyd Wright.

On August 24 we made an inspection of the house. It was a great day. Perhaps more for myself than for anyone. That night we celebrated into the wee hours of the morning. I was going through my postgraduate course with the Master. Daylight was breaking for me. When he spoke I understood, where two years before there had been a blank. He has been a great inspiration and tolerant of my ignorance. I know that I am a better man for having met him, built with him, battled with him, and learned to love him.

September 12, 1939, comes the final telegram: "DEAR E. J. IT'S PRETTY DRY HERE WE ARE WAITING AND HOPING FOR A LIFE WILL YOU? SIGNED FRANK."

September 14 I answer: "GET OVER YOUR PARCHED FEELING WATER ON THE WAY REGARDS, EDGAR."

November 15—the last letter in my file from the Master: "Dear Edgar—you were right in your surmise and I can't tell you how I appreciate your help where I guess I'll always need it most. Affection as always Frank."

1. George S. Parker was the founder and head of the Parker Pen Company, which was based in Janesville, Wisconsin, about eighty miles from Taliesin.

2. A prefabricated house sold by the Aladdin Company, manufacturer of mail-order house kits designed to be built by the buyer with little outside help.

3. Wright was punning on the name of Carl F. Thumm, an engineer who worked for Kaufmann. See Richard L. Cleary, *Merchant Prince and Master Builder: Edgar J. Kaufmann and Frank Lloyd Wright* (Pittsburgh: The Heinz Architectural Center, Carnegie Museum of Art, 1999), p. 42.

4. Here Kaufmann indicated that he wanted to insert an image of the letterhead of Walter J. Hall & Son.

5. During the construction, Hall lived in a temporary wooden shack on the terrace of the house.

UNTITLED

Liliane Kaufmann

For the past three years I have been learning to live in a Frank Lloyd Wright house. It has been an eye-opening experience and a constructive lesson in deletion.

I moved into the house with numerous misgivings, spoken and unspoken. I appreciated the architectural beauty of the exterior, but the interior seemed to me cold, barren, and monotonous. The closet space seemed inadequate and the housekeeping arrangements rudimentary, even for weekend living.

In a very short time, I decided that since I could not adapt the house to my way of living, I must adapt my way of living to the house. It proved to be surprisingly easy, and once the decision was made, my education had begun. It can be epitomized by using my own room as an example. When my eye had become accustomed to the lack of color and ornament, these two factors became apparent everywhere: I found ample color in the warm stones of my fireplace—in the stone floor and walls; the remaining plaster walls became a quiet background for two pictures at which I love to look. Lack of ornament brought out the amazing strength and loveliness of architectural line and detail. I began to glory in the sense of space and peace with which my room filled me. Leaf-laden trees or bare interlacing branches were a more-than-satisfactory substitute for curtains and draperies; a light-weight screen, easily rolled or unrolled, gave me the necessary privacy when I dressed; a sleep-shade allowed me to sleep as late as I chose in spite of wide-open, unshaded windows. At the end of three years, I resent the smallest addition to the beautiful simplicity of my room.

The matter of closet space was a revelation to me—I had grown up in a household where pile upon pile of linens, blankets, and personal clothing was a sign and symbol of good housekeeping. I have learned that the reverse is true, and I house my perfectly adequate supply of linens with the greatest ease and order. Of course, I haven't any "good" linens—no separate guest sheets and pillow cases, no guest towels. I hope never to have any again. For the first few weeks my country clothes, sweaters and coats, filled two units of hanging space and two units of sliding shelves. By a delightful process of elimination, which involved keeping only the ones I liked and really wore, I find one entire unit of shelf-space as bare as Mother Hubbard's cupboard, and one unit of hanging space only sparsely filled. I began to understand what [Rudyard Kipling's] Kim meant when he said that "a Sahib is tied by his luggage." Perhaps Frank Lloyd Wright has taught me new appreciations of literature as well as of color and proportion.

Lest anyone reading this should think that I have achieved supreme satisfaction in the matter of living and keeping house at Fallingwater, I must also list the grievances that I still harbor: I find the kitchen too small when we have crowded weekends; I have not enough space to keep china and glassware in the orderly fashion which they deserve; and I should have liked a small separate storage room for extra chairs for the dining table, extra occasional tables, additional breakfast trays for guests, etc.

Perhaps these are the vestigial remains of my previously undeveloped standards—they may disappear with the rest in another year when I have learned to live in the Wright way.

UNTITLED
Edgar Kaufmann, Jr.

The interiors of our house are planned for easy living, and in the hope that the same spirit that formed the architecture would be projected into a new field with different materials, functions, and a different scale. Naturally, we depended on Mr. Wright for designs and suggestions. He had built a background of stone piers—light gray with considerable variation into warmer tints of ocher and iron oxide red. He used the same stone for floors, with a beautiful rippled surface, just as it came from the quarry up the hill, but lightly varnished and waxed, giving a greater range of light and dark. The concrete surfaces and occasional plaster walls are finished in waterproof concrete paint, colored very light rosy ocher. Since the shapes flow in and out past the glass weather-shield, the color was held inside and out alike. The frames for glass are painted a dark iron red, called Cherokee. The window areas are left bare everywhere except for Venetian blinds in the two guest bedrooms. Against generous sweeps of these vivid yet austere materials in the winding recesses of Mr. Wright's airy caverns, we planned the furnishing of our house.

A big portion of the main furniture Mr. Wright built in—and he held certain simple features constant throughout. The shapes are large and rectangular. The wood is black walnut with sap streaks, unstained—its color value not unlike the window frames. Upholstery is latex rubber foam of varying resiliencies (which we still find very comfortable after three years of use). Echoing the cantilever of the main structure, the main blocks of the furniture (including cupboards) have been kept six inches above the floor; the supports rarely show. An expanse of one material often stops several inches short of its neighboring material. This can be seen in the first photograph where the bench back avoids the stone pier; only the top, horizontal wood surface and the seat continue through to join them. At the radiator box to the right of the dining area (right edge of photo 4) this was not possible, and the wood panel overlaps the stone instead. With these and a few more simple details, Mr. Wright gave the principal built-in elements a calm unity, and a feeling of kinship with the stone-and-concrete structure.

When we were ready to move in, some features of the big room, as Mr. Wright planned it, were lacking. His furniture layouts had always shown large carpets, even on the stairs. Five reflector floor lamps in the main room were supposed to supplement the ceiling lights of the central and dining areas. We did not yet have any movable chairs with backs or arms.

By the end of the first winter we were sure that large floor coverings would be only stuffy. This perhaps because the heating worked so well, and we had no drafts.

Natural monks' cloth covered the slats of main benches and the higher stools, and some of the square but soft back-cushions (photos 1, 2, 3)–after all, why need to scold five lively long-haired dogs every time they come in from running in the woods? Our splurge of color came in the majority of back-cushions and the double-faced ottomans on the floor–there we used the brightest red, yellow, and green we could find. Later, after trying blue, we confined ourselves to red and soft yellow and to a few down pillows in bright patterned fabrics that struck our fancy (photos 2, 3).

The coffee tables first had higher, stiffer cushions with small square tops. These we never grew to like and replaced them by the upturned stumps you see (photos 1, 2). (The chestnuts on our ridge were blighted as everywhere in the east twenty years ago, and we had been using their wood as firewood, and fences, and the stumps as tables, ever since we first came to Bear Run, fourteen years before.) To the coffee tables were added two copper-topped tables for drinks, one near the hearth for winter (photos 3, 4) (and near the kettle Mr. Wright gave us to heat wine over the fire), one near the terrace doors for summer (photo 1).

At the dining table we use peasant chairs from Tuscany, three legged, with uncarved but flamboyantly silhouetted backs. Although Mr. Wright recommended the metal chairs with circular backs and seats used in the [S. C.] Johnson [& Son, Inc.] Administration Building [Racine, Wisconsin, 1936–39], we have never been willing to replace the old ones. Through the room itself, and elsewhere, Mr. Wright suggested first the light barrel chair, made of slats, that he revised from earlier efforts for the Johnson residence ["Wingspread," the Herbert F. Johnson House, Racine, 1937–39], to be made in black walnut for our house. Later he showed us drawings of another armchair. Both seemed more formal than we wished, and the first, on sample, not loungy enough. So we started with canvas camp chairs and ended with the webbed chairs by Bruno Mathsson you see in photos 2 and 3. In photo 1 the same chair, with reading arm and pillow, is disguised by a mountain-goat-skin over the chair and a red-and-white Indian rug over the pillow. Elsewhere we have used modern chairs of Swedish or German design, or some by our friend and frequent guest [Laszlo] Gabor,[1] who also designed our outdoor chairs in webbing (photo 5). We have quite a few [Alvar] Aalto chairs too, but they seem happiest in the only rooms with curtains.

Samples of two different floor lamps were made and proved unsatisfactory. We turned to the lighting experts, and never were experts more stumped; their usual solutions were defeated everywhere, and new ones not forthcoming. Eventually, with Mr. Wright's consent, we put fluorescent strips in the radiator ledges behind the benches. (One is lighted in photo 1.) They work excellently, giving strong light for reading, and even light up the outdoor shrubbery and eaves enough to maintain some of the daytime continuity of outdoors with indoors.

1. Fallingwater, Edgar J. Kaufmann House.
Mill Run, Pennsylvania. 1934-1937. Interior

2. Fallingwater, Edgar J. Kaufmann House.
Mill Run, Pennsylvania. 1934-1937. Interior

Thus, gradually, after trial and error, our big problems have evaporated, leaving us a house we love to live in, flexible, still growing. We wanted a medium for relaxation; for this the architecture is ideal, and the furnishings, we feel, follow and heighten it to the degree we have been able to absorb and understand Mr. Wright's organic conception.

Photo 1. To the left, out of sight, is the entrance to the room (less cramped than the photo suggests), and a Capehart [record player] with record-shelves, built into one of Mr. Wright's cabinets. The speakers are in the space behind the seat, as are radiators (insulated)–the top ledge is a wood grille to let out heat and sound. On it are a French weathervane and a Mexican lacquered gourd bowl. Below on the table are objects as diverse as my grandfather's baby cup and saucer of German silver (now ashtrays), two bowls of wood by [James] Prestini, and some kitchen matches stuck in a rock slaked of its lime, picked up at the kiln on our farm. The stump has an old brass box for cigarettes, a Mexican bowl to grind chile (ashes), and the first of many nineteenth-century Western Pennsylvania potteries that are all over the house. Above, in the stonework, is set one of a pair of Chinese clay figures, whose colors blend with the stone. Mr. Wright had urged us to use Oriental art, but after we found the Western Pennsylvania pottery and the Indian crafts of the Americas, we were sure their sturdy, honest character gave more of the note of directness we wanted, and seemed equally at home in the setting. On the desk is an Aalto vase and on the shelf below are many treasured photographs by our friend Luke Swank, who took these of the interiors. Below is a huge glass lens, acting as a bowl.

The skylight has made this corner a favorite sitting spot during the day–at night it is busy with music. The skylight is also kind to our indoor plants, which grow luxuriously indeed over the stairwell that leads to the stream.

Photo 2. The front end of the living room. The windows all open, as well as the French doors on both sides. (The left-hand ones are hidden in the photo behind the pier, as is the stairwell.) Only the corners, with horizontal frames, are fixed. In the summer it becomes a roofed porch, hanging over the falls, the air cooled by the spray. Behind the long seat are radiators and lights. At each end, built-in boxes hold lemon trees, lit softly from below at night. At

4. Fallingwater, Edgar J. Kaufmann House.
Mill Run, Pennsylvania. 1934-1937. Interior

the left [*sic*], three of the higher stools, grouped in an L, are unified by a white goatskin.

Photo 3. An alcove with fixed glass, facing west. On all the benches are blankets–Mexican, Peruvian, or American Indian, so man or dog can curl up in them for a nap. On the ledge an American Indian bowl, an Aalto vase. Below, Italian glass ashtrays, a Mexican black-lacquer cigarette box, and flowers here as elsewhere from my mother's prize, the cutting garden. The low ottoman on the left is the one to the extreme right of photo 2.

Photo 4. The dining area. Two stools near the fire again joined by a fur throw. The logs near the hearth-boulder are usually piled higher, in winter to the wood shelf that separates stone from plaster. On this shelf, and on the table, simple pewter pieces from the attic of the family farmhouse in Germany. At the service hatch, a lacquered Mexican gourd. In the cavity between sideboard and wall, beer mugs. Above, on the metal shelves that bind the diverse elements of this corner, are dishes we use. On the sideboard shelves, a few plates more for looks, but mostly of the Canton blue and white we use a lot. These shelves continue down, and are masked by a pair of drop-leaf extensions to the main table–each has two leaves, so it is easy to vary the table size. On the pier hangs a copper flower container. At the window, Mexican and Indian pottery. Above the books, Peruvian weaving, dark green with red stripes. Further to the right come the stairs and the pier defining the entrance hall. The door on the left, of course, goes to the kitchen.

Photo 5. The pool of our new guest wing. There are larger trees close by. The furniture is used mainly for sunbathing and reading.

1. Laszlo Gabor was a Hungarian painter and designer, formerly resident in Vienna, where he was the business director of the Österreichische Werkbund. The Kaufmann family had helped him to immigrate to the United States in 1935, and employed him in their department store.

PLATES

Introduction

The following drawings, culled from the archives of The Museum of Modern Art and the Frank Lloyd Wright Foundation, are the surviving visual documents related to the design and planning of *Frank Lloyd Wright: American Architect*.

Plates 1 and 2 are plans worked out by Wright and the Museum's curator of architecture, John McAndrew. The first is a sketch of the plans for the first-floor galleries. The drawing has no clear orientation; McAndrew and Wright worked from all sides of the paper, turning it as they went. The busy tangle of directional lines plots the flow of galleries and the location of the Exhibition Usonian House that was to be built in the Museum's garden. Plate 2 is a blueprint showing the plans of both the first and the second floor, drawn by McAndrew, who had studied architecture and was a fine draftsman. McAndrew drew on the blueprint, altering it according to his conversations with Wright.

Plates 3 and 4 are drawings related to Wright's designs for display stands and model bases. The remainder of the plates focus on the Exhibition Usonian House, which Wright intended to construct in the Museum's Sculpture Garden. This ultimately unbuilt project was modeled on the Herbert Jacobs House (Madison, 1936–37), designed by Wright for a Wisconsin newspaper reporter and his wife, Katherine. Construction of the Exhibition House was to cost just $5,500, a reasonable sum even then; Wright believed that his design would make well-planned housing affordable to all. It incorporated advanced concepts, including an L-shaped plan, in-floor heating, and hollow-core walls that were identical inside and out. For the Museum Wright retitled his design "Exhibition Usonian House," indicating its place within his larger concepts of Broadacre City and Usonia, a coinage Wright borrowed from the nineteenth-century author Samuel Butler. Usonia was Wright's utopian vision for the Americas. Here, Broadacre City would replace the condensed, upward thrust of American urbanism of the time; it would be be decentralized, low-rise, and integrated into the surrounding landscape, and the Usonian House would be its individual living unit. Broadacre City featured prominently in the exhibition, and the Exhibition Usonian House was an integral part of the exhibition's design. McAndrew and Wright even discussed the possibility of touring not only the exhibition but, remarkably, the house itself, which they considered making fully portable, so that it could be easily disassembled and rebuilt.

—WK

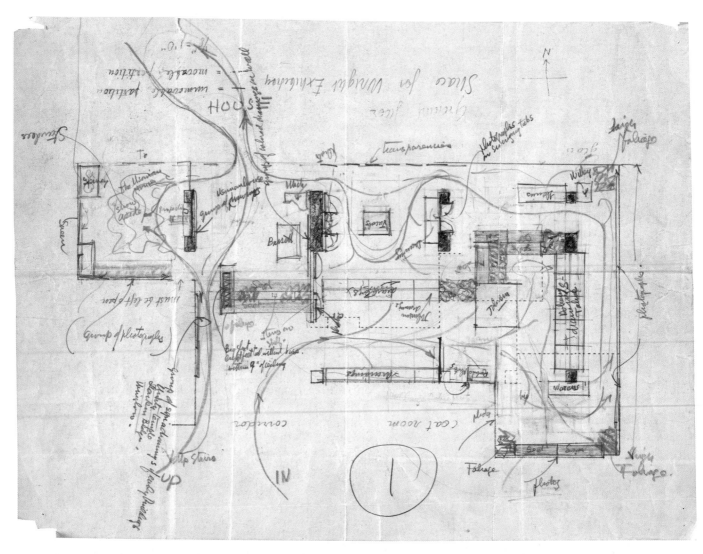

1. Frank Lloyd Wright and John McAndrew. Installation plan for the first floor of the exhibition
Frank Lloyd Wright: American Architect, The Museum of Modern Art, November 12, 1940–January 5, 1941.
Pencil and color pencil on printed paper, 12 x 16" (30.5 x 40.6 cm).
Department of Architecture and Design Study Collection, The Museum of Modern Art, New York

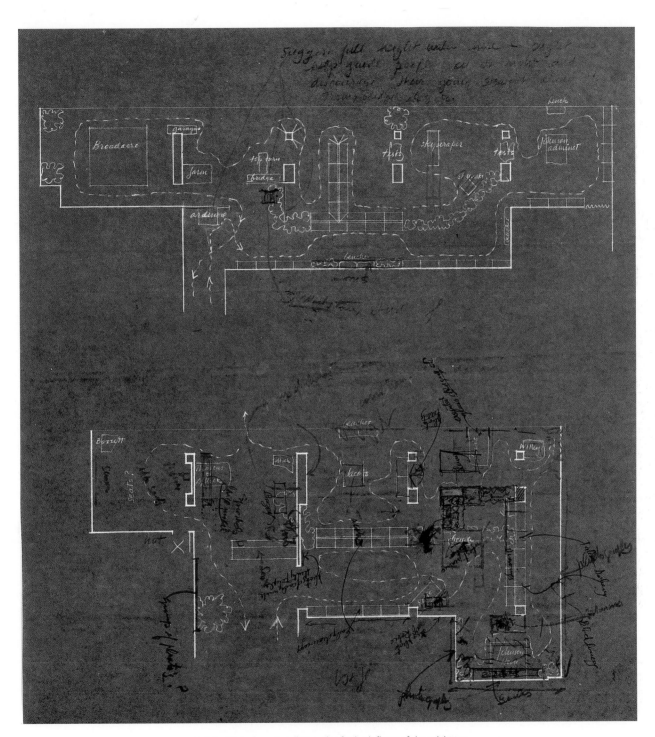

2. John McAndrew. Installation plan for both floors of the exhibition
Frank Lloyd Wright: American Architect. Blueprint, 18⅝ x 17" (47.3 x 43.2 cm).
Frank Lloyd Wright Foundation

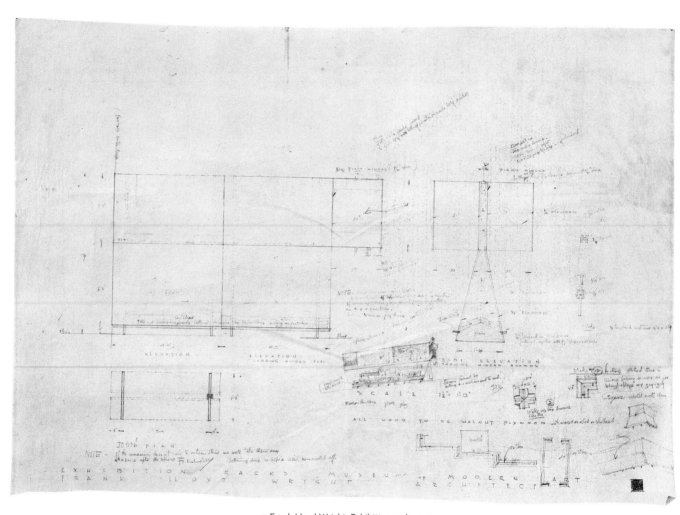

3. Frank Lloyd Wright. Exhibition racks. 1940.
Pencil on tracing paper, 25¼ x 36¼" (64.1 x 92.1 cm). Frank Lloyd Wright Foundation

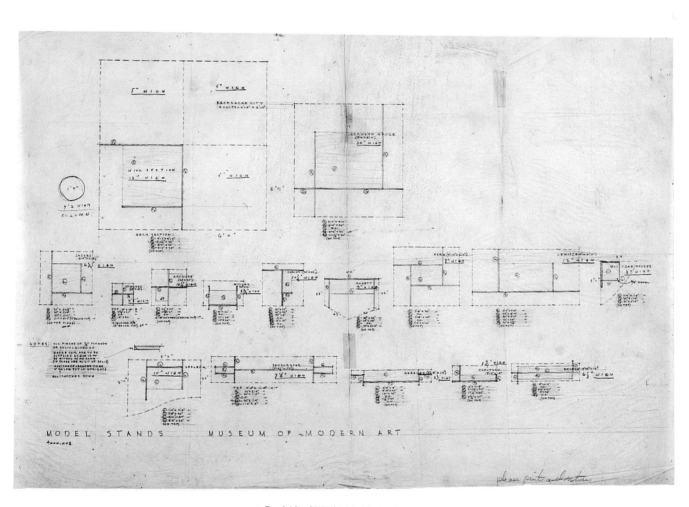

4. Frank Lloyd Wright. Model stands. 1940.
Pencil on tracing paper, 24 x 36" (61 x 91.4 cm). Frank Lloyd Wright Foundation

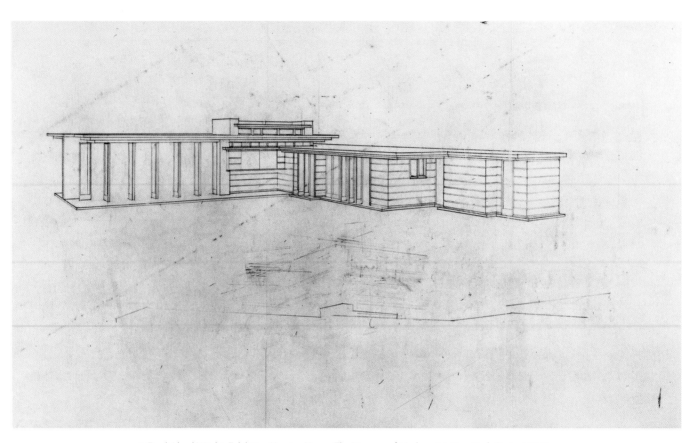

5. Frank Lloyd Wright. Exhibition Usonian House, The Museum of Modern Art, New York. Project, 1940.
Perspective and elevation. Pencil on tracing paper, 13 x 22⅜" (33 x 56.8 cm). Frank Lloyd Wright Foundation

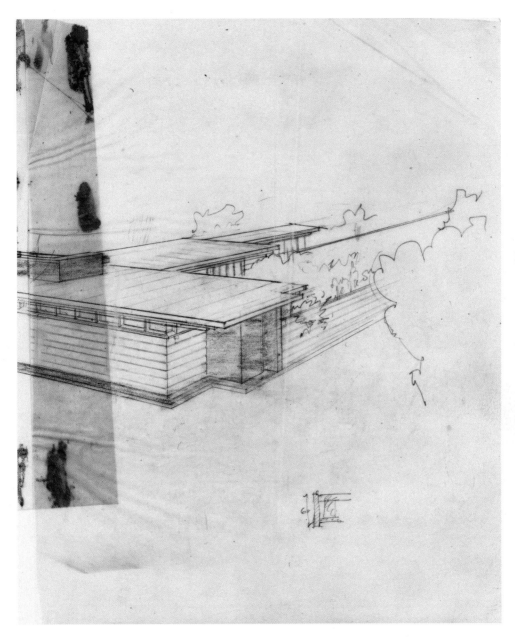

6. Frank Lloyd Wright. Exhibition Usonian House, The Museum of Modern Art, New York. Project, 1940.
Perspective. Pencil on tracing paper, 16⅛ x 13¾" (41 x 34.9 cm). Frank Lloyd Wright Foundation

7. Frank Lloyd Wright. Exhibition Usonian House, The Museum of Modern Art, New York. Project, 1940.
Cutaway perspective. Pencil on tracing paper, 16³⁄₄ x 36¹⁄₄" (42.6 x 92.1 cm). Frank Lloyd Wright Foundation

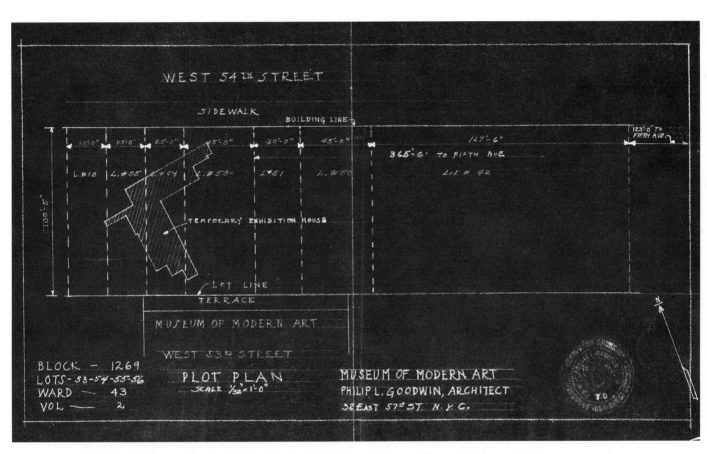

8. Philip L. Goodwin. Plot plan for Frank Lloyd Wright's Exhibition Usonian House, The Museum of Modern Art, 1940.
Blueprint, 8 3/8 x 14" (21.3 x 35.6 cm). Department of Architecture and Design Study Collection, The Museum of Modern Art, New York

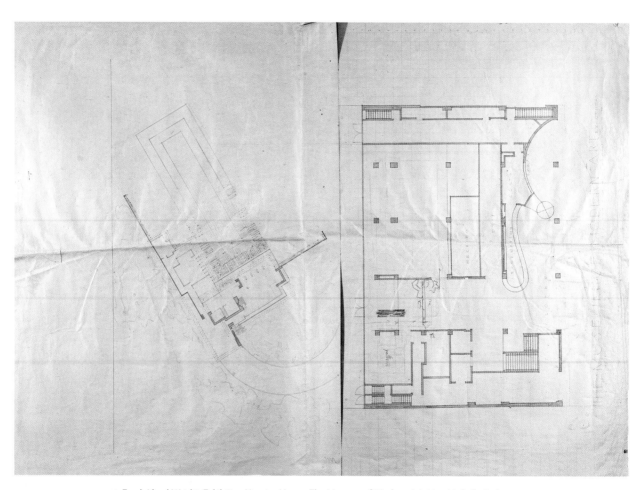

9. Frank Lloyd Wright. Exhibition Usonian House, The Museum of Modern Art, New York. Project, 1940.
Plot plan. Pencil on tracing paper, 29 1/8 x 35 3/4" (74 x 90.8 cm). Frank Lloyd Wright Foundation

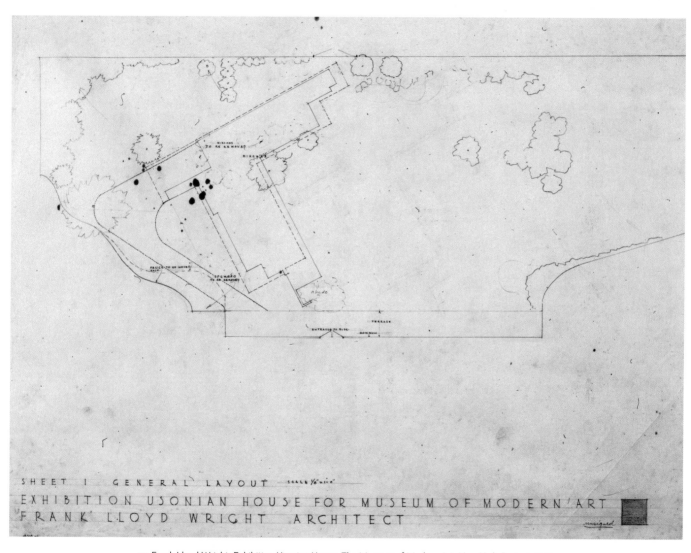

SHEET 1 GENERAL LAYOUT   SCALE ⅛"=1'-0"

EXHIBITION USONIAN HOUSE FOR MUSEUM OF MODERN ART
FRANK LLOYD WRIGHT ARCHITECT

10. Frank Lloyd Wright. Exhibition Usonian House, The Museum of Modern Art, New York. Project, 1940.
Site plan. Pencil on tracing paper, 26⅝ x 36¼" (67.6 x 92.1 cm). Frank Lloyd Wright Foundation

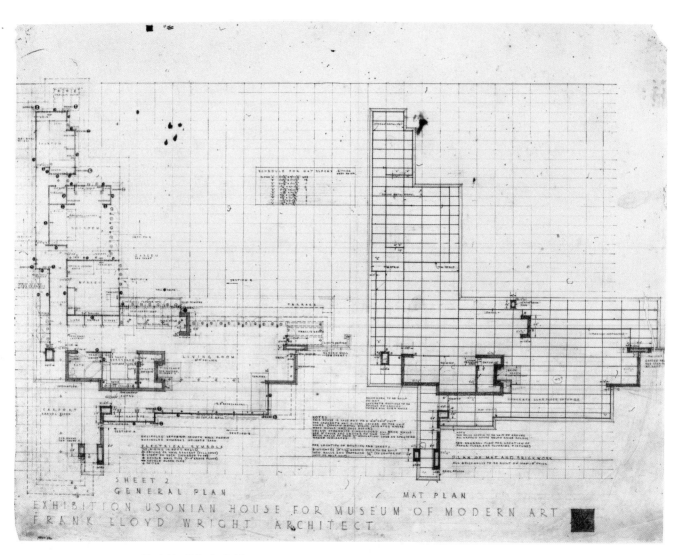

11. Frank Lloyd Wright. Exhibition Usonian House, The Museum of Modern Art, New York. Project, 1940.
General plan and mat plan. Pencil on tracing paper, 28⅛ x 36¼" (71.4 x 92.1 cm). Frank Lloyd Wright Foundation

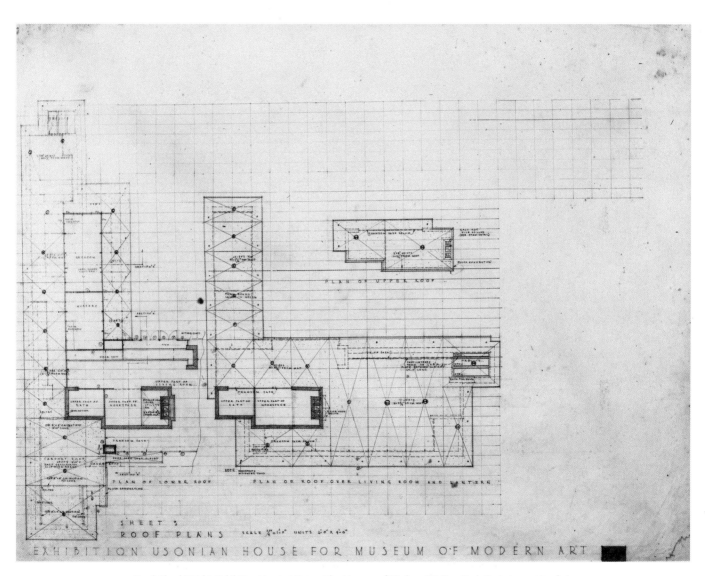

12. Frank Lloyd Wright. Exhibition Usonian House, The Museum of Modern Art, New York. Project, 1940. Roof plans.
Pencil on tracing paper, 29½ x 36¼" (74.9 x 92.1 cm). Frank Lloyd Wright Foundation

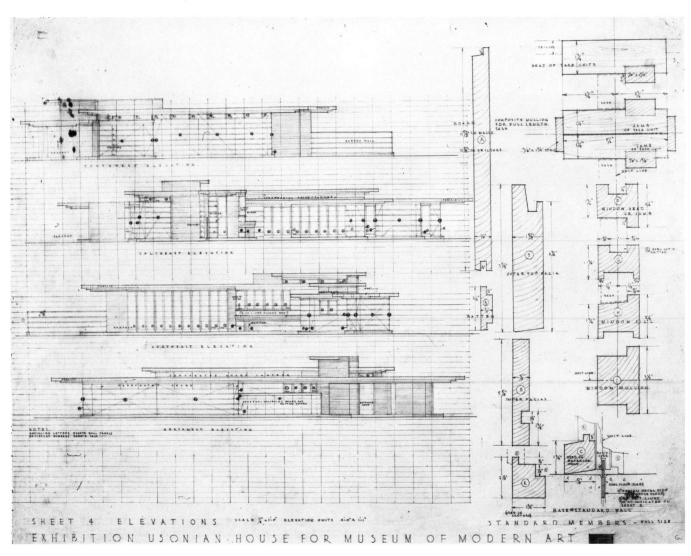

13. Frank Lloyd Wright. Exhibition Usonian House, The Museum of Modern Art, New York. Project, 1940.
Elevations and details. Pencil on tracing paper, 29⅛ x 36¼" (74 x 92.1 cm). Frank Lloyd Wright Foundation

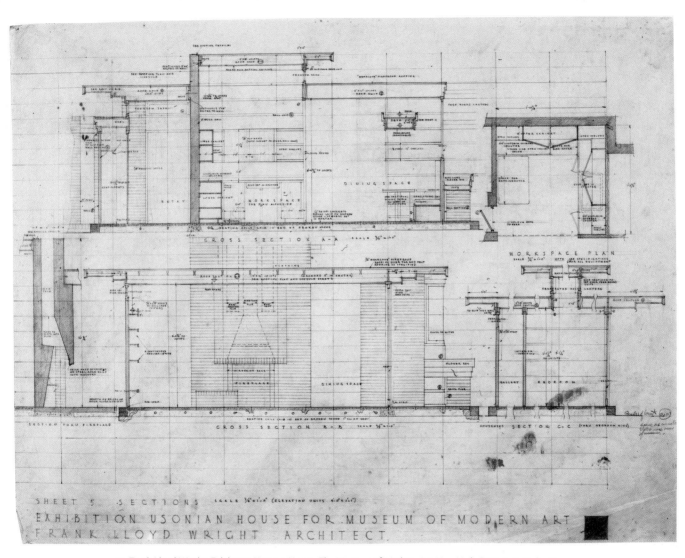

14. Frank Lloyd Wright. Exhibition Usonian House, The Museum of Modern Art, New York. Project, 1940. Sections.
Pencil on tracing paper, 28⅝ x 36¼" (72.7 x 92.1 cm). Frank Lloyd Wright Foundation

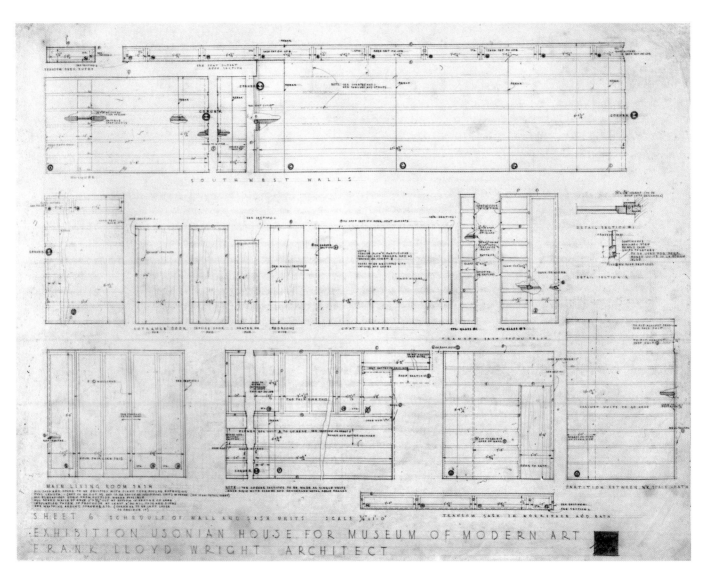

15. Frank Lloyd Wright. Exhibition Usonian House, The Museum of Modern Art, New York. Project, 1940.
Schedule of wall and sash units. Pencil on tracing paper, 28⅝ x 36¼" (72.7 x 92.1 cm). Frank Lloyd Wright Foundation

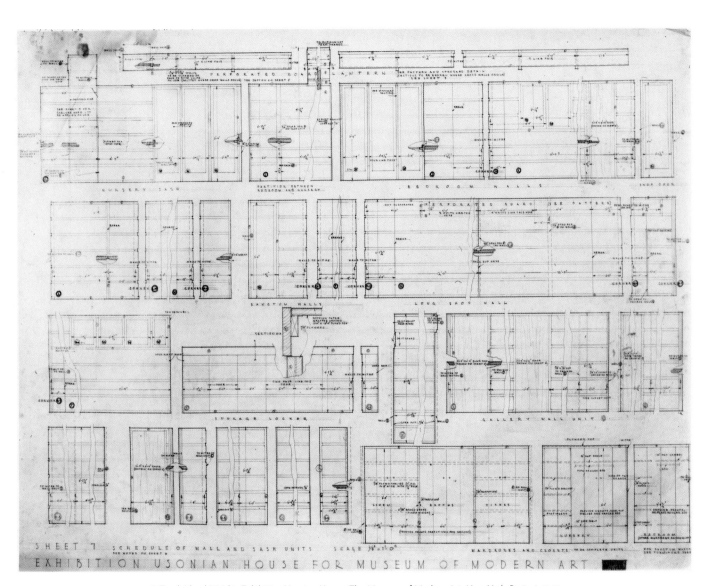

16. Frank Lloyd Wright. Exhibition Usonian House, The Museum of Modern Art, New York. Project, 1940.
Schedule of wall and sash units. Pencil on tracing paper, 29⅝ x 36¼" (74.6 x 92.1 cm). Frank Lloyd Wright Foundation

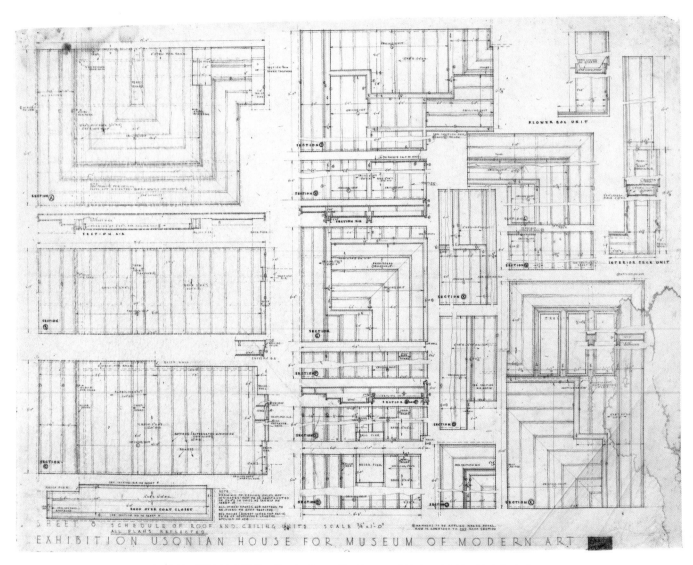

17. Frank Lloyd Wright. Exhibition Usonian House, The Museum of Modern Art, New York. Project, 1940.
Schedule of roof and ceiling units. Pencil on tracing paper, 29 x 36" (73.7 x 91.4 cm). Frank Lloyd Wright Foundation

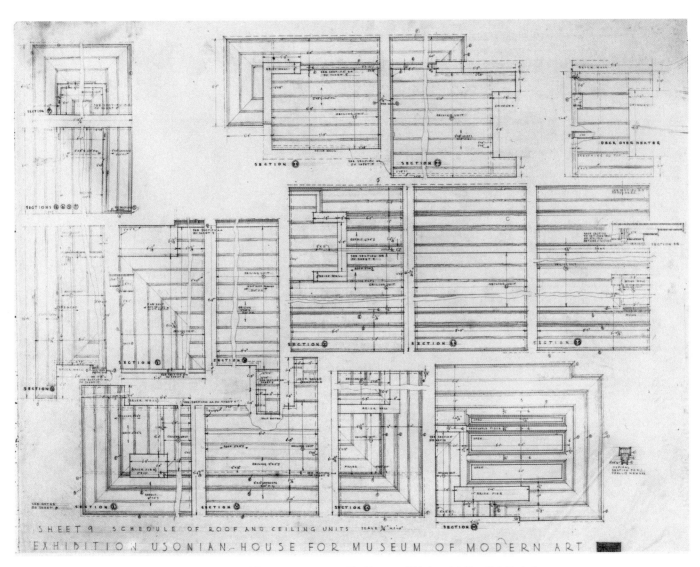

18. Frank Lloyd Wright. Exhibition Usonian House, The Museum of Modern Art, New York. Project, 1940.
Schedule of roof and ceiling units. Pencil on tracing paper, 29⅛ x 35¼" (74 x 89.5 cm). Frank Lloyd Wright Foundation

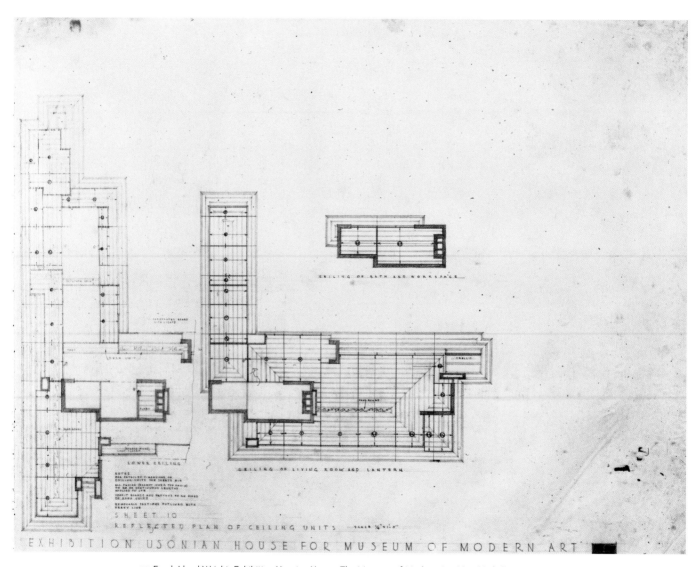

19. Frank Lloyd Wright. Exhibition Usonian House, The Museum of Modern Art, New York. Project, 1940.
Reflected plan of ceiling units. Pencil on tracing paper, 29¼ x 35⅞" (74.3 x 91.1 cm). Frank Lloyd Wright Foundation

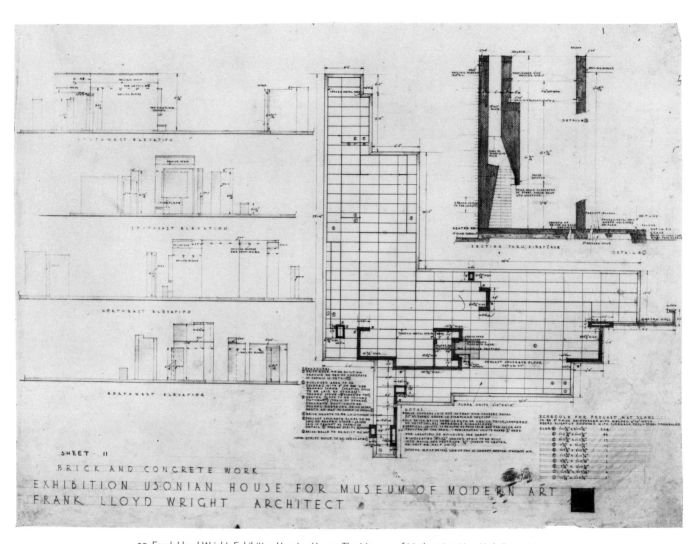

20. Frank Lloyd Wright. Exhibition Usonian House, The Museum of Modern Art, New York. Project, 1940.
Elevations, plan, and section of brick and concrete work.
Pencil on tracing paper, 26¼ x 35⅞" (66.7 x 91.1 cm). Frank Lloyd Wright Foundation

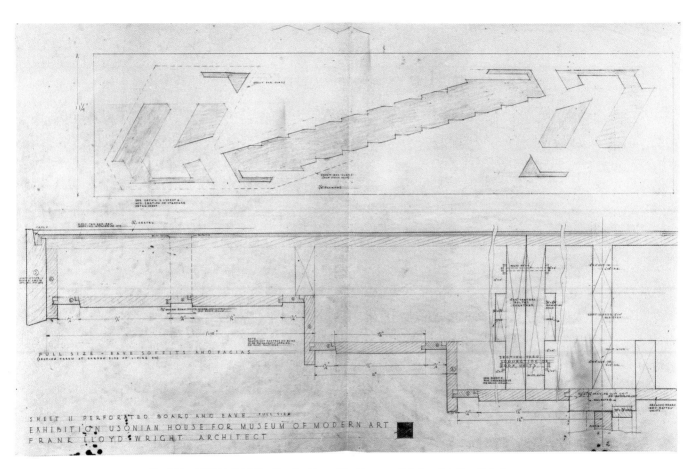

21. Frank Lloyd Wright. Exhibition Usonian House, The Museum of Modern Art, New York. Project, 1940.
Perforated board and eave (details). Pencil on tracing paper, 34 x 54¼" (86.4 x 137.8 cm). Frank Lloyd Wright Foundation

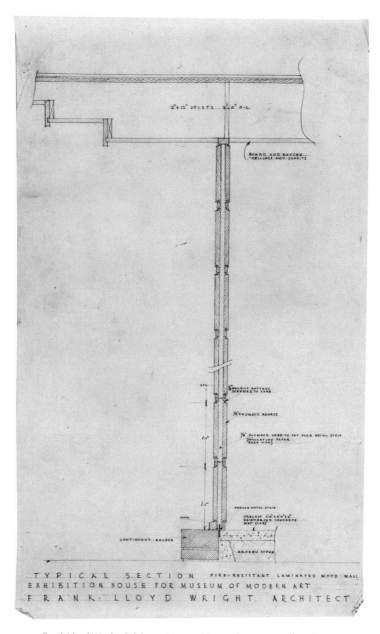

22. Frank Lloyd Wright. Exhibition Usonian House, The Museum of Modern Art,
New York. Project, 1940. Typical section. Pencil on tracing paper,
30⅛ x 18" (76.5 x 45.7 cm). Frank Lloyd Wright Foundation

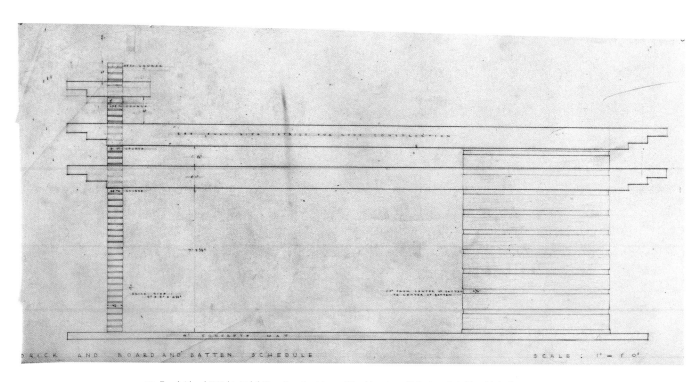

23. Frank Lloyd Wright. Exhibition Usonian House, The Museum of Modern Art, New York. Project, 1940.
Brick and board and batten schedule. Pencil on tracing paper, 16³/₄ x 34⁵/₈" (42.6 x 87.3 cm). Frank Lloyd Wright Foundation

APPENDIX

Introduction

This appendix contains five documents from The Museum of Modern Art Archives relating to *Frank Lloyd Wright: American Architect*. The first is the "Exhibition Outline," drawn up by John McAndrew and developed with Wright as a plan for the show's contents and structure. The first floor, organized in sections around the theme "Reforming the House," was to demonstrate how Wright's vision of organic architecture differed from traditional housing, and was to culminate in the Exhibition Usonian House that Wright designed for the Museum's garden. The second floor was to be organized by material and to display much of Wright's public work. The exhibition roughly followed the outline, including on the second floor several models relating to Broadacre City, Wright's ideal urban plan.

The second document, "Illustrations," seems to be the list of plates intended for the catalogue, and offers insight into which of Wright's buildings were considered important enough to warrant reproduction. The word "cuts" probably refers to the number of images to be sent to the printer: where we see, for example, one cut for four portraits, those portraits would presumably have been "ganged"—laid out as they were to appear on the page and made into one image for the printer, a cheaper method than asking the printer to make four separate reproductions. There is no indication as to the meaning of the asterisks.

The third and fourth documents list the architectural models included in the exhibition. The first of this pair includes brief descriptions of each project, presumably written by McAndrew, and lists the models in the order in which they appeared in the Museum. The second list clarifies which models appeared on which floor. Headed "MODELS, PANELS, etc. to be packed and returned to: Mr. Frank Lloyd Wright," it includes other exhibition materials besides architectural models. The model of the Robie House, which appears on List 1 but not on List 2, belonged to the Museum, so was not returned to Wright.

All of these sections are transcriptions of individual documents in the Archives—copied as they appear in these functional writings, with no attempt to correct dates, names, or other spellings. The final item in the Appendix, however, is not a transcription but an amalgam of several different documents such as registrar's receipts, the only records of the materials present in the Museum for the exhibition. The exhibition had no formal checklist; instead, installing in haste, Wright, his assistants, and McAndrew picked and chose on the spot from the hundreds of drawings, photographs, and photostats sent to the Museum. We do not know for certain, then, the show's exact contents, but we publish this imprecise catalogue in the interest of providing as much information as possible on *Frank Lloyd Wright: American Architect*. It is likely to be more inclusive than the exhibition was, but it may help to demonstrate what both Wright and the Museum considered the definitive objects of his oeuvre circa 1940.

—WK

EXHIBITION OUTLINE

First Floor
Reforming the House

> (illustrated by photos, plans, drawings and models of houses from the earliest through the newest) * means picture in the exhibition

points to be stressed: the human approach

> simplification
>
> the open plan
>
> new forms, plastic composition
>
> relation to nature
>
> ↓
>
> ORGANIC ARCHITECTURE

1. The Human Approach

Sympathetic study and understanding of the daily needs of the inhabitants is the basis of the house plan.

> Show on drawings of plans how the *space is organized for convenience* and comfort. Plan-diagrams of different use-zones (sleeping, eating and cooking, etc., etc.) shown with different colored tones, and with circulation routes dotted in with colored arrows. (perhaps this is a good place for the Zoned House)
>
> * 1 early house plan—Roberts?
> * 1 middle period plan—Millard?
> * 1 very recent plan

2. Simplification

> "5 lines instead of 3 is stupidity
> 9 pounds instead of 5 is obesity."
>
> Compare an early FLLW house with an average contemporary
>
> > * Cheney House and its neighbor
> > * plan of simple early house and confused contemporary, point out elimination of useless elements
> >
> > > a. no unnecessary walls dividing into compartments
> > > b. no space wasted in corridors and vestibules
> > > c. etc., etc.
> >
> > leading up to the
> >
> > * Bassett House, *one space articulated for use*. This will lead directly into 3.

3. The Open Plan

Repeat *One Space Articulated for Use* and show its evolution in FLLW

    * Winslow, * Heller, * Susan Dana, * D. D. Martin, * Coonley, * Jones,

    * Kaufman, *** etc.—plans emphasizing the main living-space (a tone

      shaded over everything else). Sequence of plans to show development.

Statement of how this invention of FLLW has passed into modern architecture

all over the world, and has become a fundamental of sound modern planning

    THE OPEN PLAN GIVES NEW SPACE FOR LIVING

    **** big photos of spacious interiors

    EVEN IN SMALL HOUSES

    *** other interior photos

Living demands are the basis of plan and of space organization, and these are

the basis of—

4. New Forms

Given physical form, the living space (which has been evolved from a study of the family's needs as shown) becomes a new kind of architecture

    * Willets House—date big

The new house does not look like the old house, but the change is not one of mere

"style" or "fashion," but the inevitable result of new thinking

Show sequence from:

    * no attic, to

    * low roof, to

    * flat roof

from * no cellar, to

    * low base, to

    * flat concrete mat

from * single guillotine window cut into heavy wall, to

    * casement, to

    * group of casements, to

    * band of windows, to

    * windows all over as in concrete block houses, to

    * walls of glass—one of the newest houses

plane surfaces

    ** early

    ** late

Synthesis of these and similar elements into one unified

PLASTIC COMPOSITION

    Form is organized for use, and *at the same time* is organized into

    plastic composition

      2 models   }   let these speak for

      *** several enlargements   themselves

5. Relation to Nature
>   *** about 10 fine photographs with short titles showing a variety
>   of adaptation to natural settings (* Prairie, * Millard, * Tahoe, * San
>   Marcos, * Taliesin in the Desert, * Kaufmann, * Oboler, etc., etc.)

Then a brief statement of *ORGANIC ARCHITECTURE* summing up what has gone before and leading on to the house in the garden

Second Floor

Recapitulation of the principles of Organic Architecture, and a new statement of its inseparable relation to construction and materials, ending up with the heading—

>   IN THE NATURE OF MATERIALS

Divide exhibition material on this floor into groups—each group showing the character of one material—

>   For example *Concrete*
>   >   show variety of handling in important buildings and projects
>   >   arranged in approximate chronological order
>   >   * Unity Church
>   >   * Imperial Hotel
>   >   * Millard and original Jones scheme
>   >   * St. Marks (and Temple Heights?)
>   >   * Johnson (and Capitol-Journal)
>   >   * Kaufmann & Sturges
>   >   * Kansas City Church?
>   Similar arrangements for Wood
>   >   >   Masonry
>   >   >   Glass   * Luxfer Prism
>   >   >   >   * Ribbon windows in prairie house
>   >   >   >   * Fenestration in a concrete block house
>   >   >   >   * St. Marks
>   >   >   >   * Insurance Skyscraper
>   >   >   >   * Johnson Administration
>   >   Metal, etc
>   >   etc., etc.

A short summation—stressing that Form depends on Use and Materials, but has to be organized into a plastic design by the architect. Result is Organic Architecture.

All these principles must act together in a fine building. This is even more important in a whole community. Broadacre City and auxiliary models in last two bays of 2nd floor.

ILLUSTRATIONS

cuts	page	illustrations
1	1	4 Portraits
3	2–3	C. H. McAfee project for house, Kenilworth, Ill. 1894
		W. H. Winslow House, River Forest, Ill. 1894
3*	4–5	Own studio, Oak Park, Ill., 1895
		Warren Hickox house, Kankakee, Ill., 1900
4	6–7	Frank Thomas house, Oak Park, Ill., 1901
		Arthur Heurtley house, Oak Park, Ill., 1902
		Prairie house, Ladies Home Journal project, 1901
		Ward W. Willits house, Highland Park, Ill. 1902
4	8–9	E. A. Gilmore house, Madison, Wis., 1908
		W. R. Heath house, Buffalo, N.Y., 1904–5
		D. D. Martin house, Buffalo, N.Y., 1904
		A. P. Johnson house, Lake Delavan, Wis., 1905
4	10–11	Alex Davidson house, Buffalo, N.Y., 1908
		Frank J. Baker house, Wilmette, Ill., 1909
		Oscar Steffens house, Chicago, Ill., 1909
		Avery Coonley house, Riverside, Ill., 1907–10
4	12–13	Avery Coonley house, Riverside, Ill., 1907–10
		Avery Coonley playhouse, Riverside, Ill., 1912
5	14–15	Unity Church, Oak Park, Ill., 1905–7
		Administration Bldg., Larkin Co., Buffalo, N.Y., 1904–5
3	16–17	Project for own house, Florence, Italy, 1910
		Como Orchard Summer Colony (partially constructed)
		Bitter Root Mts., Mont., 1900–09
		Midway Gardens, Chicago, Ill., 1913–4
2	18–19	Taliesin III, Spring Green, Wis., 1925
4	20–1	Taliesin III, Spring Green, Wis., 1925

2*   22-23   Mrs. George Millard house, Pasadena, Cal., 1921 ext. & int.

2*   24-25   Richard Lloyd Jones house, Tulsa, Okla., 1931
                          San Marcos in the Desert, project, Chandler, Ariz., 1929

2*   26-27   Tahoe Summer Colony, Lake Tahoe, Cal., 1923
                          St. Mark's in the Bowery, N.Y.C., 1920

3   28-29   Edgar Kaufmann house, Bear Run, Pa., 1937
                          "   " guest house, Bear Run, Pa., 1939

3*   30-31   Herbert Jacobs house, Madison, Wis., 1937
                          Suntop Homes, Ardmore, Pa., 1939

2*   32-3   Dr. Paul R. Hanna house, Palo Alto, Cal., 1938
                          George D. Sturges house, Los Angeles, Cal., 1939

4   34-5   James B. Christie house, Bernardsville, N.J., in prep. 1940
                          Gregor Affleck house, Bloomfield Hills, Mich., " " 1940
                          Bernard Schwartz house, Two Rivers, Wis., 1940
                          Arch Oboler house, Los Angeles, Cal., in prep. 1940

2   36-7   Taliesin West, Phoenix, Ariz., 1938-40
                          S. C. Johnson Co., Racine, Wis., 1937 int. & ext.

2   40   Johnson Co. & Taliesin III

MODELS IN THE ORDER OF THEIR APPEARANCE IN THE EXHIBITION, FRANK LLOYD WRIGHT, AMERICAN ARCHITECT

(beginning at left on first floor and continuing in same order on second floor)

PRESS BUILDING, San Francisco, 1911. Project for a concrete skyscraper more modern in design than any skyscraper yet built at the time.

ROBIE HOUSE, Woodlawn Avenue, Chicago, 1908. Perhaps the masterpiece of the "Prairie Houses"—typical in its low lines and continuous bands of windows.

"WINGSPREAD," Herbert Johnson Cottage near Racine, Wisconsin, 1938. The latest and largest of the "Prairie Houses."

MARCUS HOUSE, A project for Dallas, Texas, 1935. 4 bold arms support a colossal awning against the Texas sun.

FIRST DESIGN FOR A HOUSE FOR DEAN MALCOM WILLEY, Minneapolis, Minn., 1933. A comfortable low-cost house of wood construction.

"GLENLLOYD," Lloyd Lewis House, Libertyville, Illinois, 1940 (now in construction)

SYDNEY BAZETT HOUSE, Hillsborough, California, 1940. The whole plan is based on clusters of hexagons, like a honeycomb.

A DEVELOPMENT OF 40 ACRES for eight professors from Michigan State Teachers College, East Lansing, Michigan. A community of "Usonian Type" houses all of moderate cost.

HERBERT JACOBS HOUSE, Madison, Wisconsin, 1937. The first "Usonian" House and one of the most famous of all the houses—$5,500.

TOWER FOR ST. MARK'S-IN-THE-BOUWERIE, New York, 1924. A skyscraper of copper and glass.

SUNTOP HOMES, Ardmore, Pa., 1939. Brick and stone quadruple dwelling, each house renting for $55 a month.

MARTIN PENCE HOUSE, Honolulu, 1938 (project). Cylinders of laminated plywood, constructed like old-fashioned cheese-boxes.

ADMINISTRATION BUILDING FOR S. C. JOHNSON CO., Racine, Wisconsin, 1938. In the main hall stand the famous "dendriform" columns of reinforced concrete—daring and surprisingly slender (9″ diameter at bottom, 35′ high).

SECTION OF COLUMN (at base) from the Johnson Administration Building

GREGOR AFFLECK HOUSE, Bloomfield Hills, Michigan, 1940 (now in construction). Brick and wood, with living room and terrace thrust boldly over a pool.

SAN MARCOS WATER GARDENS, Chandler, Arizona, 1929. Project for a group of tourist cabins. Wood and canvas construction for rainless climate.

BROADACRE CITY. The model of the general scheme for an ideal decentralized city is supplemented by the following detail models at larger scale:

Garage Concentration for minimum houses

Integrated farm unit

"Top turn" highway intersection

Highway intersection

MODELS, PANELS, ETC. to be packed and returned to:

Mr. Frank Lloyd Wright
Taliesin
Spring Green
Wisconsin

On First Floor

Press Building, San Francisco (skyscraper of reinforced concrete)
"Wingspread" Herbert Johnson Cottage (near Racine, Wisconsin)
Marcus House (a project for Dallas, Texas)
First Design for a House for Dean Malcolm Willey, Minneapolis
"Glenlloyd" Lloyd Lewis House, Libertyville, Illinois
Sydney Bazett House, Hillsborough, California
A Development of 40 Acres for Eight Professors from Michigan State Teachers College,
        East Lansing, Michigan
Herbert Jacobs House, Madison, Wisconsin
Concrete block
Three panels with lettering
Laminated wall section—Jacobs House

On Second Floor

Broadacre City
Broadacre City—Garage Concentration for Minimum Houses
Broadacre City—Integrated Farm Unit
Broadacre City—"Top Turn" highway intersection
Broadacre City—Highway Intersection
Gregor Affleck House, Bloomfield Hills, Michigan
Section of Column (at base) from Johnson Administration Building
Administration Building for S. C. Johnson Co., Racine, Wisconsin
Martin Pence House, Honolulu
Suntop Homes, Ardmore, Pennsylvania
San Marcos Water Gardens, Chandler, Arizona
Tower for St. Mark's-in-the-Bouwerie, N.Y.
Panel: "A New Freedom"
Panel: "Organic Architecture"
Panel: Over doorway "Principle is the only safe..."
Panel: Over doorway "Broadacre City"
Perforated Board—Rosenbloom House

FRANK LLOYD WRIGHT, AMERICAN ARCHITECT: CATALOGUE OF THE EXHIBITION

This catalogue is based on four documents prepared by the office of Dorothy Dudley, Museum Registrar:

"PHOTOGRAPHS to be packed and returned to: Mr. Frank Lloyd Wright . . . "

"DRAWINGS, PHOTOSTATS, PHOTOGRAPHS, etc. to be packed and returned to: Mr. Frank Lloyd Wright . . . " (six pages)

"DRAWINGS, PHOTOSTATS, PHOTOGRAPHS, etc. to be packed and returned to: Mr. Frank Lloyd Wright . . . " (three pages)

"PROJECT ORDER NO 620. MODELS, PANELS, etc. to be packed and returned to: Mr. Frank Lloyd Wright . . . "

In addition, it incorporates the contents of the two lists of models given earlier in the Appendix, and three documents listing photographs only:

"BOSTON PHOTOGRAPHS TO BE USED IN FLW SHOW"

"NEW TWENTY INCH ENLARGEMENTS IN WRIGHT SHOW"

"TWENTY INCH ENLARGEMENTS MADE FOR THE FRANK LLOYD WRIGHT SHOW"

All of these documents lie in the Registrar Exhibition Files, Exh. #114, The Museum of Modern Art Archives, New York.

Some of the lists were clearly compiled in advance of the exhibition, others during it or in preparation for its closing. Accordingly, many items logically appear on more than one list, often—but not always—with enough accompanying information to identify the overlap. At the same time, given the circumstances in which the show was installed, the lists themselves are certainly incomplete; they make no reference, for example, to color transparencies known to have been on display. They are also vague, describing the materials in highly various degrees of detail. The catalogue, then, should be considered a careful but inevitably imprecise attempt to arrive at something that we do not believe ever existed: a complete and accurate list of the materials present in the Museum for the exhibition. Even were such a list possible, it would not reflect the contents of the exhibition exactly, since more arrived in the Museum than was actually put on display.

The projects are organized chronologically by their year of completion, then alphabetically under each year. The project names used are those recognized in the Frank Lloyd Wright scholarship. In listings of drawings, where the documents identify the medium it follows the entry in parentheses. In listings of photographs, where the documents identify the photographer the name follows the entry in parentheses. Other identifying information for individual objects and images is given a consistent format and sequence but otherwise supplied as it appears in the documents. The catalogue is followed by a list of items for which too little information is supplied to identify the project to which they belong.

1893

William H. Winslow House, River Forest, Ill.
  Drawings
    Perspective and plan
  Photographs
    One unspecified

1894

A. McAfee House, Kenilworth, Ill. Project
  Drawings
    Perspective (watercolor)

1895

Francis Apartments, Chicago, Ill.
  Drawings
    Detail: entrance
    Perspective: main entrance

1896

Luxfer Prism Office Building, Chicago, Ill.
Project
  Drawings
    Study

1900

Warren Hickox House, Kankakee, Ill.
  Photographs
    One unspecified

1901

Lexington Terrace Apartments, Chicago, Ill.
Project
  Drawings
    Perspective: court
    Perspective: development
    Plan (mounted print)

1902

Ward W. Willits House, Highland Park, Ill.
  Photographs
    One unspecified

1903

Railway Stations, Chicago Suburbs, Ill.
  Drawings
    One unspecified

1904

Larkin Company Workmen's House, Buffalo,
N.Y. Project
  Drawings
    Two elevations and plans

Darwin D. Martin House, Buffalo, N.Y.
  Photographs
    One unspecified

Wood and Plaster House, Highland Park, Ill.
Project
  Drawings
    Perspective (ink)
    One unspecified

J. A. Scudder Lodge, Desbarats, Ont. Project
  Drawings
    Perspective (ink)

H. J. Ullmann House, Oak Park, Ill. Project
  Drawings
    Plan (ink)

1905

Thomas P. Hardy House, Racine, Wisc.
  Drawings
    Perspective

A. P. Johnson House, Lake Delavan, Wisc.
  Photographs
    One unspecified

Unity Temple, Oak Park, Ill.
  Drawings
    Plan and perspective
  Photographs
    One unspecified

Yahara Boathouse, Madison, Wisc. Project
  Drawings
    Perspective

1906

Larkin Company Administration Building, Buffalo, N.Y.

Drawings

    Decorative detail

    Southeast elevation

    Southwest elevation

    East elevation and plan

    South elevation and plan

    Perspective

    Plan

Photographs

    One interior

    One unspecified

Elizabeth Stone House, Glencoe, Ill. Project

Drawings

    Perspective (ink)

Burton Westcott House, Springfield, Ohio

Photographs

    One unspecified

1907

Larkin Company Exposition Pavilion, Jamestown, Va.

Drawings

    Perspective and plan (ink and pencil)

F. F. Tomek House, Riverside, Ill.

Drawings

    Perspective (pencil and crayon)

1908

Avery Coonley House, Riverside, Ill.

Drawings

    Window details

Photographs

    Exterior, entrance side

    Two exteriors, garden side

    Exterior, wing of house

    Interior

R. W. Evans House, Chicago, Ill.

Photographs

    One unspecified

E. A. Gilmore House, Madison, Wisc.

Photographs

    One unspecified

Frederick C. Robie House, Chicago, Ill.

Model

Drawings

    Perspective and plan

Photographs

    Exterior

    Two unspecified

1909

Hiram Baldwin House, Kenilworth, Ill.

Photographs

    One unspecified

Bitter Root Inn, Darby, Mont.

Drawings

    Perspective (ink)

Oscar Steffens Cottage, Chicago, Ill.

Drawings

    Perspective

Photographs

    One unspecified (color)

Mrs. Thomas Gale House, Oak Park, Ill.

Drawings

    Perspective (ink)

1910

Frank Lloyd Wright House and Studio, Fiesole, Italy. Project

Drawings

    Perspective (ink and crayon)

1911

Avery Coonley Greenhouse, Riverside Ill. Project

Drawings

    One unspecified

Avery Coonley Kindergarten, Riverside, Ill.
Project
    Drawings
        Elevation

Arthur E. Cutten House, Downer's Grove, Ill.
Project
    Drawings
        Bird's-eye perspective

1911
Sherman M. Booth House, Glencoe, Ill.
    Drawings
        Elevation
        Perspective (color)
        Perspective
        Plan

Lake Geneva Inn, Lake Geneva, Wisc.
    Drawings
        Bird's-eye perspective
    Photographs
        Of rendering

Frank Lloyd Wright House and Studio,
Goethe Street, Chicago, Ill. Project
    Drawings
        One unspecified

1912
Avery Coonley Playhouse, Riverside, Ill.
    Drawings
        Five color perspectives
        Five elevations
        Plan
    Photographs
        One unspecified
        Two unspecified (sepia)

1913
Carnegie Library, Pembroke, Ont. Project
    Drawings
        Perspective (ink)

Midway Gardens, Chicago, Ill.
    Drawings
        Design for tympanum mural
        First sketch, perspective
        Interior: furniture elevations
        Two for railing
        Six sections and elevations
    Photographs
        Four details
        One unspecified

The San Francisco Call Building, San
Francisco, Calif. Project
    Model

1914
Embassy for the U.S.A., Tokyo. Project
    Drawings
        Perspective

Francis W. Little House ("Northome"),
Deephaven, Minn.
    Drawings
        Perspective (ink)

Spaulding Gallery for Japanese Prints,
Boston, Mass.
    Drawings
        Perspective
        Two sections

1915
American System-Built Houses for the
Richards Company
    Drawings
        Fourteen unspecified

Cinema, San Diego, Calif. Project.
    Drawings
        Perspective (watercolor)

1916

Ernest Vosburgh House, Grand Beach, Mich.

Drawings
    Perspective
    Plan

1917

Frederick C. Bogk House, Milwaukee, Wisc.

Drawings
    Two designs for rug
    Sketch: corner window

Stephen M. B. Hunt House, Oshkosh, Wisc.

Photographs
    One unspecified

1920

A. D. German Warehouse, Richland Center,
Wisc.

Drawings
    Perspective (color)

1921

Aline Barnsdall House ("Hollyhock House"),
Los Angeles, Calif.

Drawings
    Bird's-eye perspective
    Perspective: theater
Photographs
    Exterior
    Exterior detail
    Interior with fireplace
    Rendered perspective
    Rendered perspective: theater
    Nine unspecified

1923

Doheny Ranch Resort, Beverly Hills, Calif.
Project

Drawings
    Perspective (color): general view
    General view
    Perspective: house and garage
    Perspective and plan
    Perspective and plan: house

Imperial Hotel, Tokyo, Japan

Drawings
    Analysis of structure
    Construction details
    Two decorations for ladies' parlor
    Detail: banquet hall
    Four elevations
    Foundation plan
    General perspective
    Plan: main floor
    Plan: bathroom
    Plan: temporary annex
    Plan, elevation, and section:
        temporary annex
    Section: bathroom
    Study: gate lodge
Photographs
    Detail: court
    Gate lodge
    Two room interiors
    Temporary annex

Kindergarten and Playhouse for Aline
Barnsdall ("Little Dipper"), Los Angeles, Calif.
Project

Drawings
    Two perspectives
    Plan

Alice Millard House ("La Miniatura"),
Pasadena, Calif.

> Drawings
>> Perspective (color)
>> Plan
> Photographs
>> One unspecified

1924

Charles E. Ennis House, Los Angeles, Calif.

> Drawings
>> Perspective
> Photographs
>> Detail

Samuel Freeman House, Los Angeles, Calif.

> Drawings
>> Bird's-eye perspective
>> Perspective (color)
> Photographs
>> Detail

Lake Tahoe Summer Colony, Lake Tahoe,
Calif. Project

> Drawings
>> Three sketches: cabin
>> Three sketches: barge

Nakoma Country Club, Madison, Wisc. Project

> Drawings
>> Perspective (color)
>> Plan

Phi Gamma Delta Fraternity House, Madison,
Wisc. Project

> Photographs
>> One of perspective drawing

John Storer House, Hollywood, Calif.

> Drawings
>> Perspective
> Photographs
>> One unspecified

Gordon Strong Automobile Objective and
Planetarium, Sugarloaf Mountain, Md. Project

> Drawings
>> Eight sketches

1925

Mrs. Samuel William Gladney House, Fort
Worth, Tex. Project

> Drawings
>> Perspective (color)

National Life Insurance Company Building,
Chicago, Ill. Project

> Drawings
>> Cross-section
>> Elevation
>> Three floor plans
>> Interior: offices
>> Perspective

Taliesin III, Frank Lloyd Wright House and
Studio, Spring Green, Wisc.

> Drawings
>> Work song
>> Three gates
>> Plan
> Photographs
>> Corridor
>> Exterior: detail of main house
>> Exterior: roofs, trees, chimneys
>> Exterior: dining room
>> Garden wall with Buddha (Frank
>> Lloyd Wright)
>> Interior: living room corner
>> Two interiors: living room
>> Living room
>> Three unspecified
>> Roofs
>> Roofs and hills
>> Roofs and terraces
>> Roofs and terraces from roof

1928

Block House for Chandler, Chandler, Ariz.
Project
>Drawings
>>Elevation
>>Perspective
>>Plans
>>One unspecified

Davidson Produce Markets Exhibition
Pavilion, Buffalo, N.Y.
>Drawings
>>Sketches

Rosenwald School for Hampton College,
Hampton, Va. Project
>Drawings
>>Perspective (color)

1929

Ralph and Wellington Cudney House,
Chandler, Ariz. Project
>Drawings
>>Perspective

Elizabeth Noble House, Los Angeles, Calif.
Project
>Drawings
>>Elevation
>>Seven elevations (sepia print)
>>Perspective (sepia print)

Ocotilla Desert Camp, Chandler, Ariz.
>Photographs
>>Two unspecified

San Marcos Water Gardens, Chandler, Ariz.
Project
>Model
>Drawings
>>Elevations
>>Aerial perspective
>>Bird's-eye perspective
>>Perspective (color)
>>Roof plan
>>One unspecified

San Marcos-in-the-Desert Resort, Chandler,
Ariz. Project
>Drawings
>>Sketch: interior of room
>>Perspective (color)
>>Three plans

Mrs. Owen D. Young House, Chandler, Ariz.
Project
>Drawings
>>Perspective
>>Plan

1931

Richard Lloyd Jones House ("Westhope"),
Tulsa, Okla.
>Drawings
>>Perspective (pencil and crayon)
>>Two studies

St. Marks-in-the-Bouwerie Towers, New York,
 N.Y. Project
>Model
>Drawings
>>Two interior perspectives (color)
>>Two exterior perspectives (color)
>>Section and typical floor plans

1932

Capitol Journal Building, Salem, Oreg. Project
>Drawings
>>Floor plan
>>Perspective

Malcolm Willey House #1, Minneapolis, Minn.
Project
>Model
>Drawings
>>Perspective

1933

Malcolm Willey House #2, Minneapolis, Minn.
- Drawings
    - Perspective (color)
- Photographs
    - Two exterior

1934

Chapel for the Newmann Family ("Memorial to the Soil"), Cooksville, Wisc. Project
- Drawings
    - Elevation and plan
    - Two perspectives (color)

1935

Broadacre City. Project
- Models
    - Garage concentration for minimum houses
    - General scheme
    - Highway intersection
    - "Top turn" highway intersection
    - Integrated farm unit
- Three explanatory panels

Stanley Marcus House, Dallas, Tex. Project
- Model
- Drawings
    - Two perspectives
    - Plan

1936

C. H. Hoult House, Wichita, Kans. Project
- Drawings
    - Perspective
    - Perspective (color)

Robert Lusk House, Huron, S.Dak. Project
- Drawings
    - Perspective (color)
    - Perspective (pencil)
    - Plan
    - Plan and perspective

1937

Paul R. and Jean S. Hanna House ("Honeycomb House"), Palo Alto, Calif.
- Drawings
    - Two perspectives
    - Plan
    - Perspective (ink)
- Photographs
    - Dining space (Esther Born)
    - Exterior showing terrace (Esther Born)
    - Exterior showing entrance drive (Esther Born)
    - Exterior from below toward living room (Esther Born)
    - Exterior from road below (Esther Born)
    - Living room with fireplace (Esther Born)
    - Interior with desk detail (Esther Born)
    - One unspecified (Roger Sturtevant)

Herbert Jacobs House, Madison, Wisc.
- Model
- Drawings
    - Plan
    - Perspective
- Photographs
    - Exterior from garden (Roy Peterson)
    - Exterior from street (Frank Lloyd Wright)
    - Exterior: terrace (Roy Peterson)
    - Interior: living space (Roy Peterson)
- Laminated wall section

Edgar J. Kaufmann House ("Fallingwater"), Mill Run, Pa.
- Drawings
    - Perspective (color)
    - Plans and elevations
    - Site and first-floor plan
    - Study for guesthouse

Photographs
    Detail: corner fenestration
    Exterior: entrance detail
    Nine unspecified

Ben Rebhuhn House, Great Neck Estates, N.Y.
    Drawings
        Two unspecified

1938

Royal Jurgenson House, Evanston, Ill. Project
    Drawings
        One unspecified

Charles Manson House, Wausau, Wisc.
    Drawings
        Perspective (color)
        One unspecified

John C. Pew House, Madison, Wisc.
    Drawings
        Perspective
        Two plans
    Photographs
        Three exteriors

Frank Rentz House, Madison, Wisc. Project
    Drawings
        One unspecified

Taliesin West, Frank Lloyd Wright House and Studio, Scottsdale, Ariz.
    Drawings
        Perspective: front
        Perspective: rear
    Photostat
        General plan
    Photographs
        Three unspecified
        Twelve unspecified (Pedro Guerrero)
        Twelve unspecified (Pedro Guerrero?)
        Exterior: mountains in background
        Exterior

Exterior: with afternoon shadows
Exterior: detail of stone wall
Exterior: entrance

1939

Andrew F. H. Armstrong House, Ogden Dunes, Ind.
    Drawings
        One unspecified

Sidney Bazett House, Hillsborough, Calif.
    Model
    Drawings
        Three perspectives
    Photographs
        Two exteriors from below (both Esther Born)
        Exterior from garden court (Esther Born)
        Exterior showing entrance (Esther Born)
        Living room (Esther Born)

L. N. Bell House, Los Angeles, Calif.
    Drawings
        Two unspecified

Erling P. Brauner House, Lansing, Mich. Project
    Drawings
        Two plan and perspectives

Edith Carlson House ("Below Zero"), Superior, Wisc. Project
    Drawings
        Original sketch
        Perspective
        Plan

Crystal Heights, Washington, D. C. Project
    Drawings
        Six unspecified

Joseph Euchtman House, Baltimore, Md.
Drawings
Two unspecified

Goetsch-Winckler House, Okemos, Mich.
Drawings
Plan and perspective
Photographs
Exterior

C. D. Hause House, Lansing, Mich. Project
Drawings
Plan and perspective

Herbert F. Johnson House ("Wingspread"),
Wind Point, Wisc.
Model
Drawings
Ground plan
Perspective (color)
Plan: mezzanine floor
Plot plan
Presentation drawings (color)
Photographs
Interior with fireplace (Samuel
Gottscho)
Seen from distance (Samuel
Gottscho)
Terrace seen through window
(Samuel Gottscho)

S. C. Johnson & Son, Inc., Administration
Building, Racine, Wisc.
Model
Drawings
Penthouse, plan, details of columns
Two perspectives
Perspective (color)
Four plans
Plan, main floor
Section

Photographs
Four column tests
In construction
Five unspecified
One unspecified (Frank Lloyd Wright)
Section of column at base

Lloyd Lewis House ("Glenlloyd"),
Libertyville, Ill.
Model
Drawings
Perspective
Plan

Edgar Maurer House, Los Angeles, Calif.
Project
Drawings
Perspective
Original sketch plan

Sydney Newman House, Lansing, Mich.
Project
Drawings
Plan and perspective

Loren Pope House, Alexandria, Va.
Drawings
Perspective

Stanley Rosenbaum House, Florence,
Alabama
Drawings
Three unspecified
Perforated board

E. A. Smith House ("The Piedmont Pine"),
Piedmont Pines, Calif. Project
Drawings
One unspecified

Bernard Schwartz House, Two Rivers, Wisc.
Drawings
Perspective: exterior
Perspective: living space
Perspective (pencil and sepia crayon)

Perspective (sepia)
First floor plan (pencil and crayon)
Second floor plan (pencil and crayon)
Plans and isometrics
Photographs
One unspecified

Clarence Sondern House, Kansas City, Mo.
Drawings
Perspective
Plot plan

Dr. Ludd M. Spivey House, Fort Lauderdale,
Fla. Project
Drawings
Perspective (color pencil)
Perspective sketch (pencil)
Plan

C. Leigh Stevens House ("Auldbrass"),
Yemassee, S.C.
Drawings
Eight unspecified

George Sturges House, Brentwood Heights,
Calif.
Drawings
Four unspecified
Photographs
Two unspecified (Breeskin)

Suntop Homes, Ardmore, Pa.
Model
Photostats
Four unspecified
Photographs
Three unspecified

Usonia I, Lansing, Mich. Project
Model

C. R. Van Dusen House, Lansing, Mich.
Project
Drawings
Plan and perspective

1940

Gregor Affleck House, Bloomfield Hills, Mich.
Model
Drawings
Two unspecified

Design for jacket of proposed Museum
catalogue
Drawings
One unspecified (ink and crayon)

Community Christian Church, Kansas City, Mo.
Drawings
Two interior perspectives
Two perspectives (sepia)
Main-floor plan
Section A-A auditorium
Section B-B through chancel

Martin Pence House, Hilo, Hawaii. Project
Model
Drawings
Perspective (color)
Two plans
Plan and perspective

In Construction
at the Time of the Exhibition

Florida Southern College, Lakeland, Fla.
Drawings
Three unspecified

Pfeiffer Chapel, Florida Southern College,
Lakeland, Fla.
Drawings
Perspective

Arch Oboler House ("Eaglefeather"), Malibu,
Calif. Project
Drawings
Five unspecified

Rose Pauson House, Phoenix, Ariz.
Drawings
Three unspecified

Unidentified Projects

Abstraction by Robert Mosher

Concrete block

Dress Shop for Oak Park (probably the
Bramson Dress Shop, 1937)
Drawings
Perspective

Dwelling, River Forest, Ill.
Drawings
One unspecified

Garden Restaurant. Project
Drawings
One unspecified

House for the Misses Gerts (presumably a
project related to Wright's clients George
and Walter Gerts)
Photographs
One unspecified (color)

House in Oak Park
Drawings
Perspective study

Two houses
Drawings
Perspective

Ladies Home Journal Houses. N.d.
(presumably either the "Home in a Prairie
Town" or the "Small House with 'Lots of
Room in It,'" both published in *Ladies Home
Journal* in 1901, or the "Fireproof House,"
published in *Ladies Home Journal* in 1907)
Drawings
Plot plan

Ladies Home Journal House. 1900
(presumably either the "Home in a Prairie
Town" or the "Small House with 'Lots of
Room in It'")
Drawings
Perspective (ink and crayon)

Lighting
Drawings
Study

Miyanoshita Hotel
Drawings
Perspective

Three panels with lettering

Prairie Houses
Drawings
Study

Unknown house
Drawings
Perspective

Usonian House
Drawings
Perspective (color)

BIOGRAPHICAL REFERENCE

Since many names referred to in the "Letters and Telegrams" and "Original Manuscripts" sections of the book are less familiar today than they were in 1940, this reference provides brief biographical notes on a selection of the individuals mentioned in those sections.

Abbott, John E. (1908–52): Abbott began work at The Museum of Modern Art as director of the film library. At the time of the Wright exhibition he was Executive Vice-President of the Museum and worked closely with *Stephen C. Clark*, especially on financial matters.

Ashbee, C. R. (1863–1942): British architect, designer, and writer. Influenced by *William Morris* and John Ruskin, Ashbee became an influential member of the English Arts and Crafts movement. He was an early European supporter of Wright's work, visiting the architect during a U.S. lecture tour and writing the text for the 1911 edition of the *Wasmuth* Portfolio.

Asplund, Erik Gunnar (1885–1940): Swedish architect who developed a less functional, more humanly designed vision of Scandinavian modernism. From the neo-classical elements of the Stockholm Public Library (1920–28) to the more overtly modernist design of the Stockholm Exhibition (1930), Asplund's work represented a type of critical regionalism espoused by architects throughout Scandinavia in the 1930s and '40s.

Barnsdall, Louise Aline (1882–1946): Wright designed his first concrete residence, "Hollyhock House" (c. 1916–21), for Aline Barnsdall in Los Angeles. The site was to include a theater and other buildings; the theater was never built, but two additional studios were constructed under the supervision of *Rudolf M. Schindler*.

Barr, Alfred H., Jr. (1902–81): the founding director of The Museum of Modern Art. In January of 1940, he was elected to the Board of Trustees and named vice-president of the Museum. Barr was instrumental in shaping the Museum's collections and the way art was displayed and interpreted in it.

Behrens, Peter (1868–1940): German architect whose A.E.G. Turbine Factory (Berlin, 1908–9) was an icon of early modernism, in part because of its glass curtain walls. *Walter Gropius*, Mies van der Rohe, and *Le Corbusier* all worked in Behrens's studio in Berlin.

Berlage, H. P. (1856–1934): Dutch architect and urban planner. Berlage saw Wright's work during a U.S. lecture tour in 1911, and wrote several articles praising it upon his return to Europe. His own works include the Amsterdam Bourse (1897–1903) and city plans for Amsterdam and Utrecht.

Burnham, Daniel H. (1846–1912): Burnham, in partnership with *John Wellborn Root*, played an important role in the evolution of the Chicago School. Their best-known work includes such designs as the Monadnock Building (Chicago, 1889–91). Burnham was chief of construction for the World's Columbian Exposition (Chicago, 1893), whose architecture and planning demonstrated the classical

Beaux-Arts ideals that later informed his ambitious city plans for Chicago (1909) and others. He was an early mentor to Wright, who called him "Uncle Dan."

Byrne, Frances Barry (1892–1967): an apprentice of Wright's in Oak Park from 1902 to 1908. Byrne subsequently went into partnership with fellow Wright employees *Walter Burly Griffin* and *Andrew Willatzen*, then went on to establish his own practice.

Cheek, Leslie (1908–92): from 1939 to 1942, director of the Baltimore Museum of Art, where he won acclaim for his experimental exhibition designs. In the summer of 1940 *Abby Aldrich Rockefeller* invited Cheek to design an ultimately unrealized exhibition, *For Us the Living*, or "Exhibition X," which was to inform the public of the dangers of Hitler's expansion across Europe.

Clark, Stephen C. (1882–1960): a founding trustee of the Museum. In 1939, when MoMA's newly designed building opened, he was made the first chairman of the board. He worked closely with *John E. Abbott* and *Nelson Aldrich Rockefeller*, who was appointed president of the Museum at the same time.

Clarke, Hervey Parke (1899–1982): an architect of modernist houses at affordable prices, Parke believed that a small house should be designed as such, and not simply modified from older forms devised for larger dwellings. He worked in the San Francisco Bay Area, along with *John Ekin Dinwiddie*, *John Funk*, *Michael Goodman*, Harwell Hamilton Harris, and *William Wilson Wurster*.

de Klerk, Michel (1884–1923): the leader of the Amsterdam School, a group of architects that included *P. L. Kramer* and whose work dominated the government-sponsored housing built in the city between 1915 and 1930. De Klerk's buildings brought innovations to collective dwellings with a richly articulated "expressionist" architecture.

Dinwiddie, John Ekin (1902–59): a student of Wright's who went on to establish an architectural practice in San Francisco with *Eric Mendelsohn*, becoming an advocate of Bay Area Modernism.

Dow, Alden B. (1904–83): under the influence of Wright, with whom he apprenticed in the summer of 1933, Dow developed his "Unit Block" building system. He built over sixty houses in and around Midland, Michigan, and numerous others throughout the United States.

Dudok, W. M. (1884–1974): Dutch architect whose style is embodied in his Hilversum Town Hall (1928–30), in which asymmetrical compositions of rectangular blocks impart a reductive modernism and a sense of monumentality. Dudok's work is often compared with Wright's, although he denied Wright's influence.

Edelmann, John (1852–1900): an architect recognized for his use of ornament and an early mentor of *Louis Sullivan* in aesthetics and design.

Francke, Kuno (1855–1930): a professor of German literature at Harvard from 1884 to 1917. Francke visited Wright's studio in 1908 and encouraged him to visit Germany. Soon after, Wright traveled to Europe, including a stay in Berlin to work on the *Wasmuth* Portfolio.

Funk, John (1908–93): an architect who worked for *William Wilson Wurster* in the mid-1930s and built mainly around San Francisco, becoming a proponent of Bay Area Modernism.

Garnier, Tony (1869–1948): a pioneer of modernist architecture in France, Garnier was one of the first architects, along with *Auguste Perret*, to use reinforced concrete in nonindustrial buildings. His project for the "Cité Industrielle" envisioned an ideal city of the future, similar in scope and intent to Wright's later plan for Broadacre City.

Gill, Irving J. (1870–1936): developed an American modernism before the spread of the International Style in the United States. Influences from the Spanish Colonial architecture of Southern California, extensive use of reinforced concrete, lack of ornament, and clean, white walls distinguished his work from most American architectural practice of the teens and 1920s. He worked briefly alongside Wright for *Louis Sullivan*.

Goodhue, Bertram Grosvenor (1869–1924): built numerous Gothic Revival churches, including three in New York City. Like much of his late work, his monumental Los Angeles Public Library (1926), made from poured concrete, recalls Spanish Colonial, Romanesque, and Byzantine architecture as much as the Gothic.

Goodman, Michael Arthur (1903–91): a Bay Area architect. Besides his early houses, he also built several buildings on the campus of the University of California, Berkeley, where he was a professor of architecture from 1928 to 1971.

Goodwin, Philip L. (1885–1958): as an early advocate of architectural modernism in the United States, Goodwin was asked to design the new, permanent home of The Museum of Modern Art. That West Fifty-third Street building, which he designed with his partner Edward Durell Stone and completed in 1939, was one of the earliest examples of International Style architecture in New York. Goodwin joined the Museum's Board of Trustees in 1931 and was chairman of the Architecture Committee from 1935 to 1940.

Grey, Elmer (1872–1963): an architect who established his practice in Pasadena and built in and around Los Angeles. His work includes the Beverly Hills Hotel (1911) and the Pasadena Playhouse (1924), both in the California Mission style.

Griffin, Walter Burley (1876–1937): Griffin worked as a draftsman in Wright's studio from 1900 to 1906. While there, he began to design private residences in the Chicago area. Working in partnership with his wife, Marion Mahoney Griffin, also a former Wright employee, he produced numerous projects, including the city plan for Canberra, Australia.

Gropius, Walter (1883–1969): the founder of the Bauhaus School and one of the best-known modernist architects of his generation, both in his homeland of Germany and abroad. Buildings such as his Fagus Factory (1911–12) and Dessau Bauhaus (1925–26) incorporated steel skeletons and glass curtain walls, and were based on asymmetrical plans, with spaces separated according to use. Gropius relocated to the United States in 1937 and remained there for the rest of his career.

Guenzel and Drummond: Louis Guenzel (1860–1956) and William Drummond (1876–1946) were architects in partnership in the Chicago area. Drummond had worked as a draftsman for Wright from 1899 to 1909. Guenzel and

Drummond worked together from 1912 to 1915, constructing homes based on Wright's Prairie Houses.

Hall, Walter J. (1878-1952): the primary contractor in the building of Fallingwater. He was hired after Edgar Kaufmann, Jr., came upon Lynn Hall (1934), a northern-Pennsylvania gas station and inn that Hall had built in a Wrightian style. He had originally been inspired to pursue a career in architecture after seeing Wright working on the construction of the Larkin Building, Buffalo, in around 1905.

Henrich, Janet: an assistant in the Museum's Department of Architecture at the time of the Wright exhibition, who worked closely with curator John McAndrew.

Hoffman, Josef (1870–1956): Austrian artist, designer, and architect who was a member of the Vienna Secession group and cofounder of the Wiener Werkstätte in 1903. His Palais Stoclet (Brussels, 1905–11) combines the organicism of the Secessionists, in its details, with a stark white, proto-modernist geometry of form.

Howe, George (1886–1955): Beaux-Arts–trained architect who became a leading advocate of International Style modernism in the United States. With William Lescaze, he designed the Philadelphia Savings Fund Society building in Philadelphia (1929–32), one of the few American buildings in MoMA's *Modern Architecture: International Exhibition* of 1932. In 1930–31 Howe and Lescaze designed several unrealized proposals for The Museum of Modern Art. With *Philip Johnson*, Henry-Russell Hitchcock, and *Alfred Barr, Jr.*, he edited the journal *T-Square* (later *Shelter*), in which he and Wright famously debated

their approaches to a modern American architecture. He was also a member of the Museum's Architecture Committee in the 1930s.

Hudnut, Joseph (1886–1968): dean of the Harvard Graduate School of Design. In 1937 Hudnut invited *Walter Gropius* to become chair of the Department of Architecture, making the school a nexus for the dissemination of modern architecture in the United States. He wrote the introduction to the catalogue of Wright's 1940 exhibition at the Institute of Contemporary Art, Boston, *Frank Lloyd Wright: A Pictorial Record of Architectural Progress*, organized by *James S. Plaut*.

Jacobs, Herbert A. (1903–87): American newspaper journalist for whom Wright built the original Usonian House, for around $5,000 (1936). This house, with its in-floor heating, masonry core, and solid-wall construction, was the model for the house that Wright intended to build in the Museum's Sculpture Garden as part of the 1940 exhibition.

Johnson, Herbert Fisk, Jr. (1899–1978): American businessman who headed the wax-product manufacturers S. C. Johnson and Sons. In 1936 Johnson commissioned Wright to build a new administration building for the company. The great open-plan workroom is punctuated with soaring, dendriform concrete columns and clerestory windows made up of horizontally laid glass tubes. In 1937 Wright built a house for Johnson, called "Wingspread" because of its four wings radiating out of a central hub, each zoned for a different use.

Johnson, Philip Cortelyou (1906–):
Johnson's long association with the
Museum began in 1930, when he
became a member of the Advisory
Committee. From 1932 to 1934 (and
again from 1949 to 1954) he was head of
the Department of Architecture. In 1940
he was an honorary member of the
Architecture Committee and offered
financial support for Wright's Exhibition
Usonian House.

Kramer, P. L. (1881–1961): an architect of the
Amsterdam School, along with *Michel
de Klerk*, and especially known for the
many bridges he built for the
Amsterdam public works department.

Le Corbusier (1887–1965): born in
Switzerland, Charles-Édouard Jeanneret
moved to France and assumed the
name Le Corbusier when he began to
publish the avant-garde journal *L'Esprit
nouveau* (1920–25). Although he built
fewer than seventy works in his lifetime,
Le Corbusier was among the most influential architects of the twentieth century. His book *Vers une architecture* (1923)
became a manifesto for modernism,
with its famous slogan, "A house is a
machine for living in."

Loos, Adolf (1870–1933): one of the first
modernist architects. Working in Vienna,
Loos created an antiornamental architecture based on surface material and
the careful composition of space. His
polemical essay "Ornament and Crime"
(1908) attacked the previous generation's use of applied decoration and
their attempts to control the use of interior space through total design.

Mackintosh, Charles Rennie (1868–1928):
Scottish architect whose Glasgow
School of Art (1897–1909) is often
likened to Wright's early work, although
there was apparently no direct influence
in either direction. Mackintosh's architecture uses simple geometric forms,
revealed construction, and completely
designed interiors within an Arts and
Crafts sensibility.

Mackmurdo, A. H. (1851–1942): a member of
the English Arts and Crafts movement.
A student of John Ruskin and compatriot of *William Morris*, this architect's
designs for buildings, as well as for furniture and wallpaper, were important for
the development of the work of *Charles
Rennie Mackintosh* as well as Art
Nouveau.

Mallet-Stevens, Robert (1886–1945): architect and interior designer who was one
of the most commercially successful
French modernists. He designed many
shops, offices, and apartments, often
using concrete and steel as both ornament and construction material. He also
collaborated with artists, designing film
sets, for example, for Man Ray and
Ferdinand Léger.

Martin, Darwin D. (1865–1935): vice-president of the Larkin company who commissioned Wright to build the Larkin
Company Administration Building
(Buffalo, 1902–06), which before its
demolition in 1950 was among the architect's most monumental structures.
Wright also built one of the largest of
his Prairie Houses (1903–5) for Martin, a
loyal patron and client.

Maybeck, Bernard R. (1862–1957): Beaux-Arts–trained architect who built mostly in the Bay Area and developed an original, eclectic style based on Arts and Crafts ideals, apparent both in his many residential buildings and in works such as the First Church of Christ Scientist, Berkeley (1909–11).

McArthur, Albert Chase (1881–1951): architect who studied with Wright and built the Arizona Biltmore Hotel (1929) in collaboration with Wright, who, unhappy with the final design, gave him full credit for the building.

McKim, Mead and White: Charles Follen McKim (1847–1909), William Rutherford Mead (1846–1928), and Stanford White (1853–1906) formed their partnership in 1879 and became one of the best-known architectural firms in America. By the time the firm had fully dissolved, in 1919, they had built approximately 1,000 commissions. Their work epitomized the classical ideals of the École des Beaux-Arts.

Mendelsohn, Erich (1887–1953): a leader of the Expressionist movement in German architecture. In 1926, Mendelsohn visited Wright at Taliesin, where architect Richard Neutra served as interpreter. In his Einstein Tower (Potsdam, 1919–24), a research center and astronomical observatory, he used concrete and steel to create an organic form in a tribute to the technology of both modern astronomy and modern architecture.

Morris, William (1834–96): having trained as an architect, Morris founded a workshop that produced furniture, murals, wallpaper, fabric, tiles, and more. His call for a holistic approach to the arts, based on the medieval craft tradition, influenced the development of the English Arts and Crafts movement. In his collaborative approach and design principles he was a precursor of the Austrian Wiener Werkstätte and the German Deutscher Werkbund and Bauhaus school. His organic design work was also an important influence on Wright.

Morse, Edward Sylvester (1838–1925): an archaeologist whose early work brought him to Japan and who became an expert in numerous aspects of Japanese life and culture. Wright and many other American architects read his book *Japanese Homes and Their Surroundings* (1885).

Mosher, Byron Keeler (Bob) (1909–92): a member of Wright's Taliesin Fellowship who worked with *Walter J. Hall* as one of Wright's primary onsite assistants in the building of Fallingwater.

Mueller, Paul F. P. (1865?–1934): an engineer who, after working for *Louis Sullivan*, started his own company and was often hired to manage the construction of Wright's projects. He went with Wright to Japan to work on the Imperial Hotel (c. 1912–23), and also worked on projects such as Midway Gardens (1913–14) and Fallingwater (1934–37).

Mumford, Lewis (1895–1990): American architecture critic and social theorist. Mumford contributed to The Museum of Modern Art's first architecture exhibition, *Modern Architecture: International Exhibition* (1932), which featured Wright and younger Europeans. The ensuing correspondence between Mumford and Wright was mutually influential, especially as they discussed urban space and city planning.

Okura, Baron Kishichiro (1873-1928): Japanese business magnate who was the key financial backer of Wright's design for the Imperial Hotel, Tokyo.

Oud, J. J. P. (1890-1963): in the 1920s, this Dutch architect designed some of the most abstract, cubic works of early modern architecture. His contributions to the Weissenhof Housing Colony (Stuttgart, 1925-27) and his mass housing in Rotterdam include elements of both Wright and de Stijl, with which he was closely associated.

Perkins, Dwight (1867-1941): after working for *Burnham* and *Root*, Perkins shared office space with Wright as both men were beginning their respective architectural practices. They collaborated on some early projects, including the Abraham Lincoln Center in Chicago (1896-1903), built for the All Soul's Unitarian Church, where Wright's uncle, Jenkin Lloyd Jones, was the pastor.

Perret, Auguste (1874-1954): French architect who was a pioneer of concrete and steel construction and built one of the first reinforced-concrete apartments in the world, at 25b rue Franklin, Paris, in 1903-4. Working with his brother, Gustave Perret, he made many innovations in this technology.

Peters, Svetlana (1917-46): Wright's stepdaughter. The daughter of *Olgivanna Wright* by her first marriage, Svetlana was raised by the Wrights. She married William Wesley Peters, a member of Wright's Taliesin Fellowship.

Pevsner, Sir Nikolaus (1902-83): German-born architectural historian who fled to England to escape the Nazis. His book *Pioneers of the Modern Movement* (1936) was important in the introduction of modernism to Britain.

Plaut, James S. (1913-96): the director of the Institute of Contemporary Art, Boston, where he organized the exhibition *Frank Lloyd Wright: A Pictorial Record of Architectural Progress* (January 24-March 3, 1940). The ICA and The Museum of Modern Art coproduced many photographs of Wright's work that appeared in both the Boston show and the Museum's later the same year. *Joseph Hudnut*, Dean of Harvard's Graduate School of Design, wrote the introduction to the catalogue.

Purcell and Elmslie: William Gray Purcell (1880-1965) and George Grant Elmslie (1871-1952) entered into partnership in 1909. Next to Wright, they were the most prolific and established of the Prairie School architects. They built houses, banks, and various large public commissions throughout the Midwest, including the Woodbury County Courthouse (1915-17) in Sioux City, Iowa. Their collaboration ended in 1922.

Richardson, H. H. (1838-86): Richardson created a distinctively American building style by transcending his Beaux-Arts training and adopting a neo-Romanesque style using massive masonry walls. His buildings include Trinity Church, Boston (1872-77), and the Marshall Field Wholesale Building, Chicago (1885-87). His work was important to *Louis Sullivan* and *John Wellborn Root*.

Rockefeller, Abby Aldrich (1874-1948): an early American collector of modern art. Along with Lizzie P. Bliss and Mary Sullivan, she cofounded The Museum of Modern Art in 1929, and remained on the Board of Trustees throughout her life. From 1929 to 1934 she served as treasurer. She was the wife of *John D. Rockefeller, Jr.*, and the mother of *Nelson Aldrich Rockefeller*.

Rockefeller, John D., Jr. (1874–1960): the son of John D. Rockefeller, a founder of the modern oil industry, John D. Rockefeller, Jr., funded the development of Rockefeller Center and Rockefeller University in New York and established the philanthropic Rockefeller Foundation. In 1939 he donated land for the Museum's new building. He was the husband of *Abby Aldrich Rockefeller* and the father of *Nelson Aldrich Rockefeller*.

Rockefeller, Nelson Aldrich (1908–79): the son of *John D. Rockefeller, Jr.*, and *Abby Aldrich Rockefeller*, Nelson Aldrich Rockefeller was elected to the Museum's Board of Trustees in 1932, at the age of twenty-three. In 1939 he became the president of the Museum.

Root, John Wellborn (1850–91): working with *Daniel Burnham*, Root was a pioneer of the American skyscraper. The Monadnock Building, Chicago (1889–91), one of their best-known buildings, is emphatically vertical, exchanging nearly all exterior ornament for repeated rows of vertically aligned bay windows.

Schindler, Rudolf M. (1887–1953): Austrian-born architect who went to work for Wright at Taliesin in 1916. After supervising construction of the Aline Barnsdall House in Pasadena (c. 1916–21), Schindler stayed on in Los Angeles and established his own practice there. Designs such as his own house and studio (1921–22) and the Lovell Beach House (1926) demonstrate his response to the California setting.

Schmidt, Garden and Martin: Richard Ernest Schmidt (1865–1958), Hugh Mackie Gorden Garden (1873–1961), and Edgar D. Martin (1871–1951) built many commercial and industrial buildings in the Chicago area, including the Montgomery Ward & Co. Catalog House (1907–8). Before joining the partnership, Garden had worked for Wright.

Semper, Gottfried (1803–79): German architect and author of *Style in the Industrial and Technical Arts* (1860–63), one of the most influential architectural treatises of the nineteenth century. Semper's notion of the hearth as a point of origin for architecture prefigured Wright's use of a centrally located fireplace in his house plans.

Shand, Philip Morton (1888–1960): British architectural critic who translated the writings of architects *Adolf Loos* and *Walter Gropius* into English. He was a member of the MARS (Modern Architectural Research) group of architects, designers, engineers, and writers, and a participant in the early CIAM (Congrès Internationaux d'Architecture Moderne) meetings.

Silsbee, Joseph Lyman (1848–1913): the architect who was Wright's first employer, hiring him as a draftsman. *George Elmslie* and *Irving Gill* also worked for Silsbee, who built many houses in the Chicago area in the style of *H. H. Richardson*.

Stickley, Gustav (1858–1942): inspired by *William Morris*, this American designer produced simple, usually unornamented wood furniture. He published the journal *The Craftsman*, which featured design objects from the British Arts and Crafts movement and by Japanese and Native American artists.

Sullivan, Louis (1856–1924): the architect and writer whom Wright called his *"Lieber Meister"* (Beloved master). Wright worked in the Chicago office of Adler and Sullivan from 1888 to 1893. In his writing and in his architectural practice, Sullivan advocated an original style in which buildings would express their own purpose and the democratic ideals of the people.

Tallmadge, Thomas E. (1876–1940): the architect and critic who coined the term "Chicago School" and later wrote *Architecture in America* (1927), an early study of the topic.

Taylor, F. W. (1865–1915): an engineer and writer whose highly influential theories of efficiency in business and industry called for close observation of workers, the redesign of working environments to eliminate wasteful movement, and financial incentives for workers through quota-based bonuses.

Tiffany, Louis Comfort (1848–1933): designer and glassmaker associated with the American Art Nouveau movement. Nature was the primary inspiration for Tiffany's aesthetic. Son of the founder of Tiffany and Co., he inherited the business in 1902. He was an innovator in techniques of treating glass, creating nacreous, iridescent surfaces for decorative objects such as lamps and vases.

van de Velde, Henry (1863–1957): this Belgian artist, designer, and architect was a leading proponent of Art Nouveau. His expressive, organic architecture seemed to break with historical styles, and he was an early member of the Deutscher Werkbund, designing a theater with flowing concrete walls for their 1914 exhibition in Cologne.

van Loghem, J. B. (1881–1940): Dutch architect whose early work was influenced by Wright. Inspired by the Soviet Revolution, van Loghem became a dedicated socialist and spent much of his later career designing affordable mass housing.

van't Hoff, Robert (1887–1979): Dutch architect who visited Wright in the U.S. in 1914, then built several houses under Wright's influence on his return to Holland. He later became a member of the de Stijl group.

Viollet-le-Duc, Eugène-Emmanuel (1814–79): architect, scholar, and France's chief advocate for the Gothic Revival. He considered medieval architecture an inspiration for an architecture that would express the structural possibilities of its materials, including new building materials of his own time, such as iron. His writings were influential for *Louis Sullivan*, Wright, and many other modern architects.

Voysey, C. F. A. (1857–1941): architect of a series of country houses in which he rethought the British vernacular tradition. After studying design with *William Morris*, Voysey turned to architecture, simplifying traditional forms and using strip windows and large, low-hanging roofs that emphasized horizontality. Like Wright, he is sometimes considered a precursor of the International Style.

Wasmuth, Ernst: German publisher who, in 1910, brought out *Ausgeführte Bauten und Entwürfe von Frank Lloyd Wright* (Executed buildings and studies by Frank Lloyd Wright), also known as "The Wasmuth Portfolio"—a complete collection of Wright's work to date, designed in cooperation with Wright. All but thirty copies designed for American distribution were destroyed in a fire at Taliesin in 1914.

Wijdeveld, Hendrik T. (1885–1989): this Dutch architect also edited *Wendingen* (1918–31), the journal of the Amsterdam School. In 1925, Wijdeveld published a special edition on Wright, including reproductions of his designs, selections of his writing, and essays by *Lewis Mumford*, *J. J. P. Oud*, *Louis Sullivan*, and others.

Willatzen, Andrew (1876–1974): an apprentice in Wright's studio at the same time as *Frances Barry Byrne*. In partnership from 1908 to 1913, he and Byrne built many private and public works in the Seattle area.

Wils, Jan (1891–1972): Dutch architect, writer, and de Stijl member, on whom Wright's influence was so profound that he was sometimes called "Frank Lloyd Wils." Following the de Stijl principle of union among the arts, Wils designed many of his buildings in collaboration with artists.

Wright, Frank Lloyd, Jr. (1890–1978): Wright's first child with his first wife, Catherine Wright. Having studied architecture and worked on California projects of Wright's including the Aline Barnsdall House (c. 1916–21), he went on to establish a practice of his own in Southern California. He became a respected architect, designing the Hollywood Bowl (1924–28) and the Los Angeles Civic Center (1925, unexecuted).

Wright, Iovanna Lloyd (1925–): daughter of Frank Lloyd Wright and his third wife, *Olgivanna Wright*.

Wright, John Lloyd (1892–1972): Wright's second child with his first wife, Catherine Wright. Studying architecture early on, John Lloyd Wright assisted on projects such as Midway Gardens (1913–14). He continued to work as an architect and also designed children's toys, including a set of "Wright Blocks" and the well-known Lincoln Logs.

Wright, Olgivanna (1898–1985): Wright's third wife. She was born in Montenegro and was a student of the Russian mystic Gurdjieff. She met Wright in 1924, having moved to the United States. Both she and Wright divorced their present spouses; they married in 1928.

Wurster, William Wilson (1895–1973): one of the best-known of the Bay Area modern architects. He often used redwood timber in his buildings and integrated them sensitively into their site.

Yeon, John (1910–94): working primarily in and around Portland, Oregon, Yeon designed buildings that blended into their surrounding landscape. Along with that of Pietro Belluschi, his work came to define modern architecture in the Pacific Northwest.

CREDITS

Photographs

Photograph John Beinert: 52, top left.

Bulletin of the Garden Club of America: 48, top. July 1939, pp. 74–75.

Courtesy Chicago Historical Society: 17, top. Photograph Hedrich-Blessing: 30, left.

© The Cleveland Museum of Art: 30, right.

© Pedro E. Guerrero: 38; 54, bottom right. Photographs: Pedro E. Guerrero.

Courtesy Kai Gutschow: 21, center.

Courtesy Ray Morton Hall: 174.

© The Estate of Henry-Russell Hitchcock: 25, right.

Courtesy the Johnson Foundation, Racine, Wisc.: 39.

© Al Krescanko: 12. Photograph: Al Krescanko.

© The Museum of Modern Art, New York: frontispiece, 32, 77, 186, 187, back cover.

Courtesy The Museum of Modern Art, New York: 25, bottom left; 27; 34, right; 49, right. Drawn by Tina di Carlo: 49, left. Photograph Robert Damora: 54, top.

Courtesy The Museum of Modern Art Archives, New York: frontispiece, 56, 57 (pamphlet file, exh. 114), 65 (reg. exh. files, exh. 114), back cover.

Courtesy The Museum of Modern Art, Department of Architecture and Design: 46; 48, bottom; 186; 193.

© The New York Times: 51, right.

© Newsweek: 51, left. Photograph: Pat Terry.

© The Estate of Dorothy Norman: 34, bottom left.

Photographs: Luke Swank. Courtesy Claudia Elliot: 183, 184.

© Carl Van Vechten Trust: 25, top left.

Courtesy the Wellesley College Archives: 29.

Courtesy the Wisconsin Historical Society: 15, left.

© 2004 The Frank Lloyd Wright Foundation, Scottsdale, Ariz.: cover; 10; 15, right; 17, center left and right; 45, left; 58, right; 65, 74, 89, 104–5, 188–92, 194–208.

Courtesy The Frank Lloyd Wright Foundation, Scottsdale, Ariz.: 16; 17, bottom; 18–20; 21, left; 23; 34, top left; 45, right; 52, top left and bottom; 54, bottom left; 55; 58, left; 59; 168; 187.

Courtesy Robert Wojtowicz: 21, right.

Letters and Telegrams

Eugene Masselink: © 2004 The Frank Lloyd Wright Foundation, Scottsdale, Ariz.

Letters by employees of The Museum of Modern Art are © 2004 The Museum of Modern Art, New York.

The letters of John D. Rockefeller, Jr., are © 2004 The Rockefeller Archive Center, Sleepy Hollow, N.Y.

The drawings, correspondence, and writings of Frank Lloyd Wright are © 2004 The Frank Lloyd Wright Foundation, Scottsdale, Ariz.

Archives

All correspondence is from The Museum of Modern Art Archives except:

The Avery Architectural & Fine Arts Library, Columbia University: 97–98 (Wright to Hitchcock).

The Rockefeller Archive Center: 85–86 (Rockefeller to Abbott), 91–93 (Abbott to Rockefeller), 94–95 (Rockefeller to Clark), 95–96 (Clark to Rockefeller), 98–99 (Rockefeller to Clark).

The Frank Lloyd Wright Foundation: 78 (Wright to McAndrew), 79 (Behrendt to Wright), 82 (Behrendt to Wright).

Original Manuscripts

Walter Curt Behrendt as edited by Frank Lloyd Wright: © Frank Lloyd Wright Foundation.

Frank Lloyd Wright: © Frank Lloyd Wright Foundation.

Talbot Hamlin: © 2004 Talbot Fancher Hamlin.

Henry-Russell Hitchcock: © The Estate of Henry-Russell Hitchcock. Excerpt published in *Parnassus* 12, no. 8. (December 1940): 11–15.

Fiske Kimball: © Fiske Kimball Papers, Philadelphia Museum of Art Archives. Published in an earlier version in *Architectural Record*, June 1932, pp. 379–80.

Grant Manson: used by permission of John Wiley & Sons, Inc. Revised and published in Manson, *Frank Lloyd Wright to 1910: The First Golden Age* (New York: Reinhold Publishing Corporation, 1958).

John McAndrew: © The Museum of Modern Art, New York.

Richard Neutra: courtesy Dion Neutra, Architect, and Richard and Dion Neutra Papers, Department of Special Collections, Charles E. Young Research Library, University of California, Los Angeles.

Alvar Aalto: © The Alvar Aalto Foundation. Previously published in Göran Schildt, ed., *Alvar Aalto in His Own Words* (Helsinki: Otava Publishing Co., 1997).

Harwell Hamilton Harris: used by permission of The General Libraries, The University of Texas, Austin. Revised and published in *Journal of the American Institute of Architects* 18, no. 5 (November 1952): 216–19.

Mies van der Rohe: © 2004 Estate of Mies van der Rohe. Revised and published as "A Tribute to Frank Lloyd Wright," *College Art Journal* 6, no. 1 (Autumn 1946): 41–42, and in a slightly different version in Philip C. Johnson, *Mies van der Rohe* (New York: The Museum of Modern Art, 1947). The version published here is the unrevised version originally submitted to the Museum.

Edgar J. Kaufmann, Sr.: © Western Pennsylvania Conservancy/Fallingwater.

Liliane Kaufmann: © Western Pennsylvania Conservancy/Fallingwater.

Edgar Kaufmann, Jr.: © Western Pennsylvania Conservancy/Fallingwater.